REQUIEM

DIANA, PRINCESS OF WALES 1961-1997

MEMORIES AND TRIBUTES

Edited by Brian MacArthur

ARCADE PUBLISHING • NEW YORK

FIRST U.S. EDITION

ISBN 1-55970-442-X
Library of Congress Catalog Card Number 97-77561
Library of Congress Cataloging-in-Publication information is available.

Published in the United States by Arcade Publishing, Inc., New York
Distributed by Little, Brown and Company

10 9 8 7 6 5 4 3 2 1

Text design by Bet Ayer

PRINTED IN THE UNITED STATES OF AMERICA

CONTENTS

Should, in view of the complexity of securing copyright information, any copyright holder have been inadvertently overlooked, or should the copyright have been wrongly ascribed, the publisher apologises and undertakes to correct any mistakes in future editions:

INTRODUCTION

No. As Clive James wrote in the *New Yorker*, No was the first anguished and disbelieving word uttered by millions that cataclysmic Sunday morning when they heard that Diana, Princess of Wales had died in Paris, shortly after midnight, in a mangled Mercedes driven by a drunken driver. As her brother Earl Spencer declared at her funeral, she was the most hunted woman on earth. The only reason she was in Paris was to escape the paparazzi that had ruined her holiday in Sardinia – and they were the reason she dined in the security of the Ritz. She left by a back door but they still pursued her – and then took photographs at her death.

Only six hours earlier, she had called her friend Richard Kay, royal reporter of the *Daily Mail*. She was in love, she was going to see her two beloved sons on Sunday and she was as happy as he had ever known her, Kay reported. All was well with her world for the first time in years. She was thinking of completing her obligations to her charities and her campaign against anti-personnel landmines and then withdrawing from public life. Princess Diana was happy again, that was why that word No was uttered with such heartfelt disbelief.

As the opening chapter of *Requiem* demonstrates, the grief of the people was palpable (and not only in Britain). They flocked to Buckingham Palace and especially to Kensington Palace where they left flowers at the gates of her London home – and then more flowers and, as the week of grieving wore on, still more flowers until the night air outside the palaces was filled with an intense perfume. They lit candles in the wind and queued silently to sign the books of condolence.

The public was bewildered by the apparent lack of response of the Queen and the Royal Family. The Queen returned to London from Balmoral a day earlier than she had originally planned and joined the crowds outside Buckingham Palace. On the day of the funeral she bowed to the Princess's

5

hearse and as she left the palace ordered the flag be lowered to half-mast. The service in Westminster Abbey was relayed to the crowds on large screens in Hyde Park and by sound to other locations. The crowds applauded Earl Spencer's powerful and moving tribute to his sister that led, unprecedentedly, to the mourners clapping Earl Spencer in Westminster Abbey as well.

Writers paid their tributes with words instead of flowers, words that attained a nobility and eloquence rare in modern journalism. Even the most cynical were affected, as were a generation of young, feminist columnists who saw in the Princess an icon of a scorned woman who triumphed over the Establishment. Again and again, whether by friends and acquaintances, editors, journalists or historians, the same qualities were described – her beauty, simplicity, goodness and weakness; her impeccable manners; above all her compassion for the sick and suffering. All writers have willingly agreed to be included in this *Requiem*, which represents an unparalleled tribute to the significance of the Princess's life and work and the example she set of how to be a modern royal.

Journalism had many enemies even before the death of Princess Diana and newspapers were instantly put in the dock by Earl Spencer who said with evident emotion that every newspaper proprietor and every editor who had paid for 'intrusive and exploitative' paparazzi pictures of her had 'blood on their hands'. Yet although she had often been treated badly by newspapers, journalism, as this anthology amply demonstrates, served the Princess well in her death. No other event in history has been covered in so many millions of words nor with such affection and sensitivity. There was genuine shock and grief in newsrooms that Sunday and a determination on the part of every editor, reporter and writer to give their best to the evaluation of the significance of her life and her death. The sheer quality of the journalism written that day and throughout the following week – whether eloquent, angry, lyrical or critical – shines through every page of this anthology and shows what British journalism is capable of, when it really tries. The Princess's death brought dignity to front pages that only days before had been splashing paparazzi picture of 'Di and Dodi', the son of Mohamed Al Fayed who died with her in Paris and who had brought happiness to the last weeks of her life.

Journalism is often described as the first draft of history or as history on

6

the hoof. When historians come next century to dwell on the significance of Princess Diana – her impact on the British Royal Family, the fate of the Prince of Wales, the careers of her sons, the end of the British stiff upper lip and the acknowledgement that grief need not be hidden, her compassion for the sick and the suffering, the significance of all those flowers and all those candles in the wind – they will find that all the themes that will continue to dominate the debate about the Princess and her impact on the monarchy, especially after her death, are encapsulated in the journalism, written at speed and to deadlines, published in this *Requiem*.

Brian MacArthur

THE PEOPLE'S PRINCESS

Louise was suffering from muscle cancer, and together the family had decided to try to raise money for a new Day Hospice in our home town of Blackpool. When my wife Judy heard that Diana was coming to the town she wrote and asked if she'd meet Louise and she agreed.

Diana was brilliant. She just looked at Louise and said: 'I so admire you. How angry are you?' It was exactly the right question. That's when I realized how much she really understood the disease and how sufferers feel. We chatted for nearly an hour, then Judy took pictures of Louise and the Princess together. 'The only thing I'd ask,' she told us. 'is that you don't take them to Boots.' Before she left we knew we would be opening the new Louise Woolnock Day Hospice the following summer and I said wouldn't it be lovely if she could perform the official opening. She said she couldn't promise. But somehow I knew that she would come.

It was the following spring – 1991 – when we heard Diana was definitely coming. Louise didn't know it but she had just days to live. She was in indescribable pain, she was blind, she'd lost her beautiful hair, she couldn't walk and she could hardly speak.

Even so, the morning that Diana arrived for the official opening Louise developed a new light in her eyes. It was last time I saw Louise laugh. Diana walked straight up to her, gave her an enormous hug and said: 'Hello old friend.' They sat together, holding hands, talking, bursting into girlish giggles.

Exactly a week later – on 4 August 1992 – Louise died. She was only 21. I still believe she hung on for that final meeting, made herself stay alive. Their friendship meant that much.

Now I look at the photographs of them together and can hardly believe that they're both gone.

I can see them now, together again, having a little chat.

Philip Woolcock, *Express*

I was born with Turner Syndrome, which means that I would not have grown to more than 4ft 6ins naturally. It was in 1991 that I first met Diana. You may think that she was just doing her duty at the ceremony – but she was doing much, much more than that. Diana talked to me at length that day, about my problems and hopes for the future. She was genuinely interested and told me and my mum Carol to keep in touch.

Little did I realize that the moment I met her would be the start of a friendship that only ended with her death. I started to write to her and all the replies I got were handwritten and signed by Diana herself.

They meant so much and helped me get through psychological problems caused by my condition. She would not write much about herself, being much more interested in me. She gave such wonderful advice that helped me through. She would will me and my family to stay strong and believe that things would get better.

In October 1994, I told her I needed an operation in France that would help me grow to a normal height, and needed to raise £40,000. She wrote back immediately lending support. Amazingly, Diana also enclosed a personal donation towards the surgery. I cannot say how much the cheque was for, but it helped the appeal enormously.

I had the op the next April and all the time Diana was in touch by letter. She wrote that she would always be there for me. When my mum had a nervous breakdown in the difficult months of after-care, Diana wrote to *her*. The Princess was an inspiration. She didn't need to help me and very few people knew we were still in touch. She did it out of the goodness of her heart. She was a great friend in every sense of the word. She helped out with money and, more than that, the fact that she kept in touch.

Her concern for me was totally genuine. She just loved helping people in trouble, especially children. I think it was because she had had such a troubled childhood herself. That is why she understood.

I cannot believe she died. I last had a letter from her five weeks ago. She was pleased that everything was going well for me. I'm now 5ft tall and have just passed nine GCSEs. I'm starting A-levels now and hope to become a doctor – then, like Diana, I can help and care for people. I would have loved to have the chance to tell her how things are turning out.

Emma May, *Express*

It was her gestures I will always remember. She had a gift for communication that went beyond words.

We met several times at the Terence Higgins Trust, the Aids charity, where I worked. But that was just in a formal setting with lots of people there. The time that's really special to me was a Sunday evening earlier this year when she turned up to join a group of us at Westminster Abbey. The group was organized by the Dean of Westminster and was just a dozen of us gathering every week for chat. The Princess got to hear of it and phoned to ask if she could come along.

When she arrived we were all bowled over by her charm and warmth. I stood up to let her sit down and she said: 'Don't be so silly' and sat to share the seat with me. I could never imagine a member of the Royal Family sharing my seat. Later, a few of us took a walk around Westminster Abbey. But when we got to the Coronation Chair we all knew she was not destined to sit on it and the atmosphere became rather tense.

So I said: 'I think you are better off out of that family.' She laughed out loud and said: 'You are absolutely right.'

Of course, the most important thing she did for Aids sufferers was holding their hands. It was the most powerful thing – a human gesture which the world could understand. I was terribly grateful. With that gesture she changed the image of people with Aids from something scary to people you could touch and live with.

I have been terribly depressed, I am sick and have lost one of my closest friends. Her attention made me feel better.

People said she visited people like us out of a need to be loved. I think she felt like an outcast, as we Aids sufferers are. I felt she was a lonely woman. She had a withdrawn quality that lonely people have.

We felt she cared, and through her, other people came to care.

Tony Whitehead, *Express*

'I know I can give love for a minute, for half-an-hour, for a day, for a month, and I want to do that.'

Diana, 1995

A WEEK OF FLOWERS AND CANDLES

1 September

THE 'PEOPLE'S PRINCESS' RETURNS TO BRITAIN

A sombre Prince of Wales flew home from Paris with the body of his former wife Diana, Princess of Wales, last night to prepare for official mourning and a possible state funeral.

He was greeted at RAF Northolt by Tony Blair, who had earlier spoken of his utter devastation at the death of the 'People's Princess' after a car crash that also killed her companion Dodi Fayed and their French chauffeur.

At 7pm, the doors of the BAe 146 aircraft were opened and the coffin, draped in the Royal Standard surmounted by a single wreath of white lilies, was brought out and borne across the tarmac by eight RAF pallbearers, the silence broken only by the slow tread of boots.

There was no ceremony, no words spoken. Prince, Prime Minister, the Princess's two sisters, the Lord Chamberlain the Earl of Airlie, the Defence Secretary George Robertson and Lord Bramall, the Lord Lieutenant of London, stood in line with heads bowed as a brisk breeze chilled the dying light of the day.

Twelve minutes later, the coffin had been placed in the back of a hearse and driven away to a private mortuary. After a few words of thanks, the Prince returned to the aircraft for the flight back to Aberdeen and his sons at Balmoral. The Princess's body was moved to the Chapel Royal at St James's Palace just after midnight.

By then, Mr Fayed had been buried at Brookwood cemetery, Woking. His coffin, draped in black cloth with gold lettering, was flown back to Britain on his family's jet and taken to Regent's Park Mosque where 600 mourners had gathered for a simple funeral lasting just under ten minutes.

The coffin was then taken to Brookwood for a longer private family burial service. The ceremony took place just before 10pm, thus complying with

Muslim beliefs which require that burial should take place within 24 hours of death. Mr Fayed's father, the Harrods owner Mohamed Al Fayed, had been offered two plots and spent a few minutes making his choice while the six-car funeral cortège waited at the cemetery entrance.

Thousands of mourners gathered at Buckingham and Kensington Palaces and outside the Paris hospital where the 36-year-old Princess died, as political leaders from across the globe paid tribute to one of the world's best-known and most admired women. Radio and television stations scrapped their schedules and substituted continuous news programmes, and even radio stations that normally pump out rock and pop switched to more sombre music as details of the accident unfolded. Sporting fixtures were cancelled.

On the political front, a temporary truce has been declared and campaigning suspended in the Scottish and Welsh devolution polls. The Scottish referendum due on 11 September may be delayed if it is felt to be too close to the funeral – a move that might necessitate a recall of Parliament, since the dates were fixed by legislation.

President Clinton, President Mandela and Mother Teresa of Calcutta all spoke of their personal sadness at the Princess's death. The Archbishop of Canterbury, Dr George Carey, said the world had lost a 'vibrant, lovely young person,' and Mr Blair seemed to choke with emotion outside the church in his Sedgefield constituency as he said: 'I feel like everyone else in this country today. I am utterly devastated.' Baroness Thatcher said: 'A beacon of light has been extinguished.'

There was bitterness, however, from the Princess's brother, Earl Spencer, and Mr Fayed's father, who minced no words in blaming the media and paparazzi for the deaths. The couple whose romance had dominated the tabloid press for much of the summer had apparently been trying to escape a pack of paparazzi on motorcycles when their car crashed, and Lord Spencer said from his home in Cape Town that every editor and proprietor who had paid for intrusive and exploitative photographs of the Princess, encouraging ruthless and greedy individuals to risk everything in pursuit of her, had blood on their hands.

A lawyer acting for Mr Fayed said that he would bring a civil suit as soon as a judicial inquiry into the deaths had opened. He did not say at whom it would be aimed, but he strongly critized photographers hounding the couple and a spokesman for the Harrods owner said: 'There is no doubt in Mr Al Fayed's mind that this tragedy would not have occurred but for the press photographers who have dogged Mr Fayed and the Princess for weeks.' Mr Al Fayed issued a statement saying: 'This is an appalling and needless tragedy. The world has lost a Princess who is simply irreplaceable.'

The French authorities also had no hesitation in linking the accident to the photographers chasing the couple. Seven freelance photographers – six French and one of Macedonian origin – were questioned all day by police and may face criminal charges. But as the British Government faced renewed calls for privacy legislation to protect people in public life from unwarranted intrusion, it was pointed out that the tough French laws had failed to prevent the tragedy and Mr Blair's preference for self-regulation is likely to prevail.

The fatal crash happened as the Princess and Mr Fayed were driven from the Ritz, where they had dined together. Their Mercedes 600 reportedly travelling at up to 120mph, hurtled into a concrete pillar in a tunnel on the Right Bank Expressway near the River Seine shortly after midnight. Mr Fayed and the driver died instantly.

The Princess, who had massive internal injuries, was trapped in the wreckage for about an hour and a half before being taken to the Pitié Salpétrière hospital where surgeons tried for two hours to save her. The only survivor was Trevor Rhys-Jones, a bodyguard employed by Mr Al Fayed, and he was said to be in a critical condition. Witnesses complained that it took the emergency services 15 minutes to arrive and that the one police officer on the scene had made no effort to rescue the occupants of the car.

The driver was the deputy head of security at the Paris Ritz, who was known to staff as Monsieur Paul. He was not a regular driver of the powerful Mercedes and had no known training in the specialized high-speed tactics used by chauffeurs who double as security guards.

The Prince of Wales, on holiday at Balmoral with the Queen and other members of the Royal Family, was woken by a telephone call informing him of the accident. When a further call confirmed that the Princess had died, he woke Prince William and Prince Harry and broke the news to them. Mr Blair, who had been told of the accident by the British Embassy in Paris, was among the first to telephone Balmoral to offer condolences.

Buckingham Palace issued a statement saying: 'The Queen and the Prince of Wales are deeply shocked and distressed by this terrible news.'

In spite of the appalling news, the Royal Family went to morning service as usual at Crathie Kirk outside the gates of Balmoral. Princes William and Harry, outwardly calm, filed into the small granite church along with their father, the Queen and Queen Elizabeth the Queen Mother.

At lunchtime the Prince of Wales drove himself to Aberdeen airport to board a BAe 146 aircraft of the Royal Squadron to Paris, accompanied by the Princess's sisters, Lady Jane Fellowes and Lady Sarah McCorquodale. The aircraft landed at Villacoublay, a military airfield 30 minutes southwest of Paris, and the party was driven at high speed in a convoy of ten vehicles with police outriders to the hospital, where President Chirac was waiting with two of his ministers to greet the Prince.

The men shook hands, then the Prince swallowed hard as they went inside. He and the Princess's sisters were in the hospital for just under half an hour, spending a few minutes alone with the coffin in a first-floor room of the casualty unit before meeting four surgeons and four nurses who had tried to save her. Aides insisted that the body had already been formally identified by an embassy official and their decision to view the body was a personal choice. The Princess's face was reported to have been unmarked by the accident.

The arrival of the Prince's party was watched by nurses, ancillary staff and patients who stood along the narrow avenue beneath two lines of plane trees, while others leant over staircase railings and looked out of fourth-floor windows.

A small number of British and French journalists had earlier been led discreetly through back streets to a rear entrance where they were vetted and admitted by soldiers as nervous officials, sensitive to strong public feelings about journalists in the wake of the Princess's death, ushered the party in quickly. Even so, the journalists were greeted with howls of anger and shouts of 'assassins' from the crowd.

But the mood quickly calmed as the medical staff appeared, led by the anaesthetist Bruno Riou, and Alain Pavie, the thoracic and cardiac surgeon who both worked on the Princess in attempts to save her life. Pierre Coriat, head of the hospital anaesthetist unit, and Professor Jean Pierre Benazet, the emergency orthopaedic trauma surgeon, were also there.

At 5.06pm, the coffin was slowly carried from the hospital by four pallbearers, followed by two men carrying bouquets of lilies and gladioli. The Prince emerged from the building after the coffin had been placed in the steel blue Rivage hearse on which the blinds had been drawn.

Silence descended on the crowd as he strode out, looking neither to right nor left, towards his Jaguar. The cavalcade then moved off – the hearse sixth in the convoy and the Prince immediately behind – in a hail of sirens and flashing lights. When it had gone, officials bundled a black-draped coffin trolley and personal effects into a dark car and followed the convoy.

In spite of the anti-press sentiments in Paris, the royal convoy was followed from the hospital to the airport by two motorcycle film crews, with one cameraman standing on the pillion seat to film the cavalcade.

Few present remained unmoved by the sight of the Princess's last journey home. One Elysée official, who had been up since the early hours making arrangements with members of the Prince and Mr Fayed's households, shook his head and muttered '*Quel jour, quelle horreur*'.

The Times

'BOUQUETS WERE ARRIVING EVERY MINUTE'

On a warm summer afternoon, the pavement cafés of central London were as cheery as ever. At Buckingham Palace the Changing of the Guard continued as usual, though the crowd just happened to be larger and to some extent more sombre.

They stood in wonderment as the Royal Regiment of Wales marched out of the palace gates at midday, just as usual, followed by their regimental goat. People seemed to think they were watching a display of magnificent British phlegm in adversity, though it was probably a display of bureaucratic inflexibility, with no one willing to change the pageantry even in the face of tragedy.

Some people, mostly elderly, were in tears. But more were eating ice creams. Many of the tourists did not even know what had happened.

In contrast, the mood at Kensington Palace was more grief-stricken, and occasionally bitter. Shortly after lunchtime, the number of bouquets there must have approached 1,000 and more were arriving every minute. Some were lined up on the wall near the road under a sign saying 'Connoisseur

Casino'. Many more were tucked into the gilded wrought-iron gates of the palace.

They came from all manner of people: Private Heath of the Princess of Wales Royal Regiment; the Marsh Family of Chalfont St Giles; Holly, Mike and Jackie of Carmarthen; Glenda Jordan of Covington, Kentucky, the people of Pakistan, and Lee and Kev.

Dotted among the flowers were candles, teddy bears, a necklace tied around the railings, and a bottle of 1995 burgundy. Many people were weeping and a black woman lay down under a tulip tree and screamed out: 'Never! Never! Never!'

As photographers tried to take affecting pictures of two five-year-olds playing with one of the teddies, an ugly scene developed.

A young woman wearing designer black shouted at the photographers: 'Stop it! Stop it! Have some respect!'

Other photographers were jostled, as presumed accomplices in Diana's death, and advised by the police to beat a temporary retreat. Even some tourists, taking their own pictures, were abused.

One of the bouquets at Buckingham Palace carried an anonymous poem. It was not the sentimental sort usually favoured on these occasions:

I killed her. I hounded her
to the death. I followed her
every movement.
I gave her no peace. For I
bought the papers. I read the
stories and
I looked at the photographs.
They did this for me.
How can I live with that?

Matthew Engel, *Guardian*

EARL SPENCER'S STATEMENT

It was with profound shock that I heard of my sister's serious injury and subsequent death in Paris early this morning.

All those who came into contact with her, particularly over the past 17 years, will share my family's grief.

She was unique, she understood the most precious needs of human beings, particularly those that suffered, and her vibrancy and sparkle, combined with a very real sense of duty, are now gone for ever. It's heartbreaking to lose such a human being.

This is not a time for recriminations, but for sadness. However, I would say that I always believed the press would kill her in the end.

But not even I could imagine that they would take a direct hand in her death, as seems to be the case.

It will appear that every proprietor and editor of every publication that has paid for intrusive and exploitative photographs of her, encouraging greedy and ruthless individuals to risk everything in pursuit of Diana's image, has blood on his hands today.

And my heart goes out to the familes of the others killed in this incident. Above all, my thoughts are with William and Harry and with my mother and two sisters, who are showing tremendous bravery in the face of senseless tragedy.

I would ask you please at this time to respect the fact that Diana was part of a family. We, too, need space to pay our final respects to our own flesh and blood. For that, we will need privacy.

Cape Town, 31 August

THE WORLD MOURNS

TONY BLAIR: I feel like everyone else in this country today. I am utterly devastated. Our thoughts and prayers are with Princess Diana's family, particularly her two sons. Our heart goes out to them.

How many times do you remember her and in how many different ways with the sick, the dying, the children and the needy? When with just a look or a gesture that said so much – more than words – of her compassion and her humanity.

We are today a nation in a state of shock, in mourning, in grief that is so deeply painful for us.

She was a wonderful and a warm human being, although her own life was often sadly touched by tragedy. She touched the lives of so many others in Britain and throughout the world with joy and with comfort.

We know how difficult things were for her from time to time. I am sure we can only guess that.

But people everywhere, not just here in Britain, kept faith with Princess Diana.

They liked her, they loved her, they regarded her as one of the people.

She was the People's Princess and that is how she will stay, how she will remain in our hearts and our memories for ever.

PRESIDENT MANDELA: I vividly recall our meeting last year and her burning desire to assist HIV positive children. Princess Diana had indeed become an ambassador for victims of landmines, war orphans, the sick and needy throughout the world. She was undoubtedly one of the best ambassadors of Great Britain.

PRESIDENT CLINTON: Hillary and I knew Princess Diana, and we were very fond of her. We are profoundly saddened by this tragic event. Our thoughts and prayers go to her family, friends and children.

I will always be glad that I knew the Princess. I admired her work for children, Aids victims and getting rid of the scourge of landmines.

PRESIDENT YELTSIN: Diana was loved by the people of Russia. Many exceptional projects that touched the lives of ordinary people have been put into practice in Russia with her direct participation.

MOTHER TERESA: (Princess Diana gave money to the Missionaries of Charity) I am very sorry to hear about the sudden death of Princess Diana. All the sisters and I are praying for her and all the members of her family to know God's speed and peace and comfort in this moment.

She was very much concerned about the poor and her attitude towards the poor was good. That is why she came close to me. She came to Calcutta. She was taken to Sishu Bhavan [an orphanage] where we have children for adoption. We are fighting abortion with adoption. She was anxious to do something for the poor.

We never talked about her divorce. Most of the time we talked about how

18

to love God and ask God to help us to love the poor. She was a very good wife and good mother of beautiful children.

She helped me to help the poor and that's the most beautiful thing.

ARCHBISHOP OF CANTERBURY, DR GEORGE CAREY: I was shattered to hear that this vibrant person had lost her life. It is a terrible tragedy for everybody.

She seized the imagination of young and old alike. This beautiful woman was also a very vulnerable human being and out of that vulnerability and weakness, if you like, came lots of strength, her passion and her commitment to people.

I think there's a sense in which we are all grieving, because she expressed something that we all valued and loved. I knew her as someone who loved life. She was deeply committed to people, to issues, to causes. I found her a very interesting person who was very committed to people. We are reminded that death is only inches away from each one of us. Perhaps it will help us all to focus on the really important things in life, human love and relationships, and faith in God.

She had faith in God, although she wasn't the kind of person who wore religion on her sleeves. There was a deep faith there. People should pray especially for Princes William and Harry who will now grow up without a dearly-loved mother. The world has lost a vibrant, lovely young person.

The word passion seems to sum her up, commitment, to issues, to causes. She was a deeply religious person in the sense that she cared about people. She didn't associate with institutional Christianity. There was faith in her whole personality.

LORD RUNCIE, THE FORMER ARCHBISHOP OF CANTERBURY, WHO CONDUCTED THE ROYAL MARRIAGE: Diana had a great sense of eagerness to be up to the challenge of being Princess of Wales. She had a real, tender desire to be what everybody expected her to be. I treasure some of the heartfelt and sincere letters she wrote at that time. She was very tender. She needed assistance.

MOHAMED AL FAYED: This is an appalling and quite needless tragedy. The world has lost a Princess who is simply irreplaceable.

A STATEMENT ON BEHALF OF MR AL FAYED: Mr Al Fayed has lost his beloved eldest son. Mr and Mrs Al Fayed are devastated by their loss and share the sorrow of the Princess's family.

Mr Al Fayed was a great admirer of the Princess's father, the late Lord Spencer, and Lord Spencer was a tremendous friend and loyal supporter of the Al Fayeds through thick and thin. Mr Al Fayed regarded him as a brother.

Dodi had known the Princess for more than ten years and they became close when the two families had a happy holiday together in July.

Dodi was a kind, gentle and decent person who cheered the lives of those who knew him. He had a tremendous regard for Princess Diana and he cherished her friendship as did all the Al Fayed family.

The thoughts of the Al Fayed family go out to the sons of Princess Diana, to the Prince of Wales, to the Royal Family and the Princess's family. The Al Fayed family will remember for ever the enjoyable holiday they had with the Princess and her two sons in St Tropez so recently.

THE BEAUTY WHO COULDN'T TAME THE BEAST

Created as an icon by press photographs, she lived in the fizzing glare of flashguns, and now she lies dead, a victim of the insatiable lens. Behind the lens stands an industry, an apparatus of buying and selling, proprietors, profits, and, somewhere down that feeding chain, the silent millions of readers who added so handsomely to sales figures whenever Di stories appeared, and who flocked to the news-stands to see the latest blurry colour picture. Earl Spencer, her brother, was bitter about it all; she was murdered by the media, he said.

Was she? Certainly it seemed at times that the relentless pursuit of her image had driven her almost demented. Living as the harried subject of professional voyeurism is a form of modern mental torture which no one who hasn't experienced it, at least a little, can fully understand. Yet at other times Diana clearly revelled in her role as the woman that half the world wanted to watch, hear and follow. She was not mere victim. She could be a shrewd, even brilliant, exploiter of the media, both for herself and her charity causes; and it diminishes her to suggest otherwise.

All that said, her death ought to start a much-needed debate (which has to be international rather than just national) about the structure and appetites of this global industry of images and words which the public both adores and loathes. The media are omnipresent, and treated with the same mixture of enjoyment and dislike as other great powers. It was, of course, the reviled media to which people turned yesterday, unquestioningly, avid for the news.

Because of the circumstances of Diana's death, it will register as a calendar event, shocking in its suddenness. The strength of people's feelings about her are not to be doubted or slighted. 'Although I am not a royalist . . .' How many times, yesterday, people prefaced their response with this formula, distinguishing the place she held in national life from their views about the monarchy.

To many people, it is as if a light has gone out. This flawed woman shone – Tony Blair found the right word – reflecting back to us the intensity of our interest in her looks, her clothes, her loves, her charity, her modernity, her representativeness. This upper-class English girl, so narrowly formed and so unrepresentative in upbringing, became our common creation, our national possession. Her death will be sincerely mourned.

Yet if we weigh the institutional significance of the Princess's death, the balance is curiously empty. Of course her departure matters for the House of Windsor. But the monarchy is not about to dissolve or to be abolished. Instead, it is the fourth estate that this death touches most closely – the news-producers, agents of the iconography of the modern world; and not just us, but you, the consumers of news, co-participants in this frenzied dance of public, stars and audience-maximizing media.

The manner of her death raises a specific question about the harrying of superstars for their pictures. Few have ever been in Diana's league; the treatment of Hollywood stars may be bad, but they are in the image-selling business. 'Paparazzi' – today's buzz-word – must not become too easy a herd of scapegoats. The photographers' relentless pursuit of the Princess occurred because there is a wide and rich international market for their work. It is hard to see how that could ever be regulated. In theory, agreement between proprietors might stick, but it is hard to see the American supermarket tabloids or *Oggi* ceasing to find good-looking royalty interesting.

Something practical might be done to make Britain a pursuit-free zone, either by making it easier for victims to obtain injunctions or by privacy legislation. This newspaper has supported for some time the principle of a law guaranteeing privacy, noting the absurd disjunction between the scope of official privacy (i.e., for government information and officials) and a free-for-all for the rest of the world, mitigated by harsh and anachronistic libel laws. Nothing in Diana's death alters the already strong case for action on this front.

By the same measure, much in her life illustrates the reciprocal nature of media relationships: press and broadcasters need willing and co-operative subjects. The Royal Family decided a generation ago that it would manage the media. Until the late Seventies, it did so relatively successfully. Its nervous and half-embarrassed handling of the eruption of the heir to the throne's wife into superstardom was at best amateur. But there is no denying that the House of Windsor (mistakenly) chose to set out on the path that Diana subsequently followed deep into the jungle.

Of course, the media are not innocent carriers. Proprietors have agendas, editors have views of the world to propagate, reporters too often choose the lowest common denominator. But with the exception (to some extent) of the BBC, the media are commercial – we live and die by numbers. The public is well able to demonstrate its tastes in its purchases. The market for newspapers may be oddly skewed in terms of ideology, but it remains an open market; the British public does have other reputable media to choose if they are dismayed with mass-circulation newspapers.

Perhaps Diana was simply a one-off, someone whose extraordinary life since marrying Charles forbids generalizations. She grew from gauche nanny to hardened and emotional superstar in a spectacular way which lured some media people, like some ordinary Di-watchers, into a kind of insanity. She lived, and now has died, in the midst of a love affair with the public, during which her powers of seduction grew ever greater – and were put to good causes. But she was sucked up by forces which, tide-like, came to overwhelm her. Like some heroine of old, she thought she could tame the beasts – and was wrong. Some accidents have a force that feels like Fate. The smash in a Paris tunnel was one. Di, in whose life this paper was not greatly interested, enters a kind of pantheon, the Princess-martyr, murdered by the media. A cult will follow. Things weren't quite like that. She was more complicated – and so is the media. But there is enough truth in the story for many – journalists and readers too – to hang their heads. The pursuit was a kind of madness. It was cruel, too.

Independent

BRIDGET JONES'S DIARY

Sunday 31 August
9st 2, cigarettes 0, alcohol units 0.
Instants 1 (v.sad)
10am Why am I so fat with no boyfriend all on own on Sunday morning. What is wrong with self? Am just no good. Am going to go down and get paper then have fag.

10.03am Is unbelievable. Like dream or sick newspaper April Fool. Is unbelievable. Diana Dies is just not kind of thing she would do.

10.10am Am going to put on telly and they will say it has been a mistake and she is back then we will see her coming out of the Harbour Club with all the photographers asking her what it was like.

11.30am Cannot believe it. Is so scary when is obvious no one in authority knows what to do.

12.00am At least Tony Blair who seemed to say what everyone was thinking instead of repeating 'grief and shock' over and over again in manner of parrot.

13.00am Just feel so guilty that she was our national treasure and people were niggardly about her and she did not like being here. Is like great big hand coming down from heaven saying 'if you are going to squabble over her nobody is going to have her'.

13.30pm Keep having to look at newspaper headline again to make self believe it.

14.00 Really she was the patron saint of Singleton women because she started off like the archetypal fairytale doing what we all thought we were supposed to do i.e. marry a handsome Prince and she was honest enough to say that life is not like that. Also it made you feel that if someone so beautiful and gorgeous could be treated like shit by stupid men and feel unloved and lonely then it wasn't because you were rubbish if it happened to you. Also she kept re-inventing herself and sorting out her problems. She was always just trying so hard like modern women.

1pm Hmm. Wonder what people would say about me if I died?

1.01pm Nothing.

2.45 Have just had horrible realization. Was watching television with the sound down and tabloid front page came up which looked as though it might have had actual pictures of aftermath of the crash in. Realized was horrible part of me which actually wanted to see the pictures. Clearly would not buy said newspaper even if could but ugh ugh. What does this mean about me? Oh God. Am terrible.

3pm Just keep staring into space. Simply hadn't realized how much Diana was part of consciousness. Is like Jude or Shazzer being there and full of life and giggly jokes and lip gloss then suddenly being something so grown-up and horror-filled and alien as dead.

5.45 Just rang up Magda who has been to the garden centre and bought a tree and planted it for Princess Diana. Maybe could plant something in window box e.g. um basil? Could get from Cullens.

6pm Hmm. Basil does not seem right somehow.

7pm Not sure what think about everyone going to Buckingham Palace with floral tributes. Have people always done this? Is it something naff people do to try and get on the television like camping all night outside sales or good, real thing? Hm . . . Feel want to go though.

7.15pm Think going with flowers might be a bit creepy . . . but thing is really did like her. Was like having someone in heart of authority who was same as you. Also all huffer puffers criticized her re: landmines etc but if you ask me was bloody intelligent use of mad publicity. Better than doing nothing except huffing at home.

8.45pm What is point of living in capital city if cannot join in great expressions of feeling? Does not seem very English thing to do but maybe everything has changed with the changing weather and Europe and Tony Blair and it is all right to express yourself. Maybe she has changed English stuffiness.

9pm You see she was brilliant on the landmines programme. Just as good as Dimblebys Pilgers etc.

9.15 OK am definitely going to go to Kensington Palace . . . Have not got any flowers, though. Will get some from petrol station.

9.30 Petrol station has sold out. Only things like chocolate orange and custard left. Nice but inappropriate.

9.35 Bet she would like them, though.

9.45 Have chosen copy of *Vogue*, Milk Tray, 1 Instants and packet of Silk Cut. Not perfect but everyone will have bought flowers and know she liked *Vogue*.

11pm V. glad went. Felt a bit shy walking through Kensington in case people knew where was going and that was on own, but then when think about it Princess Diana was often on own.

Inside park was v. dark and gentle with everyone just walking quietly in one direction. Was no histrionics like on News. The bottom of the wall was covered with flowers and candles in the darkness and people relighting the candles that had gone out and reading messages.

Hope that she knows now after all the times she worried about not being good enough, look what everybody felt about her. Really all this should say a message to women who are worried about how they look and being rubbish and expecting so much of themselves just not to worry so much. Felt a bit embarrassed about the *Vogue* and chocolate and Instants so hid under flowers and looked at the messages which made you think that you do not have to be a spokesman for anything to be able to express things. The best one was copied from the Bible, I think, and it said in wobbly old lady's writing.

'When I was in trouble you cared about me, when I was in danger you tried to stop it, when I was sick you visited me, when people ran away you took my hand. Whatever you did for the poorest and smallest people I felt as if you did it for me.'

Independent

2 September

THE BRITISH BEGAN TO QUEUE

Uncertain what to do next, the British followed their instincts and began to queue. At eight o'clock in the morning it was possible to walk straight in to the anteroom at St James's Palace to send formal condolences on the death of Diana, Princess of Wales.

By lunchtime the official waiting time was two hours. By mid-afternoon it was three and a half hours, and the line stretched down the Mall, almost to Trafalgar Square. By 9pm the wait was seven hours, and many prepared to wait all night. Foreign tourists did not seem enthused by this prospect and turned away. The British, however, reacted differently.

The waiting crowd seemed as near as it is possible to get to a cross-section of the country: young and old; men and women; rich and poor; black and white. Many of them were carrying flowers. Only the time-pressed and the hyper-sophisticated were missing.

It did not seem as though they were responding to something terrible. It was as if we were queuing for Wimbledon or Cup Final tickets or the sales or the No. 38 bus on a particularly bad day. Or Lenin's tomb, come to that. There was a lot of humour, and banter with the police. Underneath, though, there was sense of determination: a feeling that one had to do *something*, and that this was an appropriate response.

Sensible people had brought bags of pastries; the very prudent had portable stools. One half-expected them to bring out camping stoves and start cooking lunch. As the line turned into Marlborough Road for the home stretch, the mood became a little more reverent, but only a little.

The atmosphere was not conducive to silent contemplation. Builders were drilling close by. Fire engines raced past. Planes passed overhead. The traffic in Pall Mall roared on regardless.

Eventually, we were ushered through the metal detectors, past various flunkeys who looked as if they had been hired from Harrods, in over-the-top red tail coats with brass buttons, and invited to join one final queue, leading into a long, cream-painted chamber with red drapes and subdued lighting.

'It's like going to the bank,' said the woman in front of me. And so it was. We were obviously half-expected, because the sign saying 'The Book of Condolence Queue' was not new, and had presumably lain in store since Churchill died. But the object of the exercise was a touch confused.

We were not fulfilling the old tradition of filing past the coffin. In this particular case, that would have seemed like a further act of voyeurism.

We were not paying our respects at the house. The Royal Family has not lived here since the reign of William IV. And these days most people are not quite sure what St James's Palace is for. Furthermore, this bit at the back, though handsome enough, looks rather unroyal, more like a gymnasium block at one of the finer public schools. To cap it all, there was not even a condolence book, merely five separate ringbinders, containing black-edged blank paper, placed on tables with purple cloths.

This clearly shocked everyone. They had expected something like a church visitors' book or a hotel register. There was no guidance about what to say, or how much. 'I thought you just signed your name,' said the woman in front. 'No,' said her friend, 'you've got to do a little message.'

It was not even clear who exactly we were condoling. William and Harry, of course. But who else? The Queen? Charles? Ourselves? These problems were what made the queue so slow. Many people took a long while, and composed mini-essays. Heaven knows who will ever read them. Then there was another problem. There was nowhere to put the flowers.

The habit of placing floral tributes as a response to public grief seems to have developed since the Hillsborough disaster of 1989. Every road crash, every murder, now attracts its share. It is a beautiful custom, perhaps one that could only develop in a society which has come as close as any in history to making early death a rarity.

27

But, in memory of this most rootless of human beings, there was no obvious place for the flowers to go. So a whole stack of ad hoc sites developed, including the kindergarten where she worked and the gym where she worked out. From the condolence line, the obvious alternative was down the road to Buckingham Palace. Here there was another queue, so people could either place their flowers, or simply view the thousands now on display. These were leavened with the odd curiosity: a flag of St George, a picture of Diana from the cover of *Vanity Fair,* a Queen's Park Rangers scarf.

Many more went to Harrods. Outside the Tube station, the window blinds were drawn. This was not a mark of respect: they were simply redoing the displays. The first one that was actually visible was devoted to the products of Gianni Versace.

The store was open as usual. But one of the main doors was shut and there was a real condolence book outside, supervised by a real Harrods doorman.

The scent rose from the tributes as though the pavement were the perfume counter. Behind them was the store's doormat, bearing the unfortunate store slogan: 'Enter a different world.'

Most chose to go to Kensington Palace. Here the carpet of flowers had grown to phenomenal proportions. They have been moved from under the sign saying 'Connoisseur Casino', but they stretch along the line of trees – on the grass, in the boughs, on the seats – leading to the gates of the palace itself.

And there they now cover the area of a good-sized state room. One can only guess how many in all, but it cannot be less than five thousand bunches. A nearby florist, asked how business was, replied: 'Not bad.' I think he was embarrassed.

The flowers placed on Sunday are now lost behind the weight of new arrivals. And every bus that came by disgorged dozens of passengers clutching more.

The park noticeboard has become an informal condolence book, the most moving of all. The messages are scrawled on florists' wrapping paper and scraps of notebooks and Post-it stickers. 'Dear Diana,' said one, 'your house is in heaven. Love, Laura, aged six.'

By the gates the crowd remained huge. Yet inside the gates all is silent. The royal palaces are the only buildings in London without flags at half-mast. Indeed, they are flying no flags at all. It is as though royalty is respecting Diana's memory by proving everything she claimed about their tight-lipped protocol taking precedence over humanity. The statue of William III looked on, but the family provided no other representative.

Perhaps a British revolution would be like this. There have been moments of anger, and of intense public grief. There is a report of half a rush-hour Tube carriage on the Central Line bursting into tears after a woman reading a newspaper broke down. But mostly the moments of intense mourning have been discreet.

Britain has not been indifferent, far from it. But it has been as calm as ever.

This has not been like the response to Dunblane. Those kids could have been our kids. But Diana was never a creature of our real lives. It is not likely that we would have been killed by a drunken chauffeur while being chased by a pack of photographers.

Her death, like her life, was the stuff of dream or nightmare, but not of everyday reality.

Part of nearly everyone is intensely sad. And thousands of people, more than anyone could ever have imagined, have found ways of marking that sadness. But one senses the grief is finite.

Amid all the attention only one place seemed immune. Few people went to the front of St James's Palace. There were only a couple of policemen on duty, and very few lingered behind the barriers.

Next to the octagonal turrets, built by Henry VIII, is the chapel. All that it was possible to see behind the leaded glass of the big window was a solitary lamp. Inside, though hardly anyone seemed to know it, was Diana's body.

Outside there was a lone guardsman. He stood in his sentry box, staring stiffly ahead, occasionally clicking his heels and shifting his bayonet from one hand to the other. Then, in response to some some signal deep within the mysteries of British military protocol, he would set off past the window, still staring straight ahead, hardly blinking.

And around him the Pall Mall traffic roared on regardless.

Matthew Engel, *Guardian*

3 September

LIKE PILGRIMS IN SEARCH OF A SHRINE, THEY QUEUED FOR SEVEN HOURS TO PAY THEIR RESPECTS

The queue to sign the books of condolence for Diana, Princess of Wales, ran down the Mall from St James's Palace a good half-mile to the Duke of York Steps. Here, it doubled back on itself like a snake, elongated by new mourners joining its tail.

A notice stated: 'Queuing time seven hours.' No one seemed deterred. Above them, at the top of the Duke of York Steps, the bronze statue of King George VI looked down with an expression of perplexity at this multitude come to pay their respects to the divorced wife of his grandson.

Who were they? Anyone and everyone – probably a better cross-section of the British people than you could find at any comparable event. Women outnumbered men, some holding babies, others pushing prams. Among the children, too, there were more girls than boys – all remarkably cheerful and superhumanly patient as they waited their turn to sign the books.

Some clutched bunches of flowers, others had already laid them on the banks of floral tributes outside both St James's and Buckingham Palace. Many of the bouquets had pictures of the Princess; most had poignant messages expressing love and gratitude to the 'Queen of our hearts'. They were the expressions of real grief by the unsophisticated for someone they had loved with an intensity that they had only now come to understand.

How do we account for this invasion of royal London by so many ordinary, grieving people? The most experienced commentators were at a loss for an answer. The vans and satellite dishes of the television stations skulked behind the trees in St James's Street and Green Park. Journalists shadowed by their cameramen walked up and down the queue, looking for explanation for this astonishing eruption of emotion.

Gone was the businesslike briskness that reporters often show when on the job. The cynicism so common in the profession is shamed by the sincerity of these people's feelings.

There were prayers among the messages of condolence – 'May the merciful Lord give you rest in his arms' – and a sense that here was a crowd of pilgrims in search of a shrine. The kind of comparisons that sprang into my mind were Eva Peron, St Therese of Lisieux or even the Virgin Mary.

Diana had been revered as someone ideal and remote until the ugliness and brutality of the accident in Paris brought home to the mourners both the mortality and the reality of the Princess of Wales. Now was their chance to step away from the pages of the newspapers and the screens of their television and demonstrate to themselves that their feelings were real.

Was there an element of remorse in this expression of grief? A sense of guilt that so many had treated her life as a source of entertainment? Here, in the long wait to sign the books of condolence, was a chance to atone. Was there also a desire to express a sense of solidarity with someone whose vulnerability had led her to suffer so much in her public role?

The very grandeur of the Mall, and the formal architecture of Buckingham Palace, St James's Palace and Marlborough House, was in marked contrast to the fragility of the bouquets that lay against the walls and gates. Part of Diana's attraction was the human face she gave to a Royal Family that frequently seemed remote.

She was not born a star: before her engagement to the Prince of Wales, the destiny that awaited her would have been similar to that of any other upper-class girl working in a nursery school while looking for a husband.

But even then, she had certain qualities that persisted through all that she endured. Chief among these were a modesty and simplicity that endeared her to the mass of the people.

It is easy to forget how intimidated and browbeaten people can feel by those who control their lives, such as lawyers, politicians, doctors, civil servants. It was often those who saw Diana as one of their own.

However elevated her social status, she never adopted an aura of disdain. She did not pretend to be clever or sophisticated; and, though circumstances may have obliged her to develop a certain cunning, she never lost her simplicity, modesty or natural charm.

She recognized the effect she had on the public and that in itself affected the evolution of her character. As with other charismatic figures, the success of her bond with the many made up for the failure of her relationships with the few.

The facts of her unhappy marriage are well known. It was also true that she had a turnover in personal friends. Until the advent of Dodi Fayed, her relations with men appear to have been inconsequential.

The only constant and uncritical love came from those whom she reached through her public life – not just the direct beneficiaries of the charities she patronized, but the masses who followed her life in their daily papers, sharing her happiness and her suffering as if she was a daughter or a sister or just a cousin far from home.

Her sex was all important. It was no coincidence that most of those queuing for so many hours to sign the books of condolence at St James's Palace were women. Again, just as we forget how intimidating life has become for the less-educated, so we overlook the predicament of women.

In theory they have made progress in the past 50 years: in practice their condition is often confusing. Although she was a princess, Diana's dilemmas embodied those of many ordinary women.

When she married she epitomized the blushing bride: soft, modest and retiring, ready to love, honour and obey. Then came the kind of disillusion so common to modern marriage. The husband was weak. The bond was loveless. The roof was blown off her psychological refuge: like so many women in Britain today, the Princess had to fight for her own survival and learn to live on her own.

It was therefore her own suffering, quite as much as what she did for those who suffered, that endeared her to the men and women who waited so patiently yesterday outside St James's Palace. Other members of the Royal Family, after all, such as Princess Anne or the Duchess of Kent, are well known for their acts of compassion.

The Catholic Bishops of England and Wales denounced landmines long before Princess Diana. But none of them had that mix of beauty, simplicity, goodness, weakness, pathos and glamour that was so appealing in Diana, Princess of Wales.

Nearby came the sound of bagpipes as the band struck up for the Changing of the Guard. Like a magnet, the sound drew away the bemused tourists from the genuine mourners. Groups of curious Germans followed the kilted soldiers as they marched down the Mall.

From all the major buildings visible on the skyline of London, the Union Jack flew at half-mast with one incongruous exception. From the flagstaff on Buckingham Palace itself, no flag flew at all.

Piers Paul Read, *Daily Mail*

'THEY ARE FURTHER ISOLATING THEMSELVES'

No one is bothering to ask each other what they are doing at the weekend. No one needs to. If we are not going to line the route of Diana's funeral we will be watching it on TV. A unique funeral for a unique person maybe, but already there are mutterings that it will not be unique enough. What kind of public ritual, you might ask, could possibly satisfy everyone? What has been striking about the so-called 'ordinary' members of the public who have displayed their overwhelming sense of loss is that so many of them are those who otherwise feel under-represented in society. Those who loved Diana truly were that prized political entity, a rainbow coalition of diverse groups – old and young, black and white, gay and straight.

Reporters in America have been remarking on the numbers of black and Hispanic mourners there are. Diana, it seems, spoke to everyone who has at one time or another felt marginalized. Diana the drama-queen was obviously a big gay icon, and not simply because of her work with people with Aids. She spoke somehow to life's losers while cavorting with its winners. How on earth can a state occasion, which of course this is, whether acknowledged or not, possibly represent such a diversity?

More to the point, how can the Royal Family, an institution that represents the antithesis of democracy, organize the funeral of a young woman whom people felt in their hearts to be instinctively full of democratic impulses, who consistently broke down the barriers between 'us' and 'them'?

The signs are already there that the other Royals have not, unfortunately, learnt a thing from this tragedy. Their apologists have informed us that the Royals just do things differently from normal people. Normal people think they just do things badly. The question the Firm asked of Diana when she was alive, 'Why can't she be more like us?' was always the wrong one. It should, of course, have been: 'Why can't we be more like her?'

We are now experiencing the peculiar spectacle of a Labour government gently nudging the Royal Family into the 20th century, urging it to take notice of the people's wishes. The image of royalty since the death is that they are closeted away somewhere in their cold castle, unable or uninterested in judging the public mood. One can't help wondering whose advice they are taking, for it is the wrong advice. So concerned are they with

33

keeping up appearances, they seem to have forgotten just who those appearances are for. If the public is no longer impressed by stiff upper lips, by pushing grief-stricken boys into suits and sending them off to a church service where their mother is not even mentioned; if the future king cannot even put his arm around his young sons, then what and whom is it all for? The horrible truth is that they are further isolating themselves. Charles is keeping up appearances for his parents, just as he has always done. Is he still, after everything that has happened, too weak to stand up to them?

Diana was the Princess of a young country. Both she and 'Call me Tony' Blair signalled a new informality, the end of the age of deference. Blair may do it through language and lifestyle; Diana did it physically, grabbing and hugging and touching. She literally held people to her. The establishment refuses to recognize that it is possible to be informal and still maintain dignity. Yet Nelson Mandela has done it, and Clinton has done it. Blair has done it and in many ways in their mourning for Diana, the great British public has done it.

Both Blair and Diana share a fairly middle-brow rather than high cultural taste. Diana liked Elton John and Wayne Sleep, Phil Collins and Prokofiev. If that is what she liked, then this is what she should have. That is, the funeral has both to capture the person she was as well as symbolize her huge importance. In order to do this, surely some of the protocol has to be cut through. It is already rumoured that Clinton wanted to come, but was stopped because such an honour is reserved for heads of state. The idea of putting her coffin on a gun carriage also jars. A militaristic operation seems entirely inappropriate for a woman who campaigned against landmines.

The Royal Family cannot reclaim her as one of them in death when in life they stripped her of her title. Public feeling is already running high at this hypocrisy. The Palace looks increasingly ill-equipped to deal with the desires of the people. In opening only five books in which people could give their condolences, they severely underestimated the demand. People were having to queue for up to eight hours and it was only after Richard Branson's plea on *Newsnight* that more books were fetched. Similarly, there are many who say that the route of the funeral procession is nowhere near long enough to accommodate all those who will wish to turn out to see it.

The terrible shock of Diana's death might, one would have thought, have finally catapulted the rest of the Royals into the 1990s. Yet there is little evidence of this. Instead they are desperately clinging on to old habits and old protocols in a manner that, whatever their intention, appears entirely dismissive of the public mood. Having lost its most popular member, the Firm has made the kamikaze decision to distance itself further.

There has been much talk about what a fitting memorial to Diana might be. There have been suggestions ranging from scrapping the Millennium Dome, to putting her in it, to naming hospitals, to making fires and fountains throughout the land. A fitting memorial would be a funeral that truly included the dispossessed rather than merely the great and the good. We are promised that every effort is being made to do this. Yet whatever public rituals achieve, Diana's legacy, one hopes, is also personal.

One desperately wishes that her sons will be brought up in a more open and affectionate way than their bewildered father. There are few indications that this is even possible. To say emotional literacy is not the forte of the Windsors is a gross understatement. Modernity of the most everyday kind appears beyond their reach.

Constitutional experts inform us that all is well, that the reputation of the monarchy waxes and wanes, and that that is to be expected. To that, I simply say that the life and the death of Diana were not what we expected at all; that that was then and this is now. Right now the tremendous closeness that people felt to Diana only serves to underline the enormous gulf between 'them' and 'us'. Whatever country the monarchy thinks it is ruling, it is becoming clear it is not the one that most of us actually live in.

Suzanne Moore, *Independent*

POLITICS GOES ON HOLD UNTIL AFTER SERVICE

A moratorium on politics was declared until after Princess Diana's funeral. Campaigning in the Scottish devolution referendum was included.

The cancellation of almost all activity by the main parties coincided with the announcement of a wide range of gestures of respect, ranging from the closure of shops, banks and building societies on Saturday morning to two-minute silences in various parts of the country.

The Prime Minister, Tony Blair, cancelled meetings with the Confederation of British Industry and with the TUC general secretary, John Monks, in the afternoon. He will be working at Downing Street for the rest of the week.

The Conservative leader, William Hague, said: 'I am suspending all our activities until after the funeral of the Princess. In this period, politicians of all parties should come together and reflect the national mood of unity and contemplation.'

Labour in Scotland, which is spearheading the pro-devolution compaign, confirmed that the referendum will go ahead on 11 September as planned but that campaigning will be halted until Sunday. Although publicly the pro-devolution campaigners were reconciled to the suspension, privately there was dismay at the loss of a week just as momentum had appeared to be building behind their campaign.

Scottish political leaders will meet today to reschedule debates and press conferences. The final push, supposed to begin this week with appearances from the Chancellor, Gordon Brown, and the Foreign Secretary, Robin Cook, will now be concentrated into five days.

Mr Blair had planned to arrive in Scotland for campaigning on Friday, with a break at Balmoral over the weekend. Instead, he will campaign only on the Monday.

Tam Dalyell, the Labour anti-devolution campaigner, called on the Scottish Secretary, Donald Dewar, to suspend the referendum until spring but this was rejected.

There was pressure for a national two-minute silence on Saturday. But Downing Street said this had not been discussed as part of the preparations for the funeral and indicated such silences should be left to individual initiative.

Railtrack said a two-minute silence would be observed at stations at 11am on Saturday, coinciding with the start of the funeral service.

Supermarkets such as Tesco and Sainsbury's will remain closed until 2pm on Saturday, as will other shops and building societies.

Mohamed Al Fayed has ordered that Harrods also be closed on Saturday as a mark of respect.

The Civil Aviation Authority said it was waiting for guidance from Downing Street about air traffic movements over London during the funeral. The British Airports Authority said it generally supported the idea of a period of silence at airports.

The National Trust has decided to close all its houses, shops and restaurants on Saturday until 3pm. Concerts and other pre-booked events at Trust properties will go ahead, preceded by a minute's silence.

Barclays became the first of the clearing banks to announce a decision, saying 400 branches that normally opened in the morning would stay closed.

Later, the Building Societies Association said most societies had decided not to open that day.

The NatWest Cricket Trophy final between Essex and Warwickshire scheduled for Saturday has been postponed until Sunday.

Saturday night's National Lottery draw will be postponed until Sunday morning and will take place in private, with the winning numbers published through the media afterwards.

Guardian

If only the Royals could Weep with the People

Britain is becoming less British. The displays of grief and anger about the death of Diana have been not only mass, but impassioned, florid as well as floral, public not private. There has been crying, shouting – open displays of emotion, not private reflection. This is not how the nation popularly supposed itself to behave; we are meant to be a people of gritted teeth, suppressed feelings and stiff upper lips. The great mounds of flowers – and why, by the way, do we leave them wrapped in Cellophane, not properly open? – the clipped-out photographs from magazines, the piled teddy bears, the poems and pen messages, and the snaking, loudly conversing crowds outside the palaces . . . all this seems somehow foreign to the received images of the British in public sorrow. Traditionally we think of the grave, silent faces at the Cenotaph, of military processions and of the dignified but repressed and duty-lined expressions at establishment funerals or memorial services. Compared with that buttoned-up nation, the current torrents of grief over the dead Princess seem American, or even somehow Neapolitan.

The change in public behaviour is neatly caught by the reported difference of opinion between Buckingham Palace and Tony Blair's circle at Downing Street over the right way to lay Diana to rest. All the instincts of the Windsor family seem to have been traditional, with the emphasis sombre, dignified and vaguely military. They come from a class, as well as a family, sternly schooled in public reticence; from a culture in which it is a weakness to break down in front of strangers. The Prime Minister has consciously decided, it seems, to speak for another and younger strain in British public behaviour, which rather approves of tearfulness and finds mounds of flowers and notes moving and appropriate, rather than maudlin or common. The difference is seen in the debate about how much leeway should be given for vast crowds of ordinary people to feel involved in the funeral; who should be invited to the Abbey; and whether soldiers should be prominent in the event, or people from charities patronized by Diana. It is likely that the discussions have not been as sharp or as divided as malice reports; nevertheless, some difference of tone and instinct seems to have emerged.

If so, it is a poignant and important distinction, which says much about the task of royalty at the end of this century. It is easy to see a repressive, Victorian hauteur in the Windsors; reliance on sombre pageantry which contrasts not only with Diana's thoroughly contemporary tastes, but also with the instincts of the millions of her mourners. They have learnt to let it all hang out. They are not ashamed of tears and have built flimsy, touching shrines which would have meant vastly more to her than ceremonial guards or intoning archbishops. They would not have sent their bereaved sons to ordinary Sunday church services. Their emotional expectations are a world away from the self-deprecating and contorted dignity of the Prince of Wales or the amazing, iron self-discipline of his mother, who seems almost like an ancient Roman matriarch, stern-faced and unfaltering as the family tragedies pile up around her.

The people are not, it seems, like that any more. That was why, after all, so many loved Diana: the same confessional tone and readiness to admit fault which embarrassed the Windsors and their friends so intensely was what made her, to millions, 'one of us'. She drew little smiley faces in biro on children's plaster casts, and enjoyed the corny jokes, horoscope readings and ready, hug-generous behaviour of her most substantial group of mourners. The less hung-up sections of British society, including ethnic minority Di-worshippers, gays and teenagers, have been prominent in the response. But so have millions of the stolid centre of Middle Britain.

To those brought up in the old ways of the British upper-middle classes (and the simple 'uppers' too), much of this is, in truth, a little cringe-making. But the word 'old' in the previous sentence is at least as important as the class element. Diana, after all, was hardly a proletarian infant. She goes to rest in an impeccably aristocratic family chapel. What distinguished her from Charles was not class but age: she was a child of the post-Sixties global culture. He, on the other hand, is in many ways – and given his education this is no exaggeration – still the child of Edwardian values. There is absolutely no doubt which of them the vast majority of the British people identify with. And there is absolutely no doubt that this presents the monarchy with a genuine dilemma. If the Princes grow up more like their father than their mother, the people, who have changed so much already, will not recognize them as belonging to the same country.

We applaud the louder, more emotional and sentimental sorrow, the Neapolitan style of the mourning streets. The inclusive and democratic nature of the response would have been everything she hoped for as 'Queen of hearts'. It feels curiously positive and properly cathartic, as a sombre state funeral or a muted private grieving, would not have done. Modern Britain knows that, unBritish or not, it is good to cry. The heaped flowers, even with their Cellophane, are intensely moving. So are the crowds, This is clearly becoming a populist event, far beyond the reach of official control or the carefully graded rituals of monarchy. It is growing, not shrivelling. It is only a little hyperbolic to describe the mourning of Diana as a kind of emotional revolution of the streets – St James's Palace being stormed in an utterly polite but insistent way by those determined to queue through the night to express their grief. This is an unthreatening revolution, except to the Household Gods of the stiff-upper-lips. We do not mock them. The traditions of repression and self-control are linked to those of duty and sacrifice, and are therefore admirable too; perhaps as a country we have lost a certain national dignity that became us.

Be that as it may, we have moved on, and returned in spirit to the more raucous and sentimental nation we were before Victoria's reign. That is part of the meaning of what has happened in the past few days. We hope the Windsors and their advisers are watching the mood on the streets and learning from it. What would really do the monarchy good, and show that they had grasped the lesson of Diana's popularity, would be for the Queen and the Prince of Wales to break down, cry and hug one another on the steps of the Abbey this Saturday. That such an event is unthinkable shows how great is the gap between the people mourning 'their' Princess, and the

Royal Family to which she never, quite, belonged.

Independent

French Hearts Were Full

The security guards leaning against the gates of Pauline Bonaparte's one-time palace on the Rue du Faubourg St Honoré have seen most things before. Presidents, prime ministers, film stars and generals regularly sweep in and out of the British ambassador's residence under their watchful eyes – but yesterday's was a diplomatic reception with a difference.

Sure, there were celebrities – the former Polish president Lech Walesa, the British fashion designer Stella McCartney, the ex-minister Jack Lang – but they were rare. This was a rite for ordinary people: tourists, shoppers, office workers who would never have dreamt of crossing the residence's marble floors before now. They may have queued meekly like refugees awaiting hand-outs, but their hearts and hands were full.

None of the 1,000-strong crowd of visitors brandished stiff white invitations, few were smartly dressed, and if they felt annoyed about being kept waiting in the pouring rain, they cloaked their feelings in a deeply un-French silence. Their patience eventually won them the loan of black civil service umbrellas – under which they huddled without protest.

By 5.30 in the afternoon, the mourners were threatening to use up the embassy's entire stock of books of remembrance – heavy black objects the size of huge photograph albums last used after the death in 1986 of the Duchess of Windsor.

That, a senior diplomat observed, was a very different kind of occasion with a different class, and age, of mourner.

Yesterday morning, at nine o clock, only one black book was set out for signing. By lunchtime there were three and by the evening there were five. Cue for frantic telephone calls to London for more stationery. 'We didn't realize at first how long people were going to take to write down their thoughts,' said a rueful official. 'Or how many thoughts they would have.'

The mistake was an easy one to make: most French formalities are very formal indeed. But this was not a time for simply scrawling a signature and *mes condoléances*. Poems, personal outpourings of love and grief, whole screeds of epic or impassioned rant were carefully transcribed from ragged scraps of paper with the embassy's fountain pens.

'We started timing them when we saw what was going on. Each person was taking between three and five minutes, and one took 11. If we hadn't opened new books, we would never have been able to cope,' said the official.

More to the point, perhaps, the mourners' grief would have changed to bitterness. Few had much love for the British establishment to begin with – perceiving it as the force which tried to crush their idol's spirit and tried too late to make amends with complicated ceremonial.

Take Martine Strugen, a 48-year-old office manager who spent an hour standing in line with a sumptuous bunch of white chrysanthemums on which she'd spent all the money she usually keeps for buying lunch. 'I had to come because Diana meant so much to me. I'm no royalist but she invented a new way of being royal, a new way of being English. She broke with the image I always had of England, all that stiffness and those corgis and ceremony. She fought that awful system to the end though they tried to keep her down.'

Like so many of the women waiting, Martine spoke with enthusiasm about the Princess's new-found love for Dodi Fayed – 'she looked so happy' – but her pleasure changed to embarrassment when asked how she knew so many details of the liaisons. 'The magazines. I read it in *Voici* and *Paris Match* – not that I buy them myself, you understand . . . I see them when I have my hair done.' Given the anti-paparazzi sentiments raging in France this morning, her admission was brave – and *sotto voce*.

The real anguish, however, did not concern black books. It was simpler than that and started, inevitably, with the words 'What if . . .' What if she'd been staying at the British Embassy instead of dining at the Ritz? What if she'd used an official driver instead of the hotel's man? 'It was too late,' said the official. 'By the time we realized she was even in Paris, it was too late. It was over.'

Susannah Herbert, Paris Notebook, *Daily Telegraph*

LAMENT OF AMERICA'S DI GENERATION

When, in a few weeks perhaps, Britain starts to emerge from the self-absorption of mourning, it may begin to realize that the loss of Diana, Princess of Wales, has implications that go far beyond its own shores. Abroad, Britain will be diminished by her death to an extent that Britons themselves can hardly imagine.

I have just returned from 3100 Massachusetts Avenue in leafy north-west Washington: the address of the British Embassy. The broad avenue, lined with diplomatic missions, snakes up a gradual hill from the city centre. You can be there any day of the week and there will be no one in sight, and only an occasional (diplomatic) vehicle sweeping past.

For the past 48 hours it has been the scene of a never-ending procession of slow-moving cars and pedestrians. Families, couples, groups of friends and individuals are making their personal pilgrimage to say farewell to Diana. Many carry flowers, some a small toy, others a card or a message.

There is a queue half a mile long to sign the book of condolences, but many ignore the formalities. They have their own ritual. A pause, head bowed, in front of an expanse of flowers and messages that resembles an ever-growing shrine; the tribute laid, another pause, a photograph taken for the family album.

This scene is being repeated across the United States, wherever Britain has a representation; in New York, Chicago, Houston and elsewhere. And as striking as the numbers of people arriving is the sort of people they are; not America's aristocracy-groupies, nor the celebrity-seeking 'grannies'. Nor are they predominantly expatriates, though there is a good sprinkling of them, too.

The only way to describe them is as 'ordinary' people. Many are the young and young-middle-aged – the 'Diana' generation. Couples have brought young children, groups of teenagers and students have come, not to sneer or to gawp, but to pay their respects.

There are gay and lesbian couples, demonstratively holding hands; visitors in wheelchairs or on crutches, and most extraordinary of all, in this very white part of Washington, is the proportion of blacks and Hispanics for whom upper Massachusetts Avenue is alien territory. There is anger as well as sadness in the air; one man made a bonfire at a Los Angeles newsstand of editions of the *Globe*, a tabloid newspaper, in protest at the use of 'stalkarazzi' pictures.

In the United States, people have tried to explain the intensity of public emotion by saying that Diana, with her mixed-up life, concern for her children, eating disorders, public divorce, and her resort to the confessional, was a figure Americans were able to relate to.

There have been similar public outpourings elsewhere in the world, and the complexion of the crowd appears similar.

Outside the Paris hospital where Diana died, there were more black people than you would see in most Paris crowds. Whatever the truth of Diana's life and her personal misjudgements, ordinary people abroad felt she was on their side. Formal condolences from state leaders give barely a hint of the affection and regard in which the Princess was held.

This creates for Britain abroad a problem similar to the one that now faces the Royal Family at home. The monarchy has lost at a tragic stroke all that was young, beautiful, sympathetic, accessible and even relevant about British royalty.

That is also what Britain has lost in the world. For millions of people who knew or cared little for international diplomacy, Diana was the lively, modern and humane face of Britain.

She was a global ambassador on a scale that is only now apparent.

Her death may not impair Britain's formal diplomatic effort, but it will surely diminish Britain's international image and global reach. Even a young, presidential-style leader such as Tony Blair will have a hard task to keep Britain in the same league.

Mary Dejevsky, *Independent*

4 September

'WHERE IS THE QUEEN?'

Where is the Queen when the country needs her?

She is 550 miles from London, the focal point of the nation's grief.

Her castle at Balmoral is about as far away as it's possible to get from the sea of flowers building up outside the royal palaces.

The Queen won't be in the capital until Saturday morning. She will leave the funeral that afternoon to fly back to Scotland to resume her holiday.

. The rules say that no flag can be flown at Buckingham Palace unless she is in residence.

The Queen could break the rules for Diana.

But she has overruled her most senior aides, who believe a flag **SHOULD** be flying at half-mast above the Palace – the true symbol of our Monarchy. That empty flagpole at the end of The Mall stands as a stark insult to Diana's memory.

Who gives a damn about the stuffy rules of protocol?

The people want the Monarchy to join publicly in their mourning for Diana.

Why hasn't the Queen broadcast a personal statement of sympathy to the nation? A minute of her time would mean so much.

Every hour the Palace remains empty adds to the public anger at what they perceive to be a snub to the People's Princess.

Let Charles and William and Harry weep together in the lonely Scottish Highlands. We can understand that.

But the Queen's place is with the people. She should fly back to London immediately and stand on the Palace balcony, as she did on Di's wedding day.

Then she will see and feel the overwhelming outpouring of emotion. She will taste the tears in the air. She will know what her people want.

And she can belatedly run up a flag at half-mast.

Sun, front page

Statement Issued but No Tribute to Diana

Tony Blair was forced to shore up the Royal Family yesterday in the face of growing criticism of their failure to make any public expression of grief over the death of Diana, Princess of Wales.

Mr Blair stressed they had much to cope with, not only the complex organization of the funeral but also with comforting the two Princes.

With its image in danger, Buckingham Palace finally moved to counter the divide between the Royal Family and the grieving public. It agreed a longer route for the funeral procession and more condolence books.

Crucially, it provided the first personal note since Sunday – although there was still no direct expression of grief from Prince Charles or the Queen and, most telling, no tribute to Diana herself.

Sandy Henney, press secretary to the Prince of Wales, said: 'All the Royal Family, especially the Prince of Wales, Prince William and Prince Harry, are taking strength from the overwhelming support of the public, who are sharing their tremendous sense of loss and grief.

'They are deeply touched and enormously grateful.'

Last night the family's sense of loss was emphasized by Ronald Allison, the Queen's former press secretary, who told Channel 4 News: 'They are genuinely grief stricken. They are genuinely devastated by this – the whole of the family and particularly, of course, the Prince of Wales. I am absolutely certain the funeral on Saturday will demonstrate the family's . . . real anguish and the depth of their feelings.'

The Palace also let it be known that the Princes may walk behind the funeral cortège, ignoring advice from officials that it might prove too much of an ordeal, given the estimated two million mourners lining the route.

The Princes will return from Balmoral on Friday with Prince Charles. William, aged 15, who is understood to be receiving counselling from the Bishop of London, is reportedly determined to walk behind the gun carriage carrying his mother's coffin.

The comments from Downing Street and Buckingham Palace came after a day in which members of the public, not least those queuing to sign the books of condolence, expressed increasing hostility at the response of the Royal Family so far. Much was directed at the failure to fly a flag at half-mast in Buckingham Palace; officials said there is no flag because the Queen is not in residence.

Responding to the mounting criticism about the Royal Family remaining unseen and unheard in Scotland, Ms Henney said: 'At a time when you remember a member of the family, I think you want to be at home with the family. And that's where the Royal Family are at the moment, in Balmoral.'

As preparations for the funeral were being finalized, Downing Street insisted it will be a people's event and not one for the 'great and the good'. The number of politicians will be kept to a minimum, and the emphasis will be on inviting those who worked with the Princess in charities.

Mr Blair, who spoke with Prince Charles on the telephone for 15 minutes last night, said he wanted 'to make sure we involve as many people as possible so we can express our own sense not just of national loss, of personal loss.'

The Prime Minister, whose emotional comments on Sunday are held up in contrast with the silence from Prince Charles and the Queen, said: 'I know those are very strongly the feelings of the Royal Family as well, who are trying to cope in a tremendously difficult situation.

'They are trying to make all the practical arrangements which are very complex, obviously, for the funeral, at the same time as comforting the two boys.'

A Downing Street spokesman denied there was tension between the Government and the Palace over the funeral arrangements and said it was 'unfair' of people to characterize the Royal Family as austere.

Guardian

'ON HER WAY TO A VISION OF GOD'

Death, where is your victory?
Death, where is your sting?

Saint Paul was in defiant mood when he wrote those words in his letter to the Corinthians.

No, death, you cannot defeat us. One day you will visit each one of us, we know. Not one of us can escape from you. We recoil from you, for we see in you an enemy, the ruthless destroyer of life, the foe who shows no mercy. But no, death, victory will not be yours, for we believe that Christ rose from the dead in order to open up for us a gateway to another place where union with God locks us for ever into that endless 'now' of ecstatic love. We were made for that. No, death is not the end but a new beginning.

Diana, you are now on your way to the vision of God, to a happiness this world cannot give, where true peace is to be found. Tell us: did you, early on Sunday morning, suddenly find yourself in the presence of God, realizing then, as we all must, that none of us is worthy to be in that Presence, face to face, until ready to be so?

Our Catholic faith tells us that our prayers can help the dead to be prepared for union with God. We shall pray that the last part of the journey for you, Diana, will be swift and easy.

I know that you will not mind my saying that you were like the rest of us, frail, imperfect, flawed, but we loved you still. It is thus also with God Himself. He loves us very much. He now embraces you in death. He will most surely judge you mercifully. The maimed, the sick, the young, the old, were of much concern to you. You will have discovered that in serving these, you were in fact serving Him, even if you had not realized it at the time. We have the Lord's authority for that.

> When Lord did we see you hungry and feed you,
> or thirsty and give you to drink,
> saw you a stranger . . .
> homeless, injured, sick, marginalized . . .
> As often as you did this to the least of these,
> my brothers and sisters,
> the Lord said,
> you did it to me,

records St Matthew.

There will be many greeting you now with gratitude and joy, those who have gone before you and whom you helped so generously. For us it is different. We remain behind to weep and to mourn. It is right that we should do so. A sense of loss and bereavement has been strong, the initial shock with us still. We had to do something, lay flowers at different places, queue for several hours to sign our names, the scale of this quite surprising and impressive. We expressed something deep within us through such actions. They were an unconscious prayer to God, almost, as well as a lovely tribute to you, Diana.

But for those of us who remain there is more. We are being called by this sad death to reflect on many things. The sudden awfulness of her death has been a brutal awakening to our own mortality, to a fragility of all our human joys and sorrows. We are being called to acknowledge that it is not here in this world that our ultimate happiness is to be found. Maybe the events of this last week have already awakened within us, or may yet do so, that religious instinct which leads us to seek the true meaning and purpose of our lives. Maybe God is knocking at our doors at this time seeking to be admitted into our minds and hearts.

As a nation we must discover what it is to be charitable. We must all become more sensitive to the needs of each other, more tolerant of each other's faults, less cynical about motives, less anxious to cut others down to size, more understanding of their actions, and of their difficulties as well. We should also reflect on the way we treat those prominent in public life, how much privacy we give them, what respect we accord them. There is much for us to consider. When these days of sorrow and mourning are over, life will become normal again, and so it should. But the lessons must not be forgotten.

Farewell, then, Diana.

The agonies of the heart and anguish of the mind were often your companions in life.

They were your teachers, too, for from them you learnt understanding, compassion and kindness.

These are your finest legacy to us.

Thank you for all the good you did.

Thank you for the joy you gave to many.

Thank you for being like the rest of us, flawed but loveable, and above all loved by God.

Cardinal Basil Hume, at a Requiem Mass in Westminster Cathedral

5 September

QUEEN TO DELIVER ADDRESS ON TV

The Royal Family threw tradition away yesterday when it was announced that the Queen would give an unprecedented television address to the nation about the family's grief at the death of Diana, Princess of Wales.

Stung by criticism that the monarchy had appeared aloof following the Princess's death, the announcement was one of a series made by Buckingham Palace which revealed a fundamental break with the defence that protocol dictated how the Royal Family should act.

Bowing to public pressure for a more appropriate response, the Palace said that along with the address, which will be shown shortly before 6pm, it had also been agreed that for the first time the Union flag will be flown at half-mast over the palace on the day of the funeral.

The moves are a break with tradition and have been described by royal commentators as 'cataclysmic'.

The Palace also announced at a unique on-the-record press conference that the Queen, accompanied by the Duke of Edinburgh, the Queen Mother and Princess Margaret, will now fly to London early this afternoon from Balmoral in Scotland, rather than arriving tomorrow morning by train as first planned.

More controversially, it was also revealed that no member of the Royal Family will read a lesson at tomorrow's funeral.

Last night they attended a hastily convened special service at Crathie Kirk on Royal Deeside, the family's first public appearance since Sunday.

Lieutenant Colonel Malcolm Ross, comptroller of the Lord Chamberlain's office which has been co-ordinating palace input into the funeral arrangements, said a decision had been taken to break with convention because of the nature of the 'unique day for a unique person'.

There was a welcome for the astonishing changes from many quarters.

'You have to admire her courage in circumstnaces that are very painful and difficult,' said Lord Blake, the constitutional historian.

Lord St John of Fawsley, the constitutional expert, called on the public not to be curmudgeonly and to respond positively.

Yesterday's unprecedented church service at Crathie was another break with the original timetable. The Queen, the Duke of Edinburgh, Prince Charles and the young Princes emerged from Balmoral and joined Prince Charles and Peter Phillips, son of the Princess Royal, after the Queen requested the service yesterday morning.

The family spent several minutes at the gates of Balmoral looking at the flowers and reading condolence cards. Prince Harry gripped his father's hands as he closely read many of the tributes.

Outside Balmoral, Prince Charles' press secretary, Sandy Henney, denied that the family's appearance was to answer criticism. 'This is a family going to church for prayer in view of what's happened. It was something that seemed appropriate.'

Earlier the first signs that the Royal Family had been moved by concerns that they were not responding adequately to the national mood came when Geoffrey Crawford, the Queen's press secretary, made a public statement.

'The Royal Family have been hurt by suggestions that they are indifferent to the country's sorrow at the tragic death of the Princess of Wales,' Mr Crawford said in a move described by royal commentators as highly unusual.

'The Princess was a much loved national figure, but she was also a mother whose sons miss her deeply. Prince William and Prince Harry themselves want to be with their father and grandparents at this time in the quiet haven of Balmoral.

'As their grandmother, the Queen is helping the Princes to come to terms with their loss as they prepare themselves for the public ordeal of mourning their mother with the nation on Saturday.'

The Palace said the decision to make the television address was not connected to a number of front-page headlines yesterday which accused the Queen of sticking too closely to protocol.

As well as the fact that the Queen had not spoken since a two-line statement was released on Sunday, criticism also focused on Buckingham Palace, where the flagpole has been bare all week. Members of the public who had queued for hours to sign the books of condolence asked why a flag was not flying at half-mast.

The Palace succumbed to the pressure yesterday and said that when the Queen leaves for the funeral by car tomorrow morning the Royal Standard, flown at full mast whenever the Queen is in residence, will be lowered and the Union flag flown at half-mast instead, where it will remain until midnight.

The Duke of York and Prince Edward were yesterday the first members of the family to sign the book of condolence at St James's Palace. The Palace said that the books would be closed at 6pm tonight until 2pm on Saturday, when they will be left available for signing 24 hours a day for a further week.

A Downing Street spokesman said the new arrangements were a further sign that the Royal Family was responding positively and imaginatively to the extraordinary outpouring of grief.

Guardian

THE QUEEN'S SPEECH

Since last Sunday's dreadful news, we have seen throughout Britain and around the world an overwhelming expression of sadness at Diana's death. We have all been trying in our different ways to cope. It is not easy to express a sense of loss, since the initial shock is often succeeded by a mixture of other feelings – disbelief, incomprehension, anger and concern for those who remain.

We have all felt those emotions in these last few days. So what I say to you now, as your Queen and as a grandmother, I say from my heart.

First, I want to pay tribute to Diana myself. She was an exceptional and gifted human being. In good times and bad, she never lost her capacity to smile and laugh, nor to inspire others with her warmth and kindness.

I admired and respected her – for her energy and commitment to others, and especially for her devotion to her two boys.

This week at Balmoral we have all been trying to help William and Harry come to terms with the devastating loss that they and the rest of us have suffered.

No one who knew Diana will ever forget her. Millions of others who never met her, but felt they knew her, will remember her.

I for one believe that there are lessons to be drawn from her life and from the extraordinary and moving reaction to her death.

I share in your determination to cherish her memory.

This is also an opportunity for me, on behalf of my family and especially Prince Charles and William and Harry, to thank all of you who have brought flowers, sent messages and paid your respects in so many ways to a remarkable person.

These acts of kindness have been a huge source of help and comfort.

Our thoughts are also with Diana's family and the families of those who died with her. I know that they too have drawn strength from what has happened since last weekend, as they seek to heal their sorrow and then to face the future without a loved one.

I hope that tomorrow we can all, wherever we are, join in expressing our grief at Diana's loss and gratitude for her all-too-short life.

It is a chance to show to the whole world the British nation united in grief and respect.

May those who died rest in peace and may we, each and every one of us, thank God for someone who made many, many people happy.

A GIFT FOR LOVING:
THE PRINCESS WE KNEW

Six hours before the Princess of Wales and the man she loved were killed in a paparazzi car chase, she telephoned me from Paris.

She told me she had decided to radically change her life. She was going to complete her obligations to her charities and to the anti-personnel landmines cause and then, around November, would completely withdraw from her formal public life.

She would then, she said, be able to live as she always wanted to live. Not as an icon – how she hated to be called one – but as a private person.

It was a dream sequence I'd heard from her before, but this time I knew she meant it.

In my view as someone close to the Princess for almost five years, Dodi Fayed was a significant factor in that decision. She was in love with him and, perhaps more important, she believed that he was in love with her and that he believed in her.

They were, to use an old but priceless cliché, blissfully happy. I cannot say for certain that they would have married, but in my view it was likely.

None of this would mean, she explained, an end to the good works that had become so closely identified with her. Dodi's father Mohammed Al Fayed had agreed to help finance a charity for the victims of mines and, with Dodi's encouragement, she also had sketched out the framework of a plan to open hospices for the dying all over the world.

And yet, in the midst of all this excitement, she suddenly said: 'But I sometimes wonder what's the point? Whatever I do, it's never good enough for some people.'

There was a sigh and a silence. At the other end of the line was not so much a princess as a little girl who had unburdened herself and was waiting for words of comfort and understanding.

She knew that whatever I said and whatever I might write it would always be what I thought, and sometimes, necessarily, it would be critical.

So she trusted me and revealed herself constantly as a person completely unrecognizable to her most vocal critics, many of whom had never even met her.

They saw a scheming manipulator, a plotter, shrieking for attention and demanding the world's approval and understanding.

I knew a girl of utter simplicity, even naïvety – frightened, uncertain and, as Tony Blair said in his moving tribute yesterday, delightful company, especially when off duty.

She asked me on Saturday why the media was 'so anti-Dodi'. 'Is it because he's a millionaire?' she suggested hesitantly.

You cannot be a 'manipulator' and ask a serious question like that. Anyway, I told her it had nothing to do with his money and was more involved with his father's controversial image.

She listened. 'Hmm.' Maybe for once she thought I was being diplomatically evasive. It seemed to me that she actually believed that in a world filled with the disadvantaged, being rich might be something to be ashamed of.

But this was a princess who understood so little about that aspect of the real world she left behind when she married in 1981, that the first time she insisted on paying for two coffees in an anonymous café where we had met for a chat, away from prying eyes, she tried to leave a £5 tip on top of a £2 bill.

Suddenly she brightened and we switched subjects to her 'boys', William and Harry.

'I'm coming home tomorrow and the boys will be back from Scotland in the evening,' she said. 'I will have a few days with them before they're back at school.'

It may sound thoroughly irrelevant to reiterate what was obvious to everyone, her devotion to her sons. But the significance lay in their uncomplicated love for her.

She was a bit troubled on Saturday because William had called her to say that he was being required by Buckingham Palace to 'perform' – they wanted him to carry out a photo call at Eton where he was due to begin his third year on Wednesday.

What troubled Diana, and indeed William, was that the spotlight was being shone exclusively on William, 15, and not his 12-year-old brother Harry.

She had told me on a previous occasion how hard it was for Harry being overshadowed as a second son by William, and said she tried to ensure as far as possible that everything was shared – a point endorsed by Prince Charles.

In her two sons – and latterly in Dodi – she saw the only men in her life who had never let her down and never wanted from her anything except her being herself.

It was on a return flight from Nepal early in 1993 that the Princess and I had our first serious and lengthy conversation. We had a number of mutual friends and I had met her on several previous occasions. We talked about her trip, her children, her family and mine.

It was the start of what became a friendship based on one crucial element – her complete understanding that I, as a journalist, would never sacrifice my impartiality, especially where it concerned her acrimonious differences with the Prince of Wales and certain members of the Royal Family.

Competitors and some royal advisers frequently suggested that I was in her pocket, and there was that picture of me getting out of her car in Beauchamp Place, Knightsbridge – snapped, inevitably, by a paparazzo.

Over the years I saw her at her happiest and in her darkest moments. There were moments of confusion and despair when I believed Diana was being driven by the incredible pressures made on her almost to the point of destruction.

I knew from the outset that her mines campaign would cause her as much distress as satisfaction, as her simple notion of using her own fame to save lives was thrown in her face by politicans who accused her of embarrassing the Government by meddling in things she didn't fully understand.

'What is there to understand when people are having their legs blown off?' she asked me on many occasions.

She talked of being strengthened by events, and anyone could see how the bride of 20 had grown into a mature woman, but I never found her strong. She was as unsure of herself at her death as when I first talked with her on that aeroplane and she wanted reassurance about the role she was creating for herself.

In private she was a completely different person from the manicured clothes horse that the public's insatiable demand for icons had created.

She was natural and witty and did a wonderful impression of the Queen. This was the person, she told me, that she would have been all the time if she hadn't married into the world's most famous family.

Just before last Christmas I lunched with her at a friend's house in Hampstead. We ate vegetable curry, with pulses and rice, and drank still water. Diana was intoxicating company. She never needed on that day – or any carefree day with friends for that matter – the fortification of alcohol.

After lunch she helped clear the table and stacked the dishwasher, soaked the pans and wiped the table with a damp cloth.

Then four of us went for a walk on Hampstead Heath. We were all arm-in-arm, plodding through mud after heavy rain in ordinary shoes, laughing at the state they were in. People passing us on the Heath could hardly believe they were seeing the most famous woman in the world entirely without her public make-up. She wore jeans and ankle boots. Her unstyled hair was its natural shape, flat.

But the simple soul who was the real Diana was already anticipating Christmas, which she hated because her sons inevitably spent it with their father and the rest of the Royal Family. She would be alone as usual, and told me she going away to Barbuda for a few days.

It was the solitary glum moment in a sunny afternoon, and she soon shrugged it off and began to have fun.

On Saturday she didn't talk much about Dodi, and I understood why: she was afraid that the moment too much was read into the relationship it would end. She always feared that the pressures of publicity would alienate any man in her life. 'Who would have me with all the baggage I come with?' she would say.

She had told me she regretted admitting in her famous *Panorama* interview having an affair with James Hewitt, whom she had also loved.

So why had she said it? The answer was simplicity itself. Charles had admitted adultery on television, so why shouldn't she?

Whatever the psychiatrists said about her bulimia and its roots in her disrupted childhood, Diana believed that its main cause was the poor quality of her life with Charles – 'there were three of us in this marriage so it was a bit crowded,' as she told the *Panorama* audience.

This made her gloomy enough. And yet it never pushed her to the extremes of misery she felt when commentators and the public misunderstood what she was doing.

Most of all, she hated being called 'manipulative' and privately railed against those who used the word to describe her. 'They don't even know me,' she would say bitterly, sitting cross-legged on the floor of her apartment in Kensington Palace and pouring tea from a china pot.

It was this blindness, as she saw it, to what she really was that led her seriously to consider living in another country where she hoped she would be understood.

The idea first emerged in her mind about three years ago. 'I've got to find a place where I can have peace of mind,' she said to me.

She considered France, because it was near enough to stay in close touch with William and Harry. She thought of America because she – naïvely, it must be said – saw it as a country so brimming over with glittery people and celebrities that she would be able to 'disappear'.

She also thought of South Africa, where her brother Charles has made his home, and even Australia because it was the furthest place she could think of from the seat of her unhappiness. But this would have separated her from her sons.

Everyone said she would go anywhere, do anything to have her picture taken, but in my view the truth was completely different. A good day for Diana was one where her picture was not taken and paparazzi photographers did not pursue her and clamber over her car.

'Why are they so obsessed with me?' she would ask me, and I tried to explain but never felt that she fully understood.

Millions of women dreamed of changing places with her, but the Princess that I knew yearned for the ordinary, humdrum routine of their lives.

'They don't know how lucky they are,' she would say.

On Saturday, just before she was joined by Dodi for that last fateful dinner at the Ritz in Paris, she told me how 'fed up' she was being compared with Camilla.

'It's all so meaningless,' she said, and left it at that.

She didn't say, she never said, whether she thought Charles and Camilla should marry.

Then, knowing that as a journalist I often work at weekends, she said to me: 'Unplug your phone and get a good night's sleep.'

They were her final words to me, uttered with the same warmth and consideration with which she wrote to my mother when my father died last December and then sent her tickets for the ballet I had told her my mother loved.

On Saturday evening, Diana was as happy as I have ever known her. For the first time in years, all was well with her world.

Richard Kay, *Daily Mail*

'HER LAUGHTER, HER SENSE OF FUN'

'It's a hunt, Rosa, it's a hunt. Will you really tell people what it is like?' These words were spoken to me by Diana, Princess of Wales, towards the end of our recent Greek holiday together, immediately before her last, fatal trip with Dodi Fayed.

She had talked often to me about the intrusion of the press, about what it was like to be hounded by the paparazzi and to have to fight for every second of her privacy, but this was the first time I had been caught on the other side of the lens with her, and I was horrified. It made no difference that they never found us, because, as far as the Princess was concerned, those who wrote about her did not recognize the boundary between truth and fiction.

I had turned to her in utter disbelief on the third night of our trip after watching the news. We had apparently been on the island of Khios and Oinouses. We had then gone to Mykonos, where we had taken a plane to Naxos. From there, we were due to fly to Turkey.

We had reportedly been using five boats and four helicopters, and had been the guests of the Lemos family. And yes, this must all be true, because we were then shown pictures of the ten press helicopters, and shots of the 250 journalists 'on the spot'.

Then came the announcement of an offer of 280 million drachmas from one newspaper for any photograph of the Princess. It was then that I turned to her and said: 'This is unbelievable, I must write about it!'

We had, in fact, been that day to the island of Hydra, hundreds of miles from where we were reported as being, where a charming man in a shop had sat us down and said: 'Do you realize that the whole country is looking for you?' And it was just as we were strolling back to the boat that a tourist in a café recognized her, leapt out of his chair and took some snaps. Diana was furious. 'That's it,' she said, 'All over the front pages tomorrow.'

'It's only a tourist,' I said. 'We'll be fine.' She looked at me and said: 'Just wait.' And sure enough, there we were the next day, on the front page of the *Sun*.

The lengths to which we went to avoid the paparazzi became more complicated every day. We were on a small motor cruiser, the *Della Grazzia*, with three crew. The captain, Manolis, would ring his friends around Greece to find out where the paparazzi were, and we would move in the opposite direction. We were not found, and Diana said to me that she could not remember five days abroad when she had not been discovered.

She called the boat 'our cottage' because of its size, and as soon as we went on board she disappeared down to her cabin. She reappeared ten minutes later. 'I've nested, Rosa. Have you?'

One of the aspects of the escape these five days afforded was that she could be totally herself or, as she put it to me, she could just 'be Diana'. No make-up, no hair-dying, no clothes except a swimsuit. On our way back to the port of Piraeus, she asked me to let her know when we were two hours away from arrival so that she could 'get ready' and assume her public face again. This involved ironing her own dress, which produced moans of real horror from Vassilis, the deckhand, who would obviously have considered it an honour to undertake this domestic task for her.

I promised her that I would write about 'the hunt', and would do so on our return. I was devastated when speaking to a close friend of hers this week, who had spoken to her last Saturday evening: 'Please get up early and go to Victoria Station to pick up the *Sunday Telegraph*. Rosa's article will be in it, and I want you to read it to me,' she had said. I hadn't done it: and even if I had, it would have been too late for her. The hunt was over. I feel that I let her down, and that is one of the reasons why I am writing this.

What will I remember most about Diana? It has to be her laughter, her sense of fun, her irrepressible giggle. She took her job seriously, but never herself. She saw a complete distinction between her personal life and her public duty. The tragedy is that no one else recognized this crucial divide. She was no saint, and was as frail and vulnerable as the rest of us – in fact, rather more so. She had a huge capacity for unhappiness, which is why she responded so well to the suffering face of humanity. She felt real pain, and understood real unhappiness, and this was in no way alleviated by the glitz and glamour of her public persona.

She was not particularly clever – as she famously pointed out herself – but she had an intuitive genius, and was, for want of a better phrase, a real trier. She had a unique ability to spot the broken-hearted, and she could zero in on them, excluding all hangers-on and spectators.

But this gift took its toll. She would call me on her return from an 'away day' and simply cry, totally drained and exhausted. She was relentless in her ability to give. She had huge courage, and whenever things got too much for her she would say to herself: 'Diana, remember you're a Spencer' (she was far prouder of this than of being royal), and she would then get on with whatever she had to do. She had the manners of a true aristocrat, and instantly made people feel at ease. She wrote thank-you letters more promptly than anyone else I know, and on her birthday one year, when she was alone in Kensington Palace, I rang to see if she wanted to have lunch, to which she replied 'No, I'm sitting here writing my thank-you letters.'

But what of her humour? She was a marvellous mimic. One night in Greece, she tried to get hold of Prince William. She got through to the Balmoral switchboard, and left a message as he was out. She put down the telephone, raised her eyebrows, and said: 'This is what she [the switchboard operator at Balmoral] will be saying now.' And with a glorious Scottish accent, she said: 'Och, there goes the Princess of Wales on yet another sunshine cruise.' She also did a brilliant imitation of her admirer Nelson Mandela, and of Imran Khan telling Jemima to stop giggling.

She tried to get hold of her boys again the next day, but again they were out. 'Out killing things,' she said to me, with a wry smile. But then she went on to say she couldn't understand why she was constantly being portrayed in the press as someone who didn't approve of country pursuits. 'After all,' she said. 'I was brought up in that way. I hunted when I was young. And it is all part of their heritage.'

She talked to me constantly about her sons, about her concern to protect them from their position. Her aim was to make sure they understood what it was to walk in the street as well as to live in the palace. Not to be isolated, and to be able to lead a balanced life in which the two sides, duty and private, coexisted. She told Prince William in particular more than most mothers would have told their children. But she had no choice. She wanted him to hear the truth from her, about her life, and the people she was seeing, and what they meant to her, rather than read a distorted, exaggerated and frequently untrue version in the tabloid press.

Recently she took the boys to the cinema, and they were offered something to drink. Prince Harry asked for water, but when it came it was fizzy, and he had wanted still, so he asked the lady to change it. Diana berated him afterwards. She told him that it didn't matter what it was he had wanted; he should simply have thanked her for what he had been given. She went further. She said it was that sort of behaviour that gave the Royal Family a bad name for being difficult, and that he must learn the lesson now. But of course she was not a stern mother, far from it. She was always hugging her boys, and I remember Prince Harry coming through the door of her study at Kensington Palace, and launching himself like a projectile into her arms. My heart cries out for them now.

Although sometimes erratic and often naïve in her interpretation of events, she always found time for her friends when they needed her. When I lost a baby after six months' pregnancy, she, more than anyone, knew what to say, and what to do. She was both compassionate and practical. These two qualities coexisted in her in a way I have never seen in anyone else. She instinctively found the words to ease the pain, and at the same time knew that I should name my daughter, and bury her. She always remembered her anniversary, and talked about her often. I will never, ever forget her face, her touch, her warmth and compassion on the day that we buried Natalya.

Similarly, when my daughter Domenica was born, and we learnt that she had Down's syndrome, she was at my bedside immediately with emotional support and practical help. She offered herself as her godmother, told me which doctors had experience in this field, and gave me the names of people to contact who had gone through the same thing.

But there were few around to understand how trapped she felt and how much she craved an independence that most of us take for granted. Four years ago we went to Bali on holiday, and she felt completely stifled by the police protection – those were the days when she was still Her Royal Highness.

One day, we went to a private house on a beach, and I sensed an incredible restlessness in her. I took her bodyguard to one side, and suggested that

Diana and I might have a walk alone together on the beach, and that he could sit on the balcony, and not accompany us. Diana and I walked for about two hours, she becoming quite sunburnt, and halfway through she turned to me and said: 'I haven't felt as free as this since I was 19.'

At just 20, she was totally unprepared for life in the royal court. When we were on our Greek 'cottage' she talked about those early days – about her love for her husband, about her total exhaustion after the wedding, the escape of being on *Britannia*, and then returning to the realities of her new position at Balmoral after only two weeks away. How she was suddenly Her Royal Highness, and how people were hanging on her every word – 'only I had none'.

We talked about how she 'learnt to be royal', and how, even then, she understood intuitively the importance of the human element to it all. She was completely unsnobbish and unstuffy, she never stood on ceremony, or hid her warm personality behind her title. She was utterly devoid of arrogance, either natural or acquired.

When we had originally planned our trip to Greece, we booked ourselves on an Olympic Airways flight, but a couple of days before we were due to go she rang me and said that Dodi would like us to use his jet because we would have more chance of escaping the paparazzi. I was ambivalent about this, having earlier strongly advised her not to go on holiday with the Al Fayeds (which was in fact when her romance with Dodi began), but I absolutely understood her desire for privacy. It was exactly the reason we were going away.

'Look at all this, Rosa, isn't it awful?' she giggled, as we sat in the plush pink seats, feet disappearing in the green pile carpet covered in pharaohs' heads. And on our way back, at the end of the holiday, the air hostess brought her a tin of Beluga caviar, which was a present from Dodi. 'You take this, Rosa,' she said. 'Give it to Dominic [my husband].' A pause, another giggle. 'You see, I know I'll be having some at dinner tonight.'

On her recent trip to Bosnia, Dodi had insisted that she use the jet, as he wanted to make sure she was as safe and comfortable as possible. The *Telegraph* journalist Bill Deedes flew out with her, and made some comment about her having influential friends. She looked him in the eye, and said: 'My investment portfolio from the divorce settlement is doing very well, thank you, Lord Deedes.'

And yes, she did talk to me in Greece about her relationship with Dodi , although she had not made any decisions about her future. She was happy, enjoying herself, and liked the feeling of having someone who not only so obviously cared for her, but was not afraid to be seen doing so.

Her conversations with him were full of laughter, and when he left a message on her mobile answering machine, she insisted that I listen to it, just so that I could hear 'his wonderful voice'. But about one thing she was perfectly clear. 'Whatever happens to me in this relationship, I will continue to do my work, and to help where I am needed.' She also said that, in a way, what she did would be more important than ever, because the world that Dodi inhabited was so far removed from reality.

Contrary to popular belief, she was not at all a material girl, and she became truly angry with Dodi when he would ring and recite a list of the presents he had purchased for her. 'That's not what I want, Rosa, it makes me uneasy. I don't want to be bought, I have everything I want, I just want someone to be there for me, to make me feel safe and secure.' She meant, of course, emotionally secure.

She was one of the more insecure people of this world. She achieved a veneer over her natural shyness, but she found walking into a room full of people an ordeal. The main reason she gave up so many charities of which she was patron at the time of her divorce was that she felt she was simply a figurehead, a name guaranteed to raise money. She didn't want any more to put on the evening dress, sit on a seat and wait for the amount the charity had raised to hit her desk in the form of a letter. She wanted to roll up her sleeves and get on with it. 'I want to walk into a room, be it a hospice for the dying or a hospital for sick children, and feel that I am needed. I want to do, not just to be.'

A mutual friend of ours was Father Alexander Sherbrooke. I first met him on the night I lost Natalya, and she had met him with Mother Teresa, with whom he had done much work. He buried my daughter, and then christened my third daughter, Domenica. Diana was by my side, and a constant support, day and night, throughout these intensely difficult and private moments, and so got to know Father Alexander very well.

He came to see me this week, when he described the Princess as 'a messenger of peace'. He had seen her going about her work in Mother Teresa's House for the Dying in Calcutta, and was struck by her ability to handle the suffering, diseased and dying.

He said that he, as a priest, and indeed most people, had to go through a rigorous intellectual process to summon up the courage to deal with the very disabled and afflicted. 'I have to imagine the suffering body of Christ,' he told me. 'But the Princess was completely intuitive, and saw something special in every human being.'

Earlier, I said that Diana was no saint. By this I meant that she could be very naughty. But speaking as a Roman Catholic, I can say that I saw God in her when she went about what she called her 'work'. And the vast majority of this work, principally visiting the sick and dying, was done spontaneously and in secret. Her trip to Bosnia was one of the few where she wanted cameras present, to draw world attention to an issue she cared deeply about.

Diana had told me about the importance of touch: of how just cupping her hands round someone's face gave huge comfort, and transcended all barriers of race and language. She talked a lot about Bosnia, as we chugged along. She needed to digest the horrors she had seen, to make some sense of the ghastly stories she had been told. She cried one night, while we were motoring along for three hours under the full moon, and she told me what she had witnessed.

Diana was not religious in any conventional sense, but she did have a highly developed spiritual side. On Sunday, 17 August, we had docked on the Greek mainland in a small village called Kipazissi, and we went together to the Greek Orthodox Church. While we were there we lit candles for our children, and when we left the church she turned to me and said: 'Oh Rosa, I do so love my boys.'

On her desk in her study at Kensington Palace she had a statue of Christ, which was draped with rosaries given to her by the Pope and Mother Teresa. When I was there recently I saw a note in her own hand on her desk which read: 'You can't comfort the afflicted without afflicting the comfortable.'

Diana had such a conflict of personalities within one character. She was complicated on the one hand and simple and naïve on the other. These two coexisted, sometimes awkwardly, and made her life more difficult than it should have been. Her dark side was that of a wounded, trapped animal, and her bright side was that of a luminous being. She used to bound down the stairs at Kensington Palace, arms outstretched, saying: 'Rosa, how nice to see you,' and her presence would explode and fill the rooms. It was so difficult when I went back there this week.

But as a wounded animal she could be terrifying, and her infamous *Panorama* interview was an example of that. It was born of some basic desire to hurt those who she felt had betrayed her. But she also had the ability to admit her mistakes, and she said to me that she regretted doing the programme. The sad thing is that it was her only television interview, and it was Diana at her worst. If she had found, as she appeared to have with Dodi, some emotional stability, then the luminous side of her character might have prevailed.

She frequently asked me for advice, but rarely took it. She found it difficult to accept criticism, and there was one particular occasion, on her last trip with Prince Charles to Korea, when I berated her for her sulky public behaviour down a crackling telephone line from the other side of the world. I told her she should put her personal life on hold, remember that she was representing her country, and was there as HRH The Princess of Wales, not as Diana. I didn't hear from her for four months. And then, as usually happened, she just picked up the telephone one day: 'Rosa, how are you?' and off we went again.

And on this last trip two weeks ago, we talked about so many things. She wrote to me afterwards – of course the thank-you letter was immediate. 'I loved being with you and sharing so many important moments. True friendships are hugely valuable . . . We've stuck together through hell and back.'

On Wednesday night I went to the chapel and prayed beside her coffin. Her presence was palpable, like a humming force, and my tears came. I relied upon her more than I knew. I cried for her boys, for my Domenica who will never know her dedicated and compassionate godmother, and for the loss of a true friend and companion.

And for so much more. For that magnetic life force which she harnessed so well to do so much for so many. For a power that did not rely on her beauty, but on what came from within, and which she shared freely with so many.

From the chapel I went, with my husband and two friends, to Kensington Gardens, where we walked silently among the ocean of floral tributes. I could almost hear her voice in my ear: 'Rosa, no, not all this! For me?' For she never knew how much she was loved.

My last conversation with her was by mobile telephone on the afternoon of 27 August. 'Just tell me, is it bliss?' I asked. 'Yes, bliss,' she replied. 'Bye-bye.'

When we buried Natalya, I read a poem by Rabindranath Tagore over her grave. I came across it again in an anthology I was reading on the boat, and it made me cry. 'Read it to me, Rosa,' she said, and I did:

They who are near me do not know that you are nearer to me than they are
They who speak to me do not know that my heart is full with your unspoken words
They who crowd in my path do not know that I am walking alone with you
They who love me do not know that their love brings you to my heart

Rosa Monckton, *Sunday Telegraph*

A PRINCESS AMONG THE LANDMINES

They told us that the main road we wanted to take from Tuzla was dangerous. So we made a long detour. That was three weeks ago in Bosnia, where Diana, Princess of Wales, and I were travelling together, talking to those who had been injured or bereaved by mines. The road hazard which ended her life in Paris was of another kind.

To have witnessed the way she brought comfort to these people, many in deep distress, some in tears, is to understand what we have lost, for ever.

It is not all sorrow. She was an engaging person to travel with because she had this penchant for simple jokes. When we stopped for a break, she would sometimes approach, one arm behind her back. 'Would you like a gin and tonic?' She would wait to see my eyes light up at this prospect of the unexpected, then hand over a small bottle of Evian.

We had first discussed this Bosnia trip early this year before she made the expedition to Angola in January. It had been a subject of concern to me from the early 1990s. Travelling in Asia and Africa to write about famine, refugees and other crises, I saw what a deadly enemy mines had become to some of the poorest people on Earth. The Princess of Wales shared that concern. Furthermore, she emphasized to me, her concern about mines and their victims would continue. Angola was not, she insisted, to be seen as a one-off. Where next?

Well, I told her, they will certainly not allow you to go to Cambodia because you might be kidnapped. Nor will they let you go to Afghanistan because the Taliban are shelling Kabul. Her best bet, I suggested, would be Bosnia. So it came about, and on 8 August we took off from London in a private jet and flew into Sarajevo.

If you are going to concern yourself with the consequences of man's inhumanity to man as closely as the Princess of Wales desired to do, Sarajevo is a place to go. On this first day we had no time to stop there, because of engagements in Tuzla, which was a long drive away.

So we drove straight through the city, past its huge cemeteries, up what was called Sniper's Alley, through streets of shattered offices and homes. At one point I murmured to her something about the bridge on which the Archduke had been assassinated in 1914. Otherwise we sat in silence, as she looked around her, taking it in, saying nothing, betraying no emotion.

Part of her gift in bringing comfort to those in anguish lay in this sensitive awareness of when silence is best. She was not a voluble sympathizer, quite the reverse. At some point during an outpouring of grief, she would stretch out a hand or both hands and touch the person on the arm or face.

I found some of the tales we had to hear almost unendurable. Yet I never saw her lose this calm, which plainly had a most soothing effect. As I reported at the time, she saw dreadful wounds, heard horrifying stories while maintaining the demeanour of a professional but sympathetic nurse.

Nor in the course of those three days did I see her concentration flag; and this was remarkable because the distractions were intense. The cameramen and the reporters who met her at every stop had an interest in her encounters with victims of mines, but, unlike the Angolan expedition, it was not their main interest.

She had, as it later transpired, interrupted her holiday to visit Bosnia. Much of the holiday was spent with Dodi Fayed. The pictures were public. Therein lay the main press interest. It was a test of temper, of temperament, of character and of many other things.

She would utter a faint murmur of dismay at the sight of 40 cameramen lined up outside some humble home. Then self-discipline would assert itself. It afforded an opportunity to witness, at uncomfortably close range, the dichotomy of Diana's attitude to photographers.

Defending their profession, some of them claim she was hopelessly inconsistent in her attitude to the camera. She resented their presence, so the argument goes, yet depended upon their work for the standing it gave her and her causes.

Our expedition helped me to reach a conclusion about this. She accepted the value of photographers in her life, and acknowledged the inestimable value they held for her good causes. What she found harder to stomach was the intrusive lengths to which some, in such an intensely competitive game, were ready to go and sought to take her.

She was happy to work with our own photographer, Ian Jones. He made various requests of her, with which she complied professionally. One of them, as we returned through Sarajevo, was to take some pictures of her among the shattered buildings.

They told us to keep off the grass, which might be mined. I found the experience altogether more trying than she appeared to do.

It was the unknown and the unexpected which troubled her. It is hardly a human aberration to resent being spied upon. I had a camera of my own for taking snapshots. She was fairly happy with this, but liked me to tell her when pictures were being taken. If I failed to do this, a finger would wag lightly. 'Now then . . . Lord Deedes . . .' It was one of her little jokes to persist in calling me Lord Deedes all the time. Not to be outdone, I peppered our conversations with 'ma'am's' 'What smart shoes, Lord Deedes!' she exclaimed one morning as we set off. 'Entirely for your benefit, ma'am,' I said, with heavy emphasis on the ma'am.

Because this newspaper wanted copy, I spent a lot of the time sitting beside her scribbling. 'Sorry about this,' I would say from time to time. Her response was generous. It might help, she thought, if I used her light satellite telephone to send stuff back. 'Give me your camera,' she said, 'and I shall take a picture of you, Lord Deedes, on my telephone.' For an amateur photographer, she made a good job of it.

These emotional encounters we had with victims and the bereaved left their mark on her. What often seemed a calm, soothing response to a tale of woe took more of a toll than one at first supposed. She made it hard for herself, insisting that every interview be granted at least 30 minutes. What made it even harder was the depths of bitterness sown by this civil war in former Yugoslavia. 'So many people,' I said to her, 'long to find someone who will listen while they express their inner feelings about all this – and they've found you.' Sad smile. No response.

Instead, she asked me which of the interviews during the day I felt had been the most emotional. We agreed on the answer. It had been a meeting with a young Muslim widow whose husband had been killed by a mine while he was fishing in May. The widow sat on one side of the Princess, the man's mother on the other.

The mother told us how she had been with her son in hospital, 'as he died, smiling'. The widow spoke of their short but happy marriage, and described him simply as a good man, an honest man, concluding: 'And he was only 29 when he died.'

Diana said very little. She caught up both their hands and held them. The mother explained her dream. In this, she told us, her son had returned to her, and explained that he was happy where he was. 'That might well be so,' Diana responded. It seemed at the time a perfect rejoinder. The mother's face was transformed.

There was a similar encounter in one of Sarajevo's largest cemeteries. The Princess of Wales went off alone to walk round it. As she did so, she encountered a mother tending her son's grave. There was no language barrier. The two women gently embraced. Watching this scene from a distance, I sought in my mind who else could have done this. Nobody . . . .

'I am a humanitarian. I always have been and I always will be,' she declared within my hearing during the Angola expedition when they accused her of meddling in politics. In saying that, she wrote her own epitaph, for that, I came to learn, was what she really thought about herself. Yet nobody could write about Diana, as I sometimes had to do, without being made aware of the passions which swirled around her, and will go on swirling.

She had her critics, and even in death she will continue to have them. It does her memory no service to brush that aside. There were, as this newspaper observed in an editorial last week, two Dianas; and sometimes one of them appeared to conflict with the best interests of the other.

All that said, it is surely right to dwell just now on the supreme quality of one who sought above all to help the vulnerable people in society, and who did it so well. She was good at this because she herself was vulnerable. She knew the feeling. She did not set out to be a saint.

This was a human being, with all the faults of most of us, but also with a bigger heart than most of us. As I discovered on that last mission for humanity, there was an underlying humility which, at least to me, redeems it all.

She was not a grand person setting out to bestow favours on the poor. She knew herself too well for that. Recognizing her own frailty, she was the better able to understand and to sympathize with the frailty of others. As I perceived in Bosnia, she saw herself as an equal with those she sought to comfort. That was part of her gift. As she told *Le Monde*: 'To begin with we are on the same level, on the same wavelength.' That is why she could sit in absolute silence, holding a hand, and transmit this feeling of 'we're in this together'.

A friend of long standing, Lady Barbara Bossom, called me yesterday. Her father, the Earl of Guilford, was killed on a mine in this country. 'What a wonderful memorial to Diana it would be,' she said, 'if the world could bring itself to abandon mines.'

Indeed it would, but the world, alas, does not work on those lines. More simply, Diana gave us an example, in this mechanistic world, which we should heed and try never to forget. Her instinct was so right: all those wounded people in Bosnia, crying aloud for someone to hear their tale, to hold their hand, to be able to communicate the uncommunicable.

We should tell our children and our grandchildren about her. We should say to them, the world you are about to enter remains in sore need of her gifts. Remember her.

W.F. Deedes, *Daily Telegraph*

'UNWAVERING PROFESSIONALISM'

The question I am most often asked, and used most often to deflect, is: 'What is the Princess really like?'

As with so many people before and since, the first impressions I gained of the Princess of Wales were of her immediate concern for others, her energy, informality and friendliness. It was in November 1987 on a sunny afternoon in the drawing-room at Kensington Palace and I was there to be interviewed for the post of equerry. She turned what could have been an ordeal into a pleasure and over the next nine years I repeatedly saw – and marvelled at –

her ability to communicate the same warmth and concern to people of every background on her public, private and humanitarian engagements in Britain and around the world.

Her talent of combining glamour with the dignity and responsibilities of royal duties put her in an almost unique category. In recent years, it might be forgotten that for most of her royal life she shouldered a major share of the burden of public duties.

From the grandest state occasion to the most informal (and even secret) charity meeting she applied the same unwavering professionalism. She set the highest standards for herself and expected others to do the same. To work for her was to know that every success, however slight, was noticed and appreciated, just as no oversight, however small, could be hidden from her acute and increasingly experienced eye.

The image presented to the world of beauty, poise and informed interest owed much to her natural ability and instincts. But these were far outweighed by the commitment she showed to memorizing written briefs, researching personalities and a genuine desire to expand her own knowledge on a host of challenging subjects. Her courtesy was of the purest kind – it sprang from her inner conviction that those she was seeking to serve (and there sometimes seemed no limit to their number) deserved nothing but the best. And on the rare occasions when the courtesy slipped the reasons were more often to do with an unfairness suffered by others than by concern for herself. Indeed it was her impatience with what she saw as injustice which gave those of us who worked for her the sense of being part of something uniquely worthwhile. After her office was established independently of the Prince's (a process, incidentally, accomplished without ill-feeling contrary to some reports), the pace became even more intense as if she felt that every single day had to be used to the full.

We worked hard but she had the inspiration of a born leader.

Her attention to detail lay behind much of the great successes of her life. Yet despite a formidable concern for efficiency and punctuality she would not hesitate to break a schedule to give a word of comfort. How often I saw her lighten a solemn occasion with a spontaneous gesture of warmth or concern. A memorable example was during the offical arrival formalities at Budapest airport, at the start of a tour. The President's wife, tearful with emotion on hearing her country's national anthem – played for the first time under a democratic regime – felt her hand taken by that of the Princess as they shared a silent companionship that overcame all language barriers.

Another and perhaps more typical example involved a visit to a children's hospice on a grey winter afternoon in an industrial town gripped by recession. Outside, she had a warm word for everyone who had braved the elements awaiting her arrival (never forgetting those whose shyness or even hostility kept them at the back of the crowd). Inside, she spent some of the last minutes of a dying child's life with grieving parents. There were no cameras.

A facet of her life, all too often overlooked, is her personal courage. Whether smiling on a rainy walkabout in Armagh, confronting (and shaming) hecklers in New York, putting her arm around a disfigured leper in Nepal or outfacing an assailant who lunged at her on a sunny day in England, her composure and quickness of thought never wavered.

Such was the richness and diversity of her life that she leaves everyone – friend, critic or bystander – no shortage of evidence on which to judge her.

But those who knew her may remember with gratitude a figure of genuine stature, who was heightened, not diminshed, by her moments of doubt and unhappiness.

Patrick Jephson, Private Secretary to the Princess, 1988–96, in *The Times*

'I WILL MISS HER SMILE'

The first time I met Diana, she was a winsome little girl full of energy and mischief. I had known her father, Earl Spencer, very well in the Fifties and her mother is virtually the same age as me.

By the time of our second meeting, she was married to Prince Charles. I had invited them both to my home at Ham Common for a mutual friend's birthday party, and Diana had arrived with a beaming smile and a huge bunch of flowers. She was young and clearly a little nervous, but made a concerted effort to talk to everyone. We were all charmed.

That party marked the beginning of my friendship with Diana – albeit a friendship with a difference. At first, we would meet for lunch in London restaurants but, partly because I do not particularly enjoy lunching out, we soon phased these out. With Diana, such encounters were particularly frustrating. Not only did everyone stare at our table, which made conversation virtually impossible, but laughter – already an essential ingredient in our relationship – had to be restrained.

So we changed to an arrangement which suited us both. Once or twice a month, I would lunch with her at Kensington Palace, and then if she was alone or had the boys home for the weekend, she would ring and ask whether she could come down to my home, Ormeley Lodge, for either Saturday or Sunday lunch.

Sunday lunch at Ormeley is usually chaotic. Everyone helps themselves and lunch is eaten so fast that Diana eventually started to time us. 'Right', she would say, 'today was an all-time record – 15 minutes.' Laughter would ring round the table and everyone would speak at once. No ceremony here, and Diana loved it.

She would drive down, usually managing to shake off the press, dash through the back door – often clutching a bunch of spring flowers or a bottle of my favourite bath oils from Jo Malone's shop – greet the staff (who all loved her), try to evade the mass of dogs yapping at her feet and settle down to amuse us. Few people realized just how funny she could be. Fellow lunch guests who were meeting Diana for the first time were often overwhelmed by her naturalness and quick wit. Certainly, her repartee became an essential ingredient of these Sunday lunches. After coffee, she would often offer to take the cups out to the kitchen – and just as often, I would find her there doing the washing-up.

When I took her to Pakistan to raise money for my son-in-law Imran Khan's cancer hospital, we were lent a little jet with seats that unfolded into beds. Diana became so hysterical with laughter at trying to recline her seat that she managed to fall out of it. None of us slept during the trip, which she put down to my non-stop chatter. I put it down to her: she made me laugh until my sides ached. But whereas my niece, Lady Cosima Somerset, and I arrived looking jaded and tired, Diana looked gloriously fresh and ready for the very rigid schedule she faced over the next 48 hours.

I will never forget the tenderness and sweetness she showed towards the cancer patients, particularly the children. While my daughter Jemina and I were wilting in the heat, she kept going from room to room for most of the day, determined that no patient should miss seeing her. She had only been scheduled to be there for four hours.

Afterwards, we went back to our rented house to wash and dress and prepare for the fund-raising banquet. This was an almost impossible task, as both the electricity and the water suddenly cut out. I found myself somewhat disgruntled, having to shower under a small trickle of water, with the aid of a torch. Diana fared somewhat better in her attempts to bathe, with the exception of several interruptions from the houseboy who kept appearing in her room with a copy of the Koran in one hand (a present for her) and a notepad and pen in the other. He wanted her autograph.

Later, with electricity restored, I sat down to have my hair done by a hairdresser who was shaking from the excitement and anticipation of having to do the Princess's hair next. There was, I noticed, a fair amount of banging coming from the upstairs landing. Then it stopped, and Diana called down the stairs: 'I have finished my ironing' (she would not allow anyone else to do it), 'would you like me to do yours?' The hairdresser nearly dropped her dryer.

That was Diana. She was a real trouper; not once did I hear her complain. When not comforting the sick, she was laughing her way through that exhausting visit, which ended at a fund-raising banquet where she signed autograph after autograph.

Back home, Ormeley was undoubtedly a refuge and a haven for her. Here, she could totally relax. There was no protocol, and she was surrounded by people who genuinely liked her. She teased everyone in the family, and we all teased her back as though she were part of us. She had an incredibly wicked sense of humour.

One of my most enduring memories is from her last visit this summer, when she came for lunch with the boys after returning from her trip with the Fayeds. I can still picture her, sitting on the sofa cuddling Harry – she was always cuddling him – and exchanging quips with William. We will miss her so much.

I will miss that fresh little voice on the telephone, always rather humbly asking me if we were busy at the weekend. I will miss her radiant smile as she burst through the door – it was always a burst – and hugged us all, so full of life and happiness at the thought of a few hours' escape from what I know to have been a lonely existence.

She had her faults, like all of us, but they were not part of my relationship with her. I rarely advised her, although maybe I should have done so. Nor did we discuss certain aspects of her private life; I felt I was there for her to have a bit of fun and relaxation and love. I never shopped or went on sunshine holidays with her. There was no need. My home was simply the rock or the haven that she could turn to for escape, where she knew she would never be betrayed.

During my husband's illness and subsequent death, Diana showed her usual concern and compassion towards the children and myself. She was always the first to ring us, to check we were all right. After Jimmy's death, she wrote three beautiful letters – to Jemima, myself and my youngest son Benjamin, who is at Eton with William.

God bless her and let her rest in peace at last.

Annabel Goldsmith, *Daily Telegraph*

'AN INCANDESCENT FLAME IN MY HEART'

In August 1993 my mother took her own life at the age of 52. In her final months, my mother was more beautiful than she had ever been and, like Diana, her beauty could never age. When Diana metamorphosed from a pretty but unformed young women into a luminous beauty I recognized my mother in her eyes and in her smile.

I became friends with Diana in January 1996. My husband, John Somerset, and I had separated that month and this particular Saturday I had left my children – Lyle aged five and Romy aged three – at their father's family home of Badminton in Gloucestershire for the first time. As I drove up the M4 to see Annabel Goldsmith, my aunt, I sobbed as if I would never stop.

I arrived at Ormeley Lodge, Richmond, to find Annabel's arms open as always to embrace me like her own daughter. Diana was also there. The three of us were alone for lunch, which was rare at that time, Annabel's home being open house on a Sunday. We sat down, Annabel on my left and Diana opposite me. I started to cry again.

As I looked across at Diana I saw for the first time in someone else's eyes true empathy. The parallel of our experience was exact. As I cried I told her that I felt as if the umbilical cord between myself and my children had been cut again and the pain was excruciating. I was beginning to mourn the loss of what had for decades been a great part of my life. I had formed a deep bond with Badminton and everybody who belonged there. Badminton had healed the pain of losing Wynyard, my father's estate near Durham, where I spent my childhood.

At Badminton, through my children, I had relived my own childhood. We shared the privilege of being surrounded by beauty and the space and freedom to create a secret world. In Diana's eyes I saw that I was understood. All she said was 'Cosi, you will get used to it.' At a moment of great pain in my life I fell in love with this girl.

The following month Diana was accompanying Annabel to Lahore to visit Imran Khan's cancer hospital. Annabel's daughter, Jemima, had recently moved to Lahore with Imran and so the three of us – Annabel, Diana and me – decided to travel together.

From the moment we boarded the plane we started laughing. We had planned our beauty sleep but realized that we were not going to sleep a wink. The pull-out beds were inadequately designed and mine was worst of all. Both Diana and Annabel tried out my bed and then we started giggling uncontrollably. It was like a dormitory farce.

We arrived early at Lahore and, in desperation, Diana asked the pilot if he could go into a holding pattern. She disappeared into one of the bathrooms, emerging 15 minutes later looking breathtaking. Suffice to say I didn't.

We spent 48 hours in Lahore during which I saw for the first time her extraordinary gift. The gift was to spread joy and to heal pain. I believe that she was able to heal people, emotionally and perhaps physically.

On the journey home we were much more pensive. Although we laughed a lot, we were both very conscious that our cocoon was about to be broken by reality. When we reached London we all shared a car, dropping Annabel off first, then Diana at Kensington Palace and finally me back home in Wandsworth. I felt immediately bereft and Diana told me the next morning on the telephone that she felt the same. What we had experienced was real intimacy and companionship, and from that moment I felt that she was my sister and that we had both been adopted into Annabel's ever-growing family.

The next day was very difficult for me. I missed Diana and I felt very alone. My doorbell rang around lunchtime and a driver handed me a huge box. I opened the parcel to find a beautiful candle set in a clay pot.

With it was a letter from Diana which said: 'I hope this candle lights some of your darkest moments.' I cried. This was the first time that she comforted me in this almost telepathic way. The candle became a symbol of hope and I would light it every evening for six months.

From then on we spoke every day on the phone and met usually once a week, for lunch at her home. I found our lunches almost like a mutual therapy session, full of silences and outpourings. We shared the experience of being separated from our husbands and uncertain about what the future held. We had both broken away from large, powerful families and therefore we had lost our protection. Both of us were considered 'hysterical, unbalanced, paranoid, foolish'. We were cast out but now we at least had each other.

Our mutual interests included the spiritual and the psychic. Diana did not believe conventionally in God but she and I both sought an explanation for life's endless chaos, pain and drama. The point of seeing psychics is that one has a sense that life is predestined.

Last year was a rough year for me and in May I suddenly felt that I wanted to get away and find some sun. Without my children, my weekends had changed from the busiest time to the quietest and time was hard to fill.

I called Diana and said would she come with me to La Residencia in Majorca and she said she could not think of anything nicer. We left on a Friday. As we arrived in Majorca a storm broke and we drove through torrential rain to the hotel. It rained endlessly until we left on Sunday morning. Diana and I shared a suite in the hotel, where we remained closeted because of the rain.

We talked about everything, from our childhoods, to our marriages, to our children. I thought Diana was a remarkable mother. She showed me by example that it was possible to break the imposed cycle of a family's emotional character.

If she could do it, then perhaps I could. There were also a lot of girlie conversations. Although Diana was so beautiful, she was quick to notice other women. She would say: 'Look at that girl, isn't she pretty?' She was always giving compliments and they were thoughtful and well-observed. She wouldn't just say: 'You look beautiful today.' She would say: 'God, that shirt looks beautiful, it really matches your eyes.' She noticed everything.

We made use of every hotel facility that weekend. We would bump into each other coming out of more and more outlandish treatments, seaweed on our eyebrows or covered in the debris of a clay bath and say: 'Oh, but you must have the . . .'

In fact, we grew confused about which treatments we had had. At Sunday lunch we became, once again, helpless with laughter. The guests were quite elderly and it was very quiet in the dining-room. But one of the staff had put *'Je t'aime'* on the music system and it was relayed into the dining-room with all the moans and groans at full volume. It seemed louder and more comic because of the genteel quietness. We also seemed to be the only two who noticed it.

After lunch we roped our new friend Helmut, the hotel manager, into driving us to the airport. As we left the gates of La Residencia we were pursued by paparazzi, a few of whom were on motorbikes.

Helmut assumed a James Bond-like attitude and negotiated the mountain roads with the convoy in close pursuit. When we hit a dual carriageway a motorbike drew alongside the car. The man on the pillion had a camera which he pointed right up against the car window. I felt as if Diana had almost been assaulted, but she remained ice cool. Her coolness was shocking to me, for I had been sure that the car would crash. If we had had a less skilful driver than Helmut, it could well have done.

As always, the next day a letter from Diana was delivered to my home. In it she thanked me for choosing to spend a girlie weekend with her. She also thanked me for putting up with the hassles that went with travelling with her.

I have a very poignant memory of Diana on the day that her divorce came through officially in August 1996. We met at Ormeley for lunch. It was a Saturday, and as I walked up to the swimming pool to find her and Annabel, she came towards me, crying. I put my arms around her and held her. We did not say anything.

The letter I got on the following Monday was very moving. It said: 'Thank you for being there over this most difficult weekend. You are the only person in the world who understands . . .'

One weekend that same summer, she came and spent the afternoon sunbathing in my garden in Wandsworth. When she came to my house, I was impressed again by how easy it was to be with her. How comfortable our silences were.

There was one particular evening which stands out in my memory. It was in the winter of 1996 and my friend Taki gave a dinner party for myself and Diana, I went to KP and then she drove me on to Taki's house. We were both in very high spirits. As we drove there, I felt a sense of two women who had finally broken free of other people's rules.

The dinner party was great fun and after dinner Taki had invited a group of people to join us. The room was very full. Diana and I went downstairs to put on make-up and to chat. She was just a girl at a dinner party. This must have been so rare for her, although it was common for me. When we went back upstairs we sat on the floor cross-legged. We held hands while we talked to other people. It was a gesture of solidarity.

After that dinner she drove me to a wine bar where I was meeting my brother. I said come with me and she did. But she left five minutes later. I felt guilty, aware that I had not fully realized the parameters of her existence. Her life could never be like mine. I was freer.

My love for Diana came from my gratitude for the gift she gave me. She walked with me down an otherwise desperately lonely path. In all the darkest moments somehow she sensed my need for comfort without my having to ask. And the power of that will never leave me. What she will always be for me, as for millions of others, is an incandescent flame in my heart.

Knowing Diana has changed my life and continues to do so. She offered me a generous and unconditional friendship. Many children from broken homes, as Diana and I were, never get over the sense of rejection. The abandonment sets the tone for the whole of one's emotional life. It affects one's judgement of people and even compels one to repeat mistakes. Diana showed me that you had a choice. You could stop the wheel. I marvel at the beauty of Diana in her final years. She was so strong and sensual. She showed everyone, and especially women, that freedom has its rewards. Tragically, she also paid its final price.

Cosima Somerset, *Daily Telegraph*

'She Wanted above all to Help Those who Had No Voice and Were Helpless'

I first met Princess Diana shortly after her wedding. Knowing that she would inevitably have to undertake an increasing number of public engagements, Prince Charles wrote to ask if I would coach his bride on public speaking. I, of course, agreed to do so most willingly.

In the beginning she was clearly nervous and my first task was to encourage a measure of self-confidence. She struck me as being genuinely shy but, despite this reticence, my overwhelming impression was of an enchanting, somewhat wicked sense of humour, most often applied to herself.

Through those meetings we became lasting friends and soon I began to find myself on the receiving end of her humour. This was usually manifested in the form of a peremptory note about some public utterance I had made in which she would sternly and precisely echo some of my own injunctions on the subject of public speaking. Her critical remarks were not, however, limited to my speeches. Once, over lunch, she took exception to my pink and green Garrick Club tie.

'How you can continue to wear that ghastly thing, I really don't know. I'll send you something decent.'

And, of course, she did. But then she always did what she said she'd do. I asked her to become President of the Royal Academy of Dramatic Art. Unhesitatingly, she accepted, on condition that the Queen who was Patron, approved. She visited the academy several times, always laughing when she saw that I was wearing 'her' tie.

'I'm not a royalist. She doesn't mean anything to me,' one of the students might say beforehand. But, without exception, by the end of the day they would have joined her never-ending army of admirers. There were, you see, no barriers as far as she was concerned. She had this remarkable and, in my experience, unique ability to put you at your ease, making you feel, at that particular moment, that you were the one person in the world to whom she wished to talk.

Contrary to common perception, Diana was truly intelligent herself, certainly not academic but somehow profoundly intuitive, with an ability to master any brief on any subject with impressive skill.

I completed my film *In Love and War* last year and, since the story focused on the Red Cross, I asked if the organization would care to benefit from a charity premiere with the Princess of Wales as guest of honour. As Diana was already having discussions with Mike Whitlam, director-general of the British Red Cross, about the possibility of renewing her official involvement, it was agreed that I should make the approach. She immediately said that she would be happy to attend the premiere and suggested we meet to discuss the matter further.

I had helped to launch the first stage of the anti-landmine campaign some time previously and, as soon as we began to talk, it was evident that the idea of generating funds to aid the victims appealed to her enormously. This culminated in her visit to Angola under the auspices of the Red Cross, accompanied by a BBC Television crew.

Before she went, she was concerned that she might be venturing into an area of activity which might be wrongly construed as political and we debated the pros and cons very carefully. But of one thing she was certain: the obscenity of landmines should be brought to public attention. For my part, I felt that whatever the political risks, the cause more than justified a decision to go.

On her return, one somewhat condescending and pompous previous government minister described the Princess as a 'loose cannon'. We showed an excerpt from her Angola documentary at the film premiere and, in thanking Diana for her attendance, I added – not without a touch of anger – that, 'for a loose cannon, she seemed to me to have recorded a hell of a bull's-eye'.

Once again, she had judged the public mood perfectly. The whole campaign really took off. Governments around the world, led by Robin Cook's announcement that the United Kingdom will sign an agreement to ban landmines, are even now discussing such a proposal in Oslo with the idea that it might be known as the Princess Diana Treaty.

Her kindness and goodwill were, of course, by no means exhibited only in the limelight. At the recent premiere, my seven-year-old granddaughter was to present her with a bouquet. Having endlessly rehearsed her curtsy, Lucy suddenly had to cope with a souvenir programme which was thrust into her other hand at the last moment.

Although she managed to hand over both bouquet and programme, her bob was completely forgotten. When I told Diana that Lucy was mortified, she immediately turned back from the threshold of the auditorium and asked to be shown the curtsy. 'I've never seen a more perfect one,' she said. Result, one small child devoted to her for life.

Over the years, we had innumerable private and intimate conversations, touching on many diverse subjects. But, one way or another, we always seemed to come round to the same overriding concern: her sons.

She longed to give them the most normal life possible while, at the same time, ensuring that Prince William was fully prepared, ultimately, to accede to the throne.

She believed passionately that many of the old conventions had to be blown away, that her children should be allowed to witness the life led by millions of United Kingdom citizens. She did not want them to be ring-fenced by protective seclusion or red carpets. She felt the boys needed to see at first hand the deprivation, the pain and the cruelty of contemporary life. She certainly never shied away from it herself.

A few months ago, I asked her if she would come to Leicester University to open a specially designed centre for disability and the arts.

She arrived by helicopter to be greeted by crowds who had waited several hours just to catch a glimpse of her. I – as always wearing 'her' tie – introduced the appropriate dignitaries. Then, accompanied by Eleanor Hartley, the director of the centre, she began her tour.

My most poignant memory of that event is the 25 minutes she spent with a group of severely disabled young people, many with cerebal palsy and in wheelchairs, who involved her in their dance display. There were no cameras, no onlookers – just Eleanor, the dancers, their helpers and me. This I shall never forget, and neither, of course, will the dancers.

She left Leicester by helicopter, as she had arrived. On the very same day, by the time my wife and I had returned to London by car, a handwritten letter from Diana awaited us. She wanted to say how much the event had meant to her. Her courtesies were impeccable.

And now she is gone. It is impossible to estimate how many lives have been illuminated by her extraordinary personality. Judging by the numbers who have placed flowers in her memory or queued throughout the day or night to register their written condolences, she has, in her all too brief life, had an impact greater than any of us can ever recall.

During my own long life, I have been privileged to meet many exceptional humanitarians. None, however, has impressed me more profoundly than the young Princess Diana, whose tragic and untimely death has left the whole world bereft.

She was indeed the People's Princess, one who never allowed wealth or position to dull the intense compassion she felt for those whom society had abandoned or cast out. Although she herself was beautiful and fashionable, the causes closest to her heart were neither. She wanted above all to help those who had no voice and were helpless.

Her fame, which proved such a relentless burden, she put to the service of the wounded, the terminally ill and the dispossessed. In remembering her, we must continue to remember, sustain and care for them in her name. She could have no more fitting memorial.

Richard Attenborough, The Times

'No'

No, there was not much I knew about her. But I knew it well. At one period, starting either just before or just after her official separation (I can't remember, and although a glance at the dates of her letters to me would tell me, I can't bear to look at them) and ending well before her death, I lunched with her often enough to goad the lurking press into some arch speculation about whether I was helping to mastermind her PR campaign, especially on television, my area of expertise. Rather to my secret disappointment, it was taken for granted that there was no romance. (My wife, well aware that she is married to a romantic egomaniac, found that aspect particularly amusing.) When the mid-market tabloids ran a page of photographs featuring the men supposedly in Diana's life, my photograph was always among the venerable, sometimes senescent, advisers, never among the young, handsome, and virile suitors. The assumption was that although she might listen to what her privy counsellors said, she would never look at any of them twice. In my case, that assumption, unlike the one about my role as the éminence grise behind her television adventures, was dead right.

No, there was nothing between me and her beyond a fleeting friendship. Many other men knew her better. Some men knew her intimately, and now, at last, I do not envy them, because what they have in their memories must make loss feel like death. (I never thought I could be sorry for James Hewitt, but think of where he is now, deprived even of the reason for his ruin, his empty head already rotting on Traitor's Gate.) As for the man who knew her most intimately of all, the Prince of Wales, he is a man as good and honest as any I have ever met, and I know him well enough to be sure that since last Sunday he has been on the Cross, and wondering whether he will ever be able to come down. My own knowledge of her is minute compared with his and theirs, but now, for the first time, I wish I had never met her at all. Then I might not have loved her, and would not feel like this, or at any rate, would feel it less. But I did meet her, and I did love her.

No, it was not a blind love: quite the opposite. Even before I met her, I had already guessed that she was a handful. After I met her, there was no doubt about it. Clearly on a hair trigger, she was unstable at best, and when the squeeze was on she was a fruitcake on the rampage. But even while reaching this conclusion I was already smitten, and from then on everything I found out about her at first hand, even – especially – her failings and her follies, only made me love her more, because there were none of them that had not once been mine, and some of them still were. In her vivid interior drama I saw my own. I didn't find out much, but what I did find out I found out from close up, from a few feet across a little table; and I knew it certainly, and it made me love her more truly. I was even convinced (this was not for certain, but it was a deep and ineradicable suspicion) that she would get herself killed, and that conviction made me love her to distraction, as if I had become a small part of some majestic tragic poem: an obscure, besotted walk-on mesmerized by the trajectory of a burning angel. I feared for her as I loved her, and the fear intensified the love. It was too much love for so tenuous a liaison, and one of the reasons I never spoke of it in public was a cheaper fear – the simple, adolescent fear of appearing ridiculous.

No, you don't have to tell me. I am appearing ridiculous now, but it is part of the ceremony, is it not? And what flowers have I to send her except my memories? They are less than a wreath, not much more than a nosegay: just a *deuil blanc* table napkin wrapping a few blooms of frangipani, the blossom of broken bread. Last week London went quiet; the loudest human sound was the murmur of self-communion; and we are told that the same was true for half the world. In the old times, when the plague came, people would cast off their sense of self, say what was on their minds, find what had always been in their minds but had remained unsaid even to themselves, and make love to strangers. There will be no *Totentanz* this time, no orgies, no mass kicking over of the traces. But there was something of the same liberation from the very British drive to protect the self, and I will be surprised if some of the new openness does not remain. The lake of flowers submerging Kensington Palace has released a perfume that has changed the air. And although those who did not participate in the vigil might sit in judgement on us for our mass delusion, we will judge them, in our turn, for their inhuman detachment.

No, nobody could escape her image in those first long days after her death – it was as if the planet were being colonized with her replicated smile – and each time I saw it, it brought back a reality that was even lovelier. I first saw Diana – the living human being, not the image – at the Cannes Film Festival. Sir Alex Guinness was getting a lifetime-achievement award, I was to be the master of ceremonies at the dinner, and Charles and Diana had come down from London just for the evening. There was a reception beforehand. The whole British film world stood around nursing drinks. It was like watching a movie composed of nothing except cameo appearances. A bit of some TV crew's lighting rig fell on a PR girl's head and she regained consciousness in the arms of Roger Moore: she thought she was in a James Bond movie. Then Charles and Diana came in and started working the room. With astonishment, I suddenly found myself on the roster of familiar faces Diana wanted to meet. There she was, right in front of me, and I instantly realized that no kind of film, whether still or moving, had done her justice. She wasn't just beautiful. She was like the sun coming up: coming up giggling. She was giggling as if she had just remembered something funny. 'I think it's terrible what you do to those Japanese people. You are *terrible*.' She was referring to the clips from Japanese game shows which I screened on the TV programme that I hosted each week. I started to protest that they were doing that crazy stuff to each other; it wasn't me doing it to them. But she quickly made it clear that she was only pretending to be shocked. She said she never missed my show and always had it taped if she was out. While I was still feeling as if, all at once, I had been awarded the Booker Prize for fiction, the Nobel Prize in Physics, and the Academy Award for Best Actor, she switched the topic. 'Ooh. There's that odious man Maxwell over there. Don't want to meet *him* again. Yuck.'

No, she really meant it. She made a face as if she had just sucked a lemon. And that did it. I was enslaved. Looming hugely at the far side of the stellar throng, the publishing tycooon Robert Maxwell was doing his usual simultaneous impersonation of Victor Mature and King Farouk: a ton and a half of half-cured ham wrapped in a white tuxedo, his pan-scrubber eyebrows dripping condescension like spoiled lard. At the time, the old crook hadn't yet been rumbled. Some of the cleverest men in Britain were still working for him and helping to vilify anyone who questioned his credentials. But this young lady, with a head allegedly composed almost exclusively of air, had the bastard's number. On the other hand, after knowing me not much more than a minute she had just handed me a story that would have embarrassed the bejesus out of the Royal Family if I had passed it on: it would take only one phone call, and next morning the front page of every British tabloid except Maxwell's *Mirror* would consist almost entirely of the word 'Yuck'. Either she was brave to the point of insanity or else I radiated trustworthiness. I decided it must be the latter. For the air of complicity she had generated between us, in so brief a time, the best word that I can think of is 'cahoots'. We were in cahoots.

No, it couldn't last. With the two-minute mark coming up, she started regretfully signalling that our lifelong friendship would have to be temporarily put on hold. Her pursed lips indicated that although she would rather stay talking to me until Hell froze over, unfortunately her duties called her away to schmooze with far less illustrious people than me. Her mouth saying that she was looking forward to my speech, her eyes saying, 'Plant you now and dig you later,' she fluttered a few fingertips and swanned off in the direction of Sir Alec. What would she say to him? *Help me, Obi-Wan Kenobi. You're my only hope.* I wish I hadn't just thought of that.

No, I didn't see her again for a long time. But I thought of her often, and especially when I saw Charles. In those days, I was one of the outer ring of his advisers. The system worked – probably still works – like this: The inner ring of advisers are on call full time for anything. In the outer ring, you get called to the centre when the upcoming job touches on your areas of competence: in my case, television, Australia, and occasionally the arts. Flattered to get the nod, I gladly made trips to see him. Born to a life in which people magically appeared when needed, he sometimes had trouble remembering that his 15 minutes with you at Highgrove or Sandringham would cost you a whole working day, but apart from that he was impeccably sensitive, courteous, and just plain thoughtful – a quality of his which is continually underestimated, and one which will make him a great king when his turn comes, as come it must. (Diana's declaration, in her *Panorama* interview, that Charles might never reign was the single biggest mistake she ever made, but haven't *you* said foolish things about the person you loved after it all went wrong?) Our meetings, though invariably friendly and increasingly funny, were always strictly business, so it was no surprise that Diana wasn't around. But when my wife and I asked him to dinner he came alone, his wife was never mentioned, and sadly I began to realize that that was no surprise either. The word was out that they were sticking together for the sake of the monarchy and the children but were otherwise going their separate ways.

No, it couldn't go on like that. I still think it should have, and right up to the divorce I published articles in *The Spectator* saying that they owed it to all of us to stick together somehow, or else the press would be confirmed in its hideous new role as a sort of latter-day Church of England with witch-finders for priests. But I was making the fundamental mistake of being more royalist than the King. The two people at the centre of events were pursuing happiness, American style, and it was becoming more obvious all the time that they had known enough unhappiness to justify the pursuit. During Charles's fortieth birthday party, at Buckingham Palace, I met her again. There were no cahoots this time. She said that she had enjoyed my latest documentary and that she was glad to see me, but she didn't seem to be glad about anything else: the lights in her face were dimmed down to about three-quarter strength, so she looked merely lovely, at a time when her full incandescence should have been outshining the chandeliers. Charles did his formidable best to jolly everyone along. The Duchess of York chortled around in her usual irrepressible manner, a bumper car in taffeta. It was fun to go for a piss, stand in a reverse line-up of hunched dinner jackets, and gradually discover that I was the only man staring at the porcelain who was not a crowned head of Europe. But generally there was something missing, and nobody could be in any doubt what it was. She was still there physically, but her soul had gone AWOL; and without that soul the party had no life.

No life, and no future. Soon the press was piling it on, and steadily the intrusiveness got worse. It became known that she was trying to lessen the effects by getting a few media figures on her side. It was manipulation, but what else does a marionette dream of except pulling strings? So I thought I knew what it was about when she sent me an invitation to lunch at Kensington Palace. I thought there would be at least half a dozen of us there to receive the gentle suggestion that a few supportive words would not come amiss. (Even for my generation, words like 'supportive' are losing their inverted commas by now: her unashamed use of me-speak has influenced the language.) But after I was shown up the staircase to the sitting-room I found myself alone. When she came into the room, it was as if that first conversation in Cannes had been frozen by the pause button and now the button had been touched again to re-start the tape. 'Sorry there aren't any film stars,' she said. 'There's just me. Hope you don't get bored.' The cahoots were back. We sat down at a small table in the next room and immediately established the protocol that would become standard, and which I will always cherish as one of the best running gags I was ever involved in. She ate like a bird while encouraging me to eat like a wolf, as if I weren't being fed properly at home. There was a catch under the joke: that I *had* a home, she made it clear, was enviable. She envied me my long marriage. When I told her that I had been a bad husband and a neglectful father, and that my guilt had begun to erode my peace of mind, she said that I must have done *something* right, if we were all still together, so I should take comfort from that. Her own marriage, she said, was coming apart. She told me why and how. I could hardly credit my ears. Armed with nothing else except what she told me then, I could have gone to a telephone and blown the whole thing sky high. But the cahoots ruled that out. The tacit bargain was: You tell me what you can't tell anyone else and I'll tell you what I can't tell anyone else, and then neither of us can tell anyone else about what we said.

No, it wasn't mutual therapy. But I suppose it was a mind game. There must have been dozens of other people that she played it with, but she infallibly picked those who would never break the deal. (If she had chosen her lovers on the same principle, she would have given a lot fewer hostages to fortune, but desire doesn't work like that.) She would make each of her platonic cavaliers believe, or at any rate want to believe, that he was the only one. The joker in her real life doubled as the ace of diamonds in the game: it was her childhood. Everything in her tormented psyche turned on what had happened to her at the age of six, when her parents separated and left her to a loneliness that nothing could cure. Then, while I was cleaning her plate after I had cleared mine, she popped the question: 'Something like that happened to you, didn't it?' It was the Princess of Wales who was asking me, so I gave her the answer. Yes, it did. When I was six, my mother got the news that my father had been killed on the way home from the war.

No, my mother cried. No, no, oh no. I was the witness of her distress, I couldn't help her, and I had been helpless ever since. I sometimes thought, I said, that everything I had ever written, built, or achieved had been in order to offset that corrosive guilt, and that I loved the world of women because I feared the world of men. Diana touched my wrist, and that was it: we were both six years old.

No, it was no trick. It might have been a mind game, but her mind was her most vivid reality, the battlefield on which she looked for peace. It was a good mind, incidentally. Of all the poisonous dreck ever written about Diana in the newspapers, the most despicable was based on the assumption that she was stupid. Journalists who read three books a year and had scarcely two ideas to rub together about anything called her an ignoramus. The truth was the opposite. Schopenhauer ('Chopin who?' I can hear her say), who was a great reader himself, pointed out the danger of letting books get between us and experience. What Diana knew was based on experience, and she knew a lot, especially about the mind. Well aware that her own was damaged, she sought comfort from those who would admit to the same condition. She spent too much time with gurus, spiritualists, and exotic healers, but that wasn't frivolity: it was desperation. For the rest of the time, which was most of it, she had a remarkable capacity to do exactly the opposite of what she was notorious for: far from being obsessed with her own injuries, she would forget herself in the injuries of others. It was the secret of her appeal to the sick and the wounded. When she walked into a hospital ward, everyone in it recognized her as one of them, because she treated them as if they could have been her. They *were* her. She was just their souls, free for a day, in a beautiful body that walked so straight and breathed so easily. The sick, she would often say, were more real to her than the well: their guard was down, they were themselves.

No, I didn't figure all that out straight away, but as time went on it became more apparent to me that I was her patient. I missed her after that first lunch, with a mild version of the forlorn longing I have seen among friends of mine when their shrinks go on holiday. So I did something so presumptuous I still don't believe I had the brass neck to go through with it. *I asked her to lunch.* The separation was practically official by now, she was kind of up for grabs, so why not, you know, *ask her to lunch?* I made the phone call to her secretary and hung up feeling like someone who was going to get a flea in his ear the size of a hummingbird. But ten minutes later the secretary was back on the line. The Princess of Wales would be delighted. How about the Caprice?

No, I didn't get there half an hour early – only twenty minutes. I took up my elaborately casual position at the corner table, double-cleaned my fingernails with my door key, and watched the forecourt through the window. As always, she was on time to the minute. When she stepped from the chauffeur-driven car, it wasn't just the way she looked that stymied me. *No escort.* She had been threatening for a while to start going out without an escort, and now she was actually doing it, the crazy little twit. The chill of fear I felt was probably useful in making me appear cool as I rose for an air kiss that stopped every knife and fork in the room, as if time had been switched off. The rattle of cutlery started again after she sat down, and there we were, tête-à-tête. It wasn't cahoots yet, though. By this time, two camps had formed, Charles's and Diana's. Diana's people were busy calling Charles a stuffed shirt, and Charles's people were just as busy calling Diana a dingbat. I wanted to make it clear to her that I was for both of them, and against anything that would make them irreconcilable. I couldn't, either in public or in private, say a word against the Prince. Putting it in jokey form – always her preferred way of hearing a lecturette – I told her that if we were caught talking high treason she would be given the privilege of dying by the sword, whereas I, a commoner and a colonial, would be lucky if they even bothered to sharpen the axe. She laughed, said she understood completely, and made it evident that she admired Charles's qualities as much as I did. Things bubbled along nicely. Cahoots again. I got both our meals to eat as usual, and from the next table the director-general of the BBC was looking at me as if I were a combination of Errol Flynn and Neil Armstrong. He was stuck with the Home Secretary. Christ, what fun she was. But the chill of fear came back when she started to talk about the possibility of going on television with a personal interview. I knew it wouldn't be with me, but that wasn't the reason I counselled her against it. I said if that happened the two-camps thing would go nuclear, and continue until there was nothing left. She would be on the run forever, and there would be nowhere to go. Nowhere would be far enough away. She seemed convinced, but of course she was pretending. She had already decided.

No, she wasn't always the straight goods. She often pretended. She would listen to advice and warnings that – as you would later discover – had been rendered obsolete by what she had already done, and pretend to consider them. Then, when the news came out, you found that she had been watching you lead yourself up the garden path. It could hurt.

No, I don't think she was being malicious, or even mischievous. There was just a lot of stuff she couldn't share. At least once, however, she lied to me outright. 'I really had nothing to do with that Andrew Morton book,' she said. 'But after my friends talked to him I had to stand by them.' She looked me straight in the eye when she said this, so I could see how plausible she could be when she was telling a whopper. I would have been terminally cheesed off if I hadn't suspected that she knew I knew, and just didn't want to be remembered as admitting it. In the *Panorama* interview, she did admit it, so I had two reasons for feeling that historic programme as a personal wound, quite apart from my premonition that it would wound her. It multiplied her popularity, but it propelled her in the direction I had spent a lot of time telling her she should never think of going in: over the wall, out of the country, away from her protection.

No, there was no chance she would listen. She *hated* the protection. She saw the protectors as assailants. She believed, against all the evidence of her own beautiful eyes, that there was some kind of enchanted place called Abroad, where she would be understood and where she could lead a more normal life. This place called Abroad became a recurring theme in future conversations at other restaurants. Kensington Place, in Kensington Church Street near Notting Hill Gate, was one of her favourite hangouts, and she thought it funny that I always booked a table against the back wall, instead of up front, near the window. There was an acre of unshielded glass and she – *she* – wanted to sit near it. It scared me rigid. Sometimes I could barely eat my own lunch, let alone hers. But it seemed she would rather have gone down in a hail of broken glass than live in fear. She could live in her own fear – the fear of never finding happiness, of never making the pieces fit, of

Mummy and Daddy never being together again – but could never live in mine, the fear for her life.

No, she never took my advice even once. Well, just once. Before she went to Japan on her big solo diplomatic trip, she asked me what would be the best thing she could do there, apart from all the hospitals and stuff. She knew that I was a student of the Japanese language and Japanese literature, and she thought I might have some nifty scheme up my sleeve. I told her I did, but it wouldn't be easy. I told her that if she learned even a few words of the language – just the standard phrases about how pleased she was to be there – she would knock them out. I could lend her my teacher, a gentle but determined little woman called Shinko. Diana, after her standard protestations about being too thick, said she was up to it. Shinko, quietly experiencing the same emotions as I would have done if I had been asked to teach the Emperor of Japan croquet, marched up to Kensington Palace and did the job. Diana flew to Japan, addressed a hundred and twenty-five million people in their own language, and made the most stunning impact there since Hirohito told them that the war was over.

No, she didn't forget. When she got back, she called me to lunch at Bibendum. We did all our standard numbers, culminating in the hallowed dessert routine, by which I ordered one crème brûlée with two spoons and finished the rest of it before she had swallowed her single mouthful. As usual, she had finessed that deadly third glass of wine into me without my even noticing. But there was an extra petit four with the coffee. It was a little red box that opened to reveal a pair of cufflinks: gold ovals enamelled in pink with the chrysanthemum of the Japanese imperial family. '*Domo arigato gozaimash'ta*,' she said. Thank you very much for what you did. 'Did I get that right?' Yes, I told her: you got that right.

No, there is not much more. Our last lunch was at Kensington Palace and Harry was present with one of his friends, so there were no cahoots. She was putting distance between us. Later on, quietly and nicely, I was dropped from her list. I understood completely. I had wanted her to be Queen. I had wanted, when I grew old, to see her in the gradually, properly altering beauty of her middle age. I had wanted to see her beside Charles on the day when he took his proper place as the most intelligent and concerned monarch this country has ever had. I had wanted to have lunch with her once a year and do the dessert routine again. But she wanted life. She was going on to those other, faraway adventures which she knew I didn't believe in. I hoped I would hear about them someday.

No, I never saw her again. Neither will anyone now. Not even once. Never even once again.

No, I can still see her. She's leaving the Caprice, heading for the back door, because a Range Rover full of photographers has just pulled up in the street outside. She's turning her head. She's smiling. Has she forgotten something? Is she coming back?

No.

Clive James, New Yorker

'A Reservoir of Resilience and Determination'

Before long, Princess Diana will enter into legend. Millions of words will be written about her, but the woman I knew was much more than a fashion plate, an icon or even a princess.

She was a person who, like so many of us, worked to raise her children, shape her identity and use her own special gifts to make a difference in the world.

Since her tragic death last weekend, I've been thinking about what she meant to me and to all of us.

I first met Diana at official ceremonies commemorating the 50th anniversary of D-Day in June 1994. Shortly afterwards, she told a mutual friend that she wanted to talk with me.

I was eager to get to know the woman behind the dazzling smile. But, given our busy schedules, it took months to arrange a meeting. We finally got together in October for a luncheon in her honour at the British Embassy in Washington.

During the meal, we sat at a table with Colin Powell and Prince Bandar, the Saudi ambassador. They are both charmers who could take anyone's mind off her troubles. Diana bantered throughout the lunch, and then, after bidding goodbye to the other guests, we met privately.

We talked of the challenges of public life and the struggle to protect our children from the scrutiny of the world. She told me of her new hopes and plans for using her position to focus attention on the needs of suffering people.

Although she seemed vulnerable and unsure about the direction her life was taking, I sensed in her a reservoir of resilience and determination that would help her take charge of her own life and help others, despite great obstacles.

Over the next few years, we stayed in touch. I saw Diana for the last time in June of this year, when she was visiting Washington to highlight her campaign to ban anti-personnel landmines.

Over tea in the White House, she spoke passionately about her recent trip to Angola and her up-coming one to Bosnia. We shared our thoughts about the progress being made worldwide in the fight against Aids and I described the efforts to end forced prostitution in Thailand, a place she planned to visit.

I kidded her that the up-coming auction of her gowns for charity was the smartest closet-cleaning strategy ever devised.

And we talked, as always, about our children. She brought me up to date on her sons William and Harry – how quickly they were growing and how she was working to provide them with childhoods as normal as possible.

She asked me about Chelsea's college plans and wanted to know more about the American university system. Our time together passed too quickly.

A White House photographer took our picture standing in front of the portrait of one of my predecessors from more than a century ago, Frances Cleveland.

Like Diana, she was a young bride who quickly found herself drawing on her own reserves of grace and poise as she became the obsession of a national media that tracked her every move. I will always be struck by the poignancy of that photograph.

Diana and I hugged goodbye. I watched her walk away, a more outwardly confident and effective young woman than the one I had met three years before.

I was impressed by her courage and persistence in getting up and going on whenever life knocked her to the mat. And I was delighted that she appeared happier and more at peace with herself.

I will miss seeing her, miss hearing the pride in her voice as she talked of her sons, miss listening to her accounts of the people she tried to help, and miss watching her build a life of integrity on her own terms.

I am reminded of what she once said about the 'disease' of not being loved. What she meant was that the absence of love could make anyone less than fully human.

I hope all who mourn her passing will honour her memory by reaching out and bringing love and comfort to all who suffer.

Few, if any of us, will ever look as beautiful on the outside as she did, but all of us can strive to develop that inner beauty of the heart and soul that she valued and understood was more lasting and important.

Hillary Clinton, *Express*

'A STAR FROM THE BEGINNING'

Diana and I were improbable friends – women almost two generations apart, from dissimilar backgrounds, working and living in different spheres.

We were certainly not close, but we saw each other when she came to Washington and when I went to London. Over the years, friendship and affection grew. She quickly realized that I would protect her privacy.

I also spoke my mind pretty freely, which amused her and which she liked.

We first met casually. Diana's great friends, the Brazilian ambassador and his wife, Paulo-Tarso and Lucia Flecha de Lima, were her hosts for a summer vacation on Martha's Vineyard in 1994, and they brought her for a visit to my beach one day.

I went down to say hello and was immediately struck by Diana's natural, low-key charm. We seemed to enjoy each other. From that point on, we were able to have easy and candid conversations during long walks on the beach.

One day, she came to fill in at my regular tennis game, much to the delight of the rest of the group, who didn't know she was coming. They asked her what they should call her. 'Call me Diana,' she replied. 'Everyone in America does.'

She was quite a good player and funny with her partners. When one disagreed about her line call, she exclaimed: 'Whose side are you on?'

As I was driving her home after the game, she talked lovingly about her sons. 'I want them to grow up knowing there are poor people as well as palaces,' she said.

As time went on, I observed her making great efforts to be there for them. In between her appearances this spring for the Red Cross in Washington and the sale of her dresses in New York, she returned to England to see them.

As everyone knows, she played a humanizing, normalizing role in their lives, seeking to introduce them to as many of the experiences of ordinary life as she could. That loss is painful to think about, even from a distance.

If you spent time with her, you felt Diana's extraordinary strength, as well as vulnerability and her somewhat mocking and ever-present humour.

I asked her if she had ever thought of going to college now that she was alone. She found my question hard to believe, and commented with irony: 'I've already had an education.' She was right. Even though she lacked degrees, she had had a long, excruciating experience.

It is hard to believe that she was barely 20 when she was married. I freely admit that I was among the millions who got up at 5am to watch her going through the huge, public, fairy tale-like ceremony.

She was a star from the beginning. She brought something to royal behaviour: touching people and speaking frankly, both major contributions. But we all soon learned that the fairy tale had no happy ending.

Diana, Princess of Wales, evolved from the beautiful young bride into someone with a mature heart and interests. When we first met, she was already developing her own concerns, which centred on children, and people ill with Aids and cancer.

It was somewhat surprising when, at a dinner I gave for her a few months later, she brought up the question of how she was going to focus her energies.

Another guest that night, Jim Lehrer, said, 'Well, you must have stacks of requests.' She said she did, but added, 'I've got to decide.'

'Make sure it matters to you,' Jim responded. 'Because if it doesn't, you cannot make it matter to others.'

Of course, she did just that.

She knew she had the power to give love and make people feel better. But she recently told me: 'If I'm going to talk on behalf of any cause, I want to go and see the problem for myself and learn about it.' She wanted to work only in areas where she thought her presence could make a difference.

Diana had the courage to step out publicly to support causes that were risky and misunderstood. But she related to the large issues in a very personal way. When she was on the Vineyard, she discovered that a well-known Aids patient with whom she had corresponded, Elizabeth Glaser, was also on the island. Diana immediately cancelled her social plans for the next day, so she could pay her a long, private visit.

Diana's position as the divorced wife of Prince Charles, but the mother of the future king, led to a lonely life. It was understandable that her natural desire to have some fun led her to Paris the night she died.

She seemed to have a clear determination to be her own person. A friend at the Vineyard once asked if she gambled. 'Not with cards,' she replied. 'But with life.'

She was part of a celebrity culture that unfortunately breeds people who make money by exploiting luminaries such as the late Jacqueline Onassis (the only parallel to Diana in America). Mrs Onassis went to court to force one of the paparazzi to keep more of a distance from her.

One point we all have to keep clear is that the paparazzi are different from the news media and most other photographers. The problem the paparazzi present will not be solved by abridging press freedoms in an understandable upsurge of the desire to protect privacy.

Diana's death has brought the problem of celebrity culture and its coverage by all of us into sharp relief. We all need to think hard about how to solve them. This tragedy need not and should not have happened. The world should not have had to suffer the sudden extinction of a real star.

Katharine Graham, *Washington Post*

THE POWER OF COMPASSION

On my dressing table in Cairo in May 1992 was a long letter from the Princess of Wales, who had been staying at the embassy a day or two earlier. I have it in front of me. In her own hand, she described her doings in Egypt and the sufferings which she had seen. She ends: 'Please be in no doubt of my gratitude for the opportunity such a visit gives me to broaden my own horizons, or my readiness to give my support to our foreign policy in any way you think would be helpful.'

That was the tenor of all my dealings with the Princess. When I came to know her, she was already at the height of her beauty and fame. Both of these gave her pleasure, but she was not content with them as many would have been. She had discovered in herself the power of compassion – the ability to enter into the anxieties and sufferings of others, in a way which brought them strength and comfort. She wanted to use this power abroad as well as at home, for the benefit of Britain as well as of those whom she met.

That was what the Princess meant when she talked of being an ambassador for Britain. This remark ruffled sensibilities unnecessarily in the media, and in the minds of a few officals agitated by the appearance of a comet not predicted in their astronomy. But, of course, she was not talking of taking charge of an embassy. Indeed, she did not suggest any formal role, which would probably have cramped her style. The charitable causes with which she was connected made all sorts of suggestions of places she should visit. What she asked for, and got from us, was advice about which visits might work best, and where the political pitfalls lay. It was no good trying to lay down exact rules on what she should do, or who she should see, in order to fit her exact constitutional position after the breakdown of her marriage. To a foreign head of state, the Princess was a beautiful and famous representative of Britain whose company was a refreshing pleasure. They were not concerned with the legal niceties and, as far as I am concerned, her visits did nothing but good.

We must each speak of what we found – from my own experience, I cannot recognize the portrait sketched by some of a rebel radical Princess setting herself against the establishment, or leading a crusade against traditional ways of doing things. An unhappy marriage brings bitterness; bitterness produces a sense of isolation, and sometimes a desire to hurt in retaliation. But to erect out of natural resentments a great new doctrine of monarchy is unreal. Diana, Princess of Wales, used to the full the traditional manners and methods of the Royal Family. She spoke and carried herself like an English girl from the background which was in fact hers, adding the particular personal flair which made her a star.

The tragic blotting-out of that star should make us all reflect afresh on the nature of the monarchy, and our expectations of it. Kings and queens began as rulers. They were the cure to anarchy. Their *raison d'être* was to govern and to be obeyed. But, during the 19th century, the British monarch finally lost the power to rule, which had been gradually eroded since Stuart times.

No longer a ruler, the monarch became a symbol. A hundred years ago this summer, a plain, dumpy old lady, driving through the streets of London to celebrate her Diamond Jubilee at St Paul's, symbolized to huge popular acclaim the majesty of the British Empire. Queen Victoria's descendants carried on this role with considerable skill, altering the symbolism to meet the needs of each generation. We were reminded, at the anniversary of VE Day in 1995, how successfully King George VI and Queen Elizabeth symbolized Britain's resistance to aggression and ultimate victory in the last war.

But symbolism is no longer enough. The Queen carries through the role of constitutional monarch and Head of the Commonwealth in a way which gains respect and affection everywhere. In parallel, the Royal Family has attempted to symbolize a loving united family, of the kind that almost all their subjects wish to live in – though they do not always succeed. In this, the Royal Family ran into trouble.

One reason was the growth of the media, now feverish in their competition across the world, hungry for sensation, careless of the consequences of what they do. Earl Spencer has restarted the old argument about whether blame should fall on paparazzi, editors, proprietors – or readers. What is certain is the huge difficulty of maintaining a happy royal marriage under these pressures. All three marriages of the Queen's children have collapsed, most dramatically that of the Prince and Princess of Wales. The effort to provide a reassuring symbolism of royal family life has failed.

This failure has given some impetus to anti-monarchist thinking, as did a similar temporary failure in the middle of Queen Victoria's reign. The good news for those of us who are deeply committed monarchists is that an answer has once again been found. In a modern democratic society, there is a huge area of necessary activity which cannot be successfully undertaken either by the state, or by commercial enterprise. Neither the profit motive nor the rules and resources of a bureaucracy can provide either by themselves, or together, for citizens' needs, now that those needs include not just a decent standard of living for all but a decent environment, and an acceptable balance between old and new. Voluntary and charitable effort on a massive scale is needed to rescue those who fall through the gaps between commercial and state provision, to sustain minority groups or causes, to experiment with new forms of service, and to stimulate artistic creation.

Politicians of all parties have talked for years about the voluntary role of the active citizen; the present Government is following its usual practice of claiming to invent ideas which it has in fact inherited. But this is not a field in which politicians are at their best. By contrast, it is precisely here that modern royalty can shine. There is, in this arena, hard work for members of the Royal Family which can bring real satisfaction to others, and to themselves. The Princess Royal found her niche with Save the Children some time ago. Both the Prince of Wales and Diana happened on the same underlying justification for their work. Being very different people, they followed it through in very different ways.

The causes whose fortunes were transformed by the Princess have been well described in the last two days. It is worth underlining the courage which she showed in her choice of unpopular groups, such as the victims of Aids and leprosy. The efforts of Prince Charles have been more local, less glamorous, more innovative. Like his father and, during the last century, Prince Albert, he has worried his way into an understanding of many of the gaps and failures of modern Britain, and then sat down to find remedies. The different enterprises of the Prince's Trust bring a touch of royal ingenuity, and help, into thousands of lives.

In both cases, this is royalty *with a cause*, supplementing royalty *as a symbol*. But it remains royalty. The Princess was triumphant because she was both a Princess and Diana. She needed to be royal to succeed. Republicans should ponder on this. The magic of royalty remains. It has not faded into the light of common day. We have seen how perilous and difficult the magic now is to handle – but can that be a good reason for abandoning it?

Rather, it is a reason for looking as far ahead as we can, and equipping Prince William so that he, too, can put the magic to good use when his time comes. It will be many years before he has to carry the full weight of monarchy. Before then, he needs a wide education and a good measure of private fun. Later he will need to find his own causes, and learn how to turn his interest in them to good effect. He knows already that his will be a daunting task; he needs meanwhile to learn from us that it is abundantly worthwhile.

Douglas Hurd, Foreign Secretary, 1989–95, in the *Daily Telegraph*

'A NATURAL COUNSELLOR'

Diana was a natural counsellor. She knew how to pay attention, the most dignifying thing one person can do for another. Time after time over a ten-year period I watched her intuitively knowing what to do and say in order to come close to another person – often people very near to death. She knew how to make a real connection, enabling people to talk to her from their hearts about what really mattered. She could sense what someone, or even a whole group of people, might need with unfailing accuracy.

She would usually ask a simple question: 'Hello, how are *you*?' She was often very funny: 'Diana, can I kiss you?'; 'No, you can't kiss me. If you like you can kiss my hand – though you never know where it may have been.' She might climb on to the bed, crouch beside the wheelchair, or reach out to touch or to hug.

Though in all our conversations I cannot recall discussing death directly – she was far too interested in living for the moment – I think she knew instinctively that life and death are two sides of the same coin, each holding the secrets of the other. Perhaps this genius at making truly human connections, which we often label as counselling and package as a skill reserved for professionals, was simply Diana's gift for teaching the living how to die and thus how to reach for life.

She was always real and spontaneous, without any agenda, formula or need of protocol. She never rushed or left anyone out and she could make even brief moments seem spacious. She always left hope, strength and joy in her wake.

Diana was well aware that connection at this level is a two-way process and that in her giving she too received. Her last public visit to the Lighthouse happened to fall on a day of particularly hurtful allegations in the press. As she left she turned to me and said: 'This morning I arrived in a filthy mood, but I'm leaving on top of the world.'

Christopher Spence, founder and president of London Lighthouse, in *The Times*

A THRILLING
FAMILIARITY
THE PRINCESS WE MET

A Woman in Earnest

Monday, 23 June, 1997. The Four Seasons, East Fifty-second Street, between Lexington and Park. At the invitation of Anna Wintour, the editor of *Vogue*, lunch with the Princess of Wales.

Anna and I get there a bit early; the Princess is exactly on time. She wears a mint-green Chanel suit with no blouse and a stunning tan. Making her way quickly across the crowded restaurant, she has the startling phosphorescence of a cartoon creation – too blonde, too tall, too painfully recognizable. Perhaps it's her height that's unsettling. It renders her more than just an acute natural beauty. She's like a strange overbred plant, a far-fetched experimental rose.

It is immediately, and surprisingly, easy to talk to her about subjects one might have supposed were off limits. Perhaps her royal armour has begun to fall away, along with the wardrobe that is to be auctioned at Christie's in a week's time. (What remains is something different: celebrity, of the highest wattage). It's obvious that Anna has the knack of relaxing her. The two worked together on a fashion benefit for breast cancer last September, and have been close since then. Within a few Perrier minutes, we are just a couple of mates having lunch with a famous girlfriend. We talk first about Tony Blair.

'I think at last I will have somone who will know how to *use* me,' Diana says. 'He's told me he wants me to go on some missions.'

'What sort of missions?' I ask.

'I'd really, really like to go to China,' she says. 'I'm very good at sorting people's heads out.' She says this straight-facedly, and I note that, like many stars with a gift for self-projection, she is almost wholly devoid of irony. But in her case the therapized phrases point to a quality of driven earnestness. It's easy to understand how she could throw herself into a public role, and just as easy, sadly, to see why she would bore Prince Charles. Notwithstanding his sometimes thoughtful pronouncements about architecture and urban planning, the county friends he surrounds himself with are a light-weight crowd. They have a collective class unease about anything that smacks of intensity. And what few people have understood is that Diana's love for Charles, like everything else about her, was embarrassingly intense. Had she been a chilly opportunist, she might have accommodated the marital arrangement favoured by so many of her husband's friends. But her love was tenacious, desperate, uncompromising. Her temperament was not the sort to take a husband's infidelity in stride. How could Charles have known that the demure deb he married would turn out to harbour a cache of emotions out of Emily Brontë?

None of this, though, is on show in the self-possessed woman who comes to lunch. The Princess that once was – the miserable girl who went mad in her cage – must now seem to her to be from another life, along with the dress she wore to dance with John Travolta at the White House. 'I've kept a few things,' she says about the auction. 'But you know that Catharine Walker with all the bugle beads? People in England don't wear those kind of clothes any more.'

I find myself marvelling at how freely she is willing to talk about members of the Royal Family, and at how shrewd she seems to have become at press relations. She understands that in marketing terms the Windsors are a decaying brand, one that requires repositioning by a media genius – perhaps someone like Peter Mandelson, the political strategist who helped get Tony Blair elected. 'I tried again and again to get them to hire someone like him to give them proper advice, but they didn't want to hear it,' she says. 'They kept saying I was manipulative. But what's the alternative? To just sit there and have them make your image for you? Sometimes editors at newspapers would write editorials suggesting things they could do, but instead of paying attention one of the private secretaries would ring up and give the editors a rocket.'

I suggest that the antics of the Duchess of York, a.k.a Fergie, don't help the royal cause.

'No,' Diana says. 'And it's a shame for Andrew, because he really is the best of the bunch. I mean, people don't know this, but he works really, really hard for the country. He does so much, and no one pays any attention at all.

It's the same with Princess Anne. She works like a dog, and nobody cares. And I keep saying to Prince Charles, "It's no good complaining that people don't care about your work. Until you straighten your head out and get things clear, people just won't give you a break." '

We talk about her sons, William and Harry. 'All my hopes are on William now,' she says. 'I don't want to push him. Charles suggested he might go to Hong Kong for the handover, but he said, "Mummy, must I? I just don't feel ready." I try to din into him all the time about the media – the dangers, and how he must understand and handle it. I think it's too late for the rest of the family. But William – I think he has it. I think he understands. I'm hoping he'll grow up to be as smart about it as John Kennedy, Jr. I want William to be able to handle things as well as John does.'

She plainly hankers for America – for the optimism, the options, the openness. She says she would love to move here. It's as if England, for her, had become synonymous with the Palace, that grey stone pile which broke her heart. Anyway, she's grown too big for it. Her kind of fame – wild and close to out of control, the sort of stardom that belongs to Elvis and Marilyn, JFK and Jackie – is truly understandable only in celebrity's homeland. 'When all the Americans come in July for Wimbledon, you can feel the energy go up,' she says wistfully. 'It all collapses again when they leave.' She smiles. 'Well, perhaps Tony Blair will change all that.' She speaks warmly of her friendship with Katharine Graham, the wise matriarch of the Washington *Post*. It's a good sign. Mrs Graham is exactly the kind of social protector Diana has always lacked – a seasoned older woman who has been through hell herself and is not mired in the politics of English aristocratic circles. 'I love her,' Diana says. 'I really do.'

We are about to order coffee, and I ask the Princess if she regrets the loss of her chance to be Queen. I assume she will avoid answering, but she surprises me again. 'Yes, yes,' she says quickly, her eyes lowered. Then she looks up and continues, 'We would have been the best team in the world. I could shake hands till the cows come home. And Charles could make serious speeches. But' – she shakes her head – 'it was not to be.'

Listening to her, I feel a great sadness for England. She is right: they would have a been a great team. The Royal Family had already been marginalized by the time she became Princess; it seems even more so now that she is no longer fully part of it. When was the last time the occupant of

Downing Street was more charismatic in the public's mind than the occupants of Buckingham Palace? During the Blitz, perhaps, when Churchill was at the noon of his inspirational power. But seldom before, and never since – until now.

'You see, Charles is not a leader,' she says. 'He's a follower. He was born to the wrong job. He'd have been so happy with a house in Tuscany, being a host to artists. He just wasn't cut out for what he got.'

I ask if one of the problems hasn't been the fact that he has had to stand so long in the wings, waiting for his role to open up.

'It's up to him to *make* his role,' she says. 'He could do anything. That's what I have tried to do.'

I ask about her plans for the summer. For the first time, she looks a little uneasy. August, she says, will be difficult 'without the boys', who will spend most of the month at Balmoral with Prince Charles. Still, she adds, now that they attend boarding schools she is getting used to their being away.

She mentions a vexing incident that occurred only the day before: she took her sons to see *The Devil's Own*, and there was an instant uproar in the press about the film's being sympathetic to the Irish Republican Army. 'I didn't know what it was about when I took them,' she says. 'We just wanted to see a movie, and we picked it out the paper because William likes Harrison Ford. I issued a statement straight away, and I called Prince Charles and left a message. I didn't want him to think I was deliberately making trouble.' She looks pained as she says this. Her relationship with her ex-husband, one feels, is settling into divorced normalcy – at any rate, she is trying hard to make it do so. She says she especially misses the boys on the weekends Charles has custody of them. What does she do without them? 'I stay in town. If I go out, I keep my eyes down or straight ahead. Wherever I go, the press find ways to spy, you know. Often I visit a hospice.'

Again, I feel the churn of strangeness I felt an hour before, when I caught sight of that long-stemmed figure weaving towards us through the restaurant's crowd of CEO suits. After Diana's public revelations of bulimia and self-mutilation, the country-house-party set permanently ceased to be part of her world. Televised confessions, talk of therapy, admissions of pain: it was all so emotionally aggressive, so unseemly – so un-English, in a word. And then, on top of it all, this bleeding-heart stuff! In the idiom of Prince Charles's best friend, the Honourable Nicholas Soames, MP, 'Pass the port, she's not my sort.' So, while the rest of her class heads west, taking the M4 to Gloucestershire on a Friday afternoon for a jolly weekend of riding or shooting, the isolated Barbarella Princess makes her visits to cancer wards, arriving in a flashing cone of artificial light, like an alien checking out the sorrows of our world.

'Doesn't it drain you, being with dying people so much?' I ask.

'No, never,' she answers fervently. 'When you discover you can give joy to people like that, there is nothing quite like it. William has begun to understand that, too. And I am hoping it will grow in him.' There is a firmness to her voice when she says this, as if she had glimpsed the only thing she can hold fast to. She reminds me of Celia Coplestone, the shallow socialite in T. S. Eliot's *The Cocktail Party*, who, devastated by a love that isn't truly reciprocated, surprises everyone in the last act by going off to do humanitarian work in a desolate corner of Africa and becoming a kind of saint. One senses that what began as a public-relations ploy has connected deeply to her fragmented sense of self. She has found a place to channel all that unrequited love, and is learning to be sustained by it.

She describes videotapes of landmine victims that a friend brought her and says how distraught they made her feel, how determined to help. 'That's what I am for,' she says. The expression in her eyes as she says this is eerie. Then the moment passes, and she reverts to being a conventional Sloane Street girl. It had just been announced that next year's G7 conference will be in Birmingham. 'Oh, God,' she says, giggling. 'Couldn't they have thought of somewhere less dreary? Birmingham!'

Before we leave the restaurant, Anna asks her if she would ever marry again. She smiles. 'Who would take me on?' she says. 'I have so much baggage. Anyone who takes me out to dinner has to accept the fact that their business will be raked over in the papers. Photographers will go through their dustbins. I think I am safer alone.' We are out on Fifty-second Street. Two photographers dart forward as she steps into her limo. *Di! Over here! Di! Di!*

When the news came of her death, my first thoughts were of place and time – of the wrongness of any royal princess, even a divorced one, contriving to be in that place at that time. In late summer, the Paris of the rich and the titled simply closes down. The city's grandees retreat north to cool woodlands or south to sunny coasts; meanwhile, Diana's English friends and sisters tramp the Scottish heather with the children or rusticate in the Tuscan villa that Archie and Amanda lend them every year. But Paris in August? Dinner at the Ritz weeks before *la rentrée*? The fact that she was there at all was discordant, a poignant symbol of a season of panic and flight.

What of the brave new Diana I had met at lunch? I found it hard to reconcile the ascendance of Dodi Fayed in her life with the woman who had come to appreciate the subtle guidance of a Katharine Graham. Some have suggested that the Princess was thumbing her nose at the Royal Family by consorting with the scion of a clan that, in its adopted but less than welcoming country, is so redolent of social, if not financial, rejection. I prefer to see it as a relapse – a wounded and wounding gesture, triggered by the galling emergence of Camilla Parker Bowles as the no-longer unthinkable wife-in-waiting. The frantic Diana lurked beneath the shining surface after all. And, for a woman with so much baggage, at the height of summer, who was there to turn to but a generous boulevardier who had the kit she needed – the planes and the yachts and the money to make it all go away?

The final weeks of Diana's life had hinted at the possibility that she was stumbling down the path blazed by the Duke and Duchess of Windsor (whose very Paris villa had been leased by Dodi Fayed's father and elaborately renovated as if in preparation for new occupants) or, worse, that she was courting the fate of a displaced Mrs Trump. If the dalliance had culminated in remarriage – to a partner at least as inappropriate as Wallis Simpson – then one of the consequences would surely have been the end of any connection with the Crown beyond the minimum required by her status as the mother of its heir once removed. A life of luxurious exile, of meaningless wandering from one pleasure spot to the next, would have been the logical sequel. In that event, the only thing that could have redeemed her in life is the thing that has redefined her in death: her earnest, utterly unironic efforts to ease a bit of human suffering. Now she is frozen into bas-relief, forever kneeling to comfort some hurt.

Diana's death, like her life, has left the Royal Family shaken. From the abdication of Edward VIII until the wedding of Charles and Diana, the Windsors had served as the reassuringly dull continuum against which the traditional calendar of English life could be marked. A Christmas speech, a picnic in Scotland, a Remembrance Day wreath, a royal christening: the Windsors' appeal was local, modest, unsurprising. Despite plenty of global travel, they were never global stars. The Mercedes that screeched into the Seine tunnel in Paris carried with it not just a princess and her playboy but a phenomenon that for sixteen years had frightened the Royal Family, captivated the nation, and enthralled the world.

As the coffin draped with the royal standard emerged slowly from the cargo hold of the plane from Paris, Prince Charles and the Spencer sisters stood silent, watching. The only sound was the soft whirr and click of cameras. What was in the Prince's mind? Along with grief and regret, perhaps this subliminal thought: Can we ever be normal again?

Tina Brown, editor, New Yorker

THE CARING PRINCESS

When I wrote my first biography of the Prince of Wales in 1978, to mark his 30th birthday, no one had heard of Lady Diana Spencer. When I wrote my second, on his 40th birthday in 1988, she was the star of his show – and the marriage was already in trouble.

Were I to write a third next year, when Charles reaches his half-century, Diana would officially have been written out of the script – while remaining a uniquely potent player between the lines. As the mother of his children, notably the future King, the Princess would have remained a major force in Charles's future, whatever direction his personal life took.

Now fate has written her out of his life, and more importantly their children's – as indeed of all of us who knew her, whether close-up or from afar. Every family in the land, every household in the world, is feeling a sense of personal loss, as if cruelly deprived of a loved one.

As I sat in a BBC TV studio, among those invited to pay the first tributes, I found myself very moved by the pictures of passers-by drawn to the railings of Buckingham and Kensington Palaces to say their own personal farewells, perhaps leave flowers.

The sight was symbolic of the personal ambition Diana had long since achieved: to be 'the People's Princess'. She herself would have been very touched. A woman with a great capacity to give and receive love, she was loved like no other member of the Royal Family. She cared, and managed to communicate it. Love her or hate her – and the vast majority adored her – she had become a part of everyone's lives, a member of everyone's family.

I first met her when she was still 'shy Di', the blushing teenager thrust overnight into the global limelight, single-handedly rejuvenating the creaky old institution of the monarchy with her own unique personal touch. Older heads worried whether this innocent young girl, without a single O-level to her name, would be able to stand up to the stresses and strains of life in the royal goldfish bowl. And they had good reason.

Diana became the royal star far faster – and lasted far longer – than she or any of the Windsors had expected. As she has told us herself, in no uncertain terms, she was not given the support she needed by either the Royal Family or their courtiers. As a result, the presence of 'a third person in the marriage' drove her off the rails a bit, causing depression and illness.

As the marital crisis grew, heading inevitably towards divorce, those of us who wrote regularly about the couple were confronted by a choice. So intense was the war of the Waleses that one was reluctantly forced to take sides. While trying to treat each partner even-handedly, writers used to first-person treatment could not remain on good terms with both.

To me, Diana was the victim – cruelly wronged and abused – and I said so in print. Gradually, a rapport developed, as with other supportive writers. Meetings and phone calls would take place, offering her version of the ever-changing scene. People have called this manipulation of the media. But it is common practice in public life – no more nor less than is a routine part of their jobs to countless politicians and other public figures.

Diana was grateful for the support, and was pleased to say so. In 15 years as a positive public relations man for the Prince of Wales – better, I venture to suggest, than the ones he paid – I never had any such thanks. It was symbolic of the difference between them as human beings.

After her divorce, a year ago last week, Diana felt able to invite to lunch in Kensington Palace various friends and advisers who could never previously have been seen there. I was one who fell into the category.

A few months ago, I was invited to lunch on a Friday. Then came a phone call asking to put it back a few days. The Princess apologized for the postponement, and said she would give me the explanation I deserved.

When I arrived at Kensington Palace the following Wednesday, she explained that a last-minute chance had arisen to watch her friend Sir Magdi Yacoub perform a heart operation. 'How can you watch those things?' I said light-heartedly. 'I'm sure I would keel over.'

She leaned forward with fierce intensity in her eyes. 'If I am going to care for people in hospital,' she said, 'I need to know every aspect of every stage of the long treatment they have been through.' She meant it. 'The caring princess' was no phoney façade.

In private, she was very bright, very funny, with a lovely laugh and a deft line in repartee. She was no giant intellect, as she well knew, but she was savvy, smart and interested in weightier subjects than she was given credit for. In my possession is a highly articulate, handwritten letter from her discussing my hefty biography of the composer Tchaikovsky – which she read, she said, 'with tears in my eyes'.

At one point during the lunch that day – just the two of us – I asked what sort of man might one day persuade Diana to remarry. Without a moment's hesitation, she said: 'Someone who understands what I'm about.'

Which gave me the chance to ask: 'So what *are* you about?'

'I'm about caring,' she replied. 'I always have been, and I always will be. I thought I had married one caring man, but alas it didn't work out. I hope one day I might meet another.'

Maybe she had met that man in Dodi Fayed, who comes from a large caring family which – unlike her former in-laws – would have made her feel wanted and loved. Now we will never know.

Although on the surface Diana appeared to lead a charmed life, her true story is really a deeply unhappy one: traumatized by her mother's departure from her life when she was only six, traumatized again by her husband's love for another woman, trapped in a gilded cage from which she had only just begun to find means of escape.

That escape lay primarily in helping people less fortunate than herself. Her early support for Aids victims helped educate an ignorant and frightened public about the true nature of that grim disease. Her recent campaign on landmines – so foolishly denounced by members of that last, undeniably 'hopeless' government – had already changed official policy on both sides of the Atlantic.

Diana raised millions for numerous causes and charities close to her heart, in which role she is quite irreplaceable. Her presence at a charitable function could attract more people, and raise more money, than all the rest of the royals combined. As the shock of her death sinks in, the Queen and Charles may well rue the day they braved public wrath by depriving Diana of her HRH and expelling her from the Royal Family.

At least she found a little happiness at the last, in the arms of a man who appreciated her true qualities. The only continuing blight on her life in recent months – as she began to find her post-divorce feet and carve out an independent way of life – were the paparazzi who dogged her every move, denying her any vestige of the freedom of movement most of us enjoy.

Now, it seems, they have had a hand in killing her. The horror of Diana's death at just 36 will take weeks, months to sink in – but, in the stunned aftermath of the news from Paris, it takes on the grim inevitability of Greek tragedy. She had so much left to give, to so many she had yet to meet.

Anthony Holden, *Express*

'SHE GLITTERED AND THE GLITTERING SUCKED YOU IN'

My eighteen-year-old daughter called from Newcastle bus station early on Sunday morning, her voice ragged: Is it true? Is it a hoax? No, no; it's real, it's true.

Her tears were genuine – because of the shock, and hysterically thrilled – because of the excitement. The tossing out of television schedules; the constant mordant chords of the National Anthem; the worldwide clamour (Nelson Mandela! Mother Teresa! Bill and Hillary! Tom Cruise!).

This daugher is a child of the Thatcher years, born in 1979. Thatcher's children were push-chaired off to the Fairy-tale Wedding street parties and given cake to eat and tiny flags to wave, and when they see the old photographs they almost believe they remember it all. She said, 'There's never been a day of my life when Diana hasn't been in the papers.'

At eighteen, this daughter's almost old enough herself to go through a Royal Girlfriend baptism of fire, as Diana did, with scant help from the Palace and none from the press. Diana Spencer had her 20th birthday three weeks before she dragged that unconscionably over-romantic frock up the aisle on the arm of her courtier father.

Twenty is almost old enough to dress up as a virgin sacrifice (her uncle vouched for her virginity, remember? while feminists howled and begged Don't Do It, Di!) and stutter through your vows in front of 20 million people, including the Monarch, your mother-in-law. Isn't it?

I don't think so. She was clearly so young we were frightened for her as we put out more flags. She was so raw as an embryonic Royal that she had to change, and she did. We watched her turn from that gawky child into a global coverstar almost overnight.

She got The Look right almost immediately – how could she help it? In the Eighties, it was hard to resist either *Dynasty* or designer dressing and she embraced both. If you looked right in that odd decade, you *were* right. Later, with stickier and stickier dread, we watched her stumble and fall and squawk and resist until she finally flung off the ludicrous fairy-tale.

By the time she was 30 and I started to come across her now and again in her public life, she was clearly desperate. Too old to play the gamine any more, but too damaged ever to grow and mature as a woman. She had been inside the royal box too long.

When she half-scrambled out of it, in 1993, saying breathily that she needed 'more time and space in her private life' she began to lose her magic touch. She was breaking up on the inside (all that wretched inner self business – mystics, clairvoyants, magic pyramids, intestine-cleaning sessions, battered-wives meetings, gurus) and her image began to break up on the outside, too. She dumped 300-odd charities and the telly was full of admirable women swallowing hard and praising her with faint damns.

She posed for mad pictures with surgeon's masks. She leaned too heavily on staff and friends, lost them, betrayed them and desperately replaced them. She was rootless, baseless, wallowing. Dinner-parties would shriek with cynical laughter at her ambulance-chasing and shalwar-kameez-wearing. I shrieked myself. She was always great copy.

Great pictures, too. Always great: whether as docile Di, or dazzling Di, with her knowing, camera-ready face, or as desperate and demented Di, snatching at car-keys and cameras and begging to be left alone. And now there are pictures of her dying of course. And – who knows? even pictures of her dead. It's been done before.

Such a violent, shocking, pitiable death, alone in a Paris hospital. By 'alone', I mean without family. I mean with only Mohamed Fayed and the British Ambassador to Paris on the scene, because there were decisions to be taken and protocol to be observed and the Queen's Flight is not so expeditiously mustered as a Harrods helicopter for a semi-detached, not-Royal-any-more Princess.

When I heard her angry and understandably vengeful brother deliver his bitter valedictory in South Africa ('I always knew the Press would kill her one day') and tell the world's media that they had blood on their hands, I thought of the chilling line at the close of Webster's tragedy *The Duchess of Malfi*: 'Cover her face. Mine eyes dazzle. She died young.'

The pity is that we will never be able to cover her dazzling face, the most photographed in the world. Her image is as familiar to us as our own family pictures. Her almost lifesize head gleams from the London-postcard stand at mainline stations: the smile, the blue eye-liner and the Spencer tiara as iconic as a London bus. Her face will dazzle for decades like Marilyn Monroe's, and never grow old.

The icky Monroe comparison is unavoidable now. Both died at 36; both were iconic, fantasy women who were lapped with sentimental adoration from unknown millions of Ordinary Folk (not to mention drag queens and dress designers); both were charismatically beautiful and both were damaged. Both were girls sent out to do a woman's job. They failed and succeeded without ever understanding why.

The most curious thing about Diana's extraordinary life was that she was as fascinated by the star-crossed mega-celebrities, Monroe and Jackie O and Princess Grace, as any other *Hello!* reader. She understood stardom, so long as it was in two dimensions.

I had lunch at Kensington Palace after she became semi-detached , in the early Nineties. It was wildly exciting, both to get inside a fine and private palace and to meet a global icon face to face. You are shown first into a anteroom packed with stuff like a provincial museum – pictures, boxes, chests, ornaments – I hesitate to say objets d'art because there was little d'art. These were royal tshotschkes – mostly with little brass plaques or silver plates on them saying where and when they were PRESENTED TO HRH THE PRINCE OF WALES. Not necessarily *this* Prince of Wales: some of the tureens and chests were from the Raj.

Upstairs it was grand and chintzy and the pictures were all of William and Harry. This was after the separation but before the divorce. After *Diana – Her True Story* but before *Panorama*. She was still HRH, still under police protection, but desperately trying to get out from under the curious mantle of royalty, and I couldn't blame her, not after I'd seen that museum room downstairs and the grand, chintz-lined trap above, which was staffed by flunkeys in navy-blue uniforms with rows of buttons.

They appeared, summoned by bells, to pour wine and change the courses, while she batted the brittle, gossipy conversation back and forth.

She was one of the half-dozen most seductive people I have ever met. 'Seductive, yes. Not sexual,' said a former equerry. She flirted, with men, women, children. She had a curious intelligence, considering she was about as well educated as any current GCSE English-passer, part dozy Sloane, partly jet-set sharp.

She was wearing a lipstick pink suit and a lot of gilt jewellery. Her hair was sprayed stiff. She looked like the youngest and prettiest girl in your office, dressed for an afternoon wedding. But she glittered, and the glittering sucked you in.

Am I being manipulated? I kept thinking. Yes, I am. Does she know she's doing it? Yes, she does. Can she help it? I don't think so. She looked brilliantly cheerful while she was talking and suddenly melancholy when she wasn't.

It was a damned melancholy life. Her sons were no longer part of the daily fabric. At boarding school during term-time and shared during the holidays; their access to her was by now determined by her husband. Christmas and the summer holidays (spent at Sandringham and Balmoral) were nervy, petulant, wretched times her staff learnt to dread. No wonder she played Happy Families with the Fayeds. She had spent the first 19 years of her short life in the wreckage of one troubled family and the next 17 in what we have all learnt to recognize as the destructive maelstrom of another.

At the end of my lunch, a taxi arrived for me, also summoned by bells. She came down the stairs with me and out to the front door, where she hopped from foot to foot like a little girl, beaming gloriously at the cab driver, dazzling in her lipstick pink, scrunging on the gravel.

The cabbie goggled. He drove sedately down the policed driveway and then went like a rocket up Kensington High Street, shouting that he couldn't believe it, blimey, was she incredible or what? She'd made his day. What was the house like? What was I there for? Lunch? What did we eat?

He couldn't wait to phone his missis. She'd go barmy when she heard about this. He said, 'Crikey – she live in that pile all by herself? Don't she get lonely?' You bet, I said.

Vicki Woods, *Guardian*

A PERRIER WITH THE PRINCESS

From the pavement where I was standing, in the covered pathway to the restaurant in Park Lane, there was not a paparazzo to be seen. Yet, according to the manager who had brought us the warning message, there was a pack of them out there.

Inside, sitting at the table where we had just finished lunch, was a worried waitress and the Princess of Wales. Outside, I was left looking through the haze of fumes to Marble Arch and back, unable to see the slightest bulge of Japanese plastic, the faintest glint of lens, the least sound of Italian-speaking, motorbike-driving paparazzo.

Somewhat shamefacedly, I returned to the table. Just as a precaution the *Times* driver was contacted and sent round to a side entrance. The Princess continued calmly to sip her bottled water and talk about herself, her husband, his family, her work, her problems and the complex cat's-cradle which the media wove between them all.

The date was 18 May 1994, not the worst of days for the then wife of the Prince of Wales but not a good day either. Even when she arrived at the restaurant, she had worn a quick smile and a bad-news frown. There was no preamble. Her face was stretched into the faintest pattern of lines and circles and her question was wholly rhetorical: 'Well, do we know how this particular story got into the papers this morning?'

She did know. The subject of the day was the Princess's 'grooming expenses' which, according to the *Daily Mail* and others, were higher than £3,000 a week. 'My husband said it at a dinner party last week, where it got to Ross Benson and to Nigel Dempster and now there's all this stuff, she complained. Most of the 'stuff' had been helpful hints from journalists about how much her various suits and shoes might have cost and how readers might replicate them at lower prices. 'No one mentions all HIS stuff,' she smiled dryly, 'the bracelet at Christmas for me and the necklace, bought at the same time on the same bill from the same shop, which I never see.'

I paused – in some surprise. We had spoken for barely five minutes. It was already clear that this was not to be a wide-ranging conversation. Whatever else is said about Diana, Princess of Wales, in this dreadful week, let it not be said that she lacked sophistication about the media, her use of it and its use of her. She could be as 'on message' as the most disciplined, determined New Labour apparatchik. She was as charming that day as everyone always says that she is. But she did not move outside the lines that she had most clearly defined.

Inside those lines were the very aspects of her life which most people keep outside in discussion with newspaper editors – her husband, his mistress, her in-laws, her own fragile sense of herself. Within minutes I felt I was talking to someone I knew. By the time that she had toyed her way through her foie gras and lamb, I knew things about her that I did not know about my closest friends.

I should admit now that, before this lunch, I had a very low level of interest in what I would have called at that time 'our Royal soap opera'. I assumed, wrongly, that a large amount of the journalism generated by the juvenile Windsors was misleading, false, fourth-hand; or worse. I did not immediately accept the analysis which she set out with such care. But this was long before the *Panorama* interview. To read what seemed like recycled gossip about iconic characters was one thing. To hear so directly from the central player was quite another. I presume that many others in our business had the same experience.

The Princess complained of how her husband's family divided the charity world between its long-established members – a duchess for hospice, a duke for animals, a princess for children. Occasionally twisting the stem of an empty glass, she described how hard it was for her to enter where her real interests led and where the real demand for her was so high.

I had not expected her to be fond of the Dimbleby biography of her husband. But it was different again to hear her views directly. 'Did you know that it originally was supposed to contain nothing about our relationship at all? How were readers supposed to think that the children came? By immaculate conception?'

'By divine right of kings,' I ventured, trying with difficulty to enter into the spirit of this dialogue. 'Oh great, by DI-vine right,' she giggled. 'That's just what did happen.'

116

The speed with which she ran through her list of subjects would not have disgraced a bank chairman anxious to catch the Ascot train. One moment she was on the subject of John Major's allegedly feeble response to the 'could Camilla be queen?' question: 'Major and my husband are both very alike, quite BFs these days, always seeing each other.' The next moment it was how photographers could help her to present her case to the people. Next it was how stuffiness and protocol prevented her from going to John Smith's funeral: 'It may not have been a full state occasion but it became a powerful public event and no one from the Royal Family was there.'

'Did you object or try and explain that to anyone?' I asked. 'No, it would be awful to have been turned down twice,' she said.

Underlying everything was her sense of her personal contact, through the media, with the British people and the family's fear of that. 'My husband's father once sent me a long formal letter setting out the duties of the Princess of Wales. There was "much more to it than being popular", he said. I sent him back a long letter in reply. He sent me a shorter one – and so on until I finally signed off with "it's been so nice getting to know you like this". One day those letters will all be found in the archives. So will the memos by which my husband and I communicate too. Can you believe it?

She made it clear that she alone, she felt, could manage her image, her job and her family. She felt that her husband's friends were manipulating the press against her – as they had done this very day – and that her only recourse was to fight like with like. And on this day too, she had a plan.

To my horror she began to set out a complicated story about how she had helped a tramp who had fallen into Regent's Park canal and was going to see him in hospital this afternoon. This 'Diana rescues tramp' story was new to me. But I had missed enough 'royal exclusives' in my life to be far from sure that I had not just somehow missed this one too.

That prospect obviously worried her as well. I did not seem interested enough. Some bits of her story did not fit together as well as a true story should. Yet it seemed churlish to cross-examine a princess who, in any case, had such a clear and crowded agenda of her own.

It was just at this moment that we were saved by the waitress and her warning that the paparazzi – with their special guides to pricing dresses, shoes and hats – were gathered outside the main restaurant door for her exit.

The Times car was at the side. We both slipped out of the door – and into the back seat. 'University College Hospital,' I said and we drove back across Park Lane. I began to explain to our passenger that this ruse was all rather pointless since no paparazzi were anywhere to be seen. Then she pointed to the wooded area in the central reservation of the road. First one lens caught the light. Then another behind a low branch, another on a thick trunk and others she said that she saw up in the trees. There was one man that she recognized, another that she began to wave to before the moment had passed the car was on its way to the tramp.

There was then a sharp banging on the top of the car. I started with alarm. The Princess was much calmer. Sitting six feet above the road, holding no camera that either of us could see, a unicyclist was correcting his balance with a rest upon our roof.

Later that day a royal messenger delivered a thick cream letter, thanking me for the 'rescue' in an airy open hand. 'Today of all days it meant a great deal to me not to be photographed.' The next day the newspapers carried full accounts of how the Princess had saved the tramp. *The Times* carried the story too, though without any briefing from me. It seemed perhaps the least interesting part of what the Princess had said.

Peter Stothard, editor, The Times

'She Talked Hopefully about her Future'

'There are more important things to worry about than my legs,' Diana, Princess of Wales observed with that self-deprecating (or was it mocking?) smile which won over so many people determined not to be impressed – including some of us lunching with her at the *Guardian*.

It was the spring of 1996, when the Princess was visiting newspaper offices a few months before her divorce from Prince Charles. It was around the time of the Great Cellulite Controversy, which raged in the tabloids for a full week. Were those famous legs beginning to look less than perfect?

No one around the *Guardian's* lunch table had raised the topic, but it came up during the inevitable discussion on the paparazzi. Diana hated their attention, she insisted. Between 10 and 15 photographers followed her every day, looking for the photo which could earn them '£15,000' for a single shot.

She did her work-outs at three different gyms and fortunately photographers only knew one of them, she said. 'They block the road in front of the car. They like to see you vulnerable, they like to see you cry,' the Princess told us. They swore at her – vehemently. According to my notes, made soon after lunch, she used an expression like 'f and c' to make clear just how bad it sometimes was.

The Princess's instinctive rapport with diverse audiences, billionaires and landmine victims alike, was already legendary and journalists were well within her range, particularly middle-aged men. Seductive rather than sexy, someone wrote yesterday. In her pink jacket, grey blouse, black knee-length skirt – and big blue eyes – she was giving us a performance. And manipulative or not (in truth probably a bit of both) it was a formidable one.

Cabinet ministers and other heavyweight public figures lunch in Fleet Street newspaper offices. Few give such a good account of themselves. The grizzled hacks softened and succumbed. The sisterhood was impressed – and pleased to be so. In picking an innocent 19-year-old to join 'the Firm', the Windsors had bitten off more than they could chew.

What most impressed Alan Rusbridger, the *Guardian's* editor, and his colleagues – women as well as men – was how fluent Diana proved to be, how adept at handling awkward questions. Jane Atkinson, her press officer, hardly said a word at the lunch. She didn't need to.

How did she get on with the Duchess of York? Great friends, Diana said, referring to them both as 'the girls' – as in 'the girls are a problem' for the Palace. Why did the Duchess get an even worse press than she sometimes did? 'I don't have an overdraft.' Princess Anne? She worked hard, so many engagements 'it makes you tired just to read the Court Circular'. A deadpan one-liner. Then she giggled.

The substance of the royal opinions was unremarkable. Unsurprisingly she was not a republican, despite her suffering at the hands of the British Royal Family. 'It's my children's future.' But she favoured a slimmed-down version – 'Prince Charles wants to change things' – and thought the Norwegians did it well, though 'we are not Norway'. She did not want to see the Queen Mother on a bike, she explained.

Her admiration for the Queen ('I call her Mama') was evident and, we thought, sincere. So was her dislike of the Court, cold people who had been there too long and were not 'street smart'. They did not know about people losing their jobs.

There was not much laughter at Buckingham Palace. They had been jealous of the publicity she attracted from day one and found change threatening. She still rang them 'to tell them what I'm doing'. After all, the Queen's private secretary, Sir Robert Fellowes, was still her brother-in-law, married to her sister Jane. Apart from expressing a dislike of fox-hunting ('I don't like my boys doing it') Diana was discreetly loyal to Prince Charles. They always agreed about the children, so sending William to Eton has been 'our decision. He has to be close to his Grandmother.'

The Princess talked hopefully about her future as Britain's roving ambassador. 'Everything is on hold until the divorce,' the Princess said. She hoped for a normal life eventually. 'In ten years it might be better.' What if she had never married Prince Charles? 'I would have been running Relate [the marriage guidance service],' Diana said without hesitation.

There was no mention of Camilla Parker Bowles, unless she was the unnamed 'another lady' whom Diana suspected was leaking news of the divorce decision to the *Sun*. It was all deftly done. Here was a royal who knew the plot of *EastEnders* and liked to talk to people in the queue at W.H. Smith's in Kensington.

She knew the jargon, she was street smart. And, in taking her sons to meet homeless people, she hoped they would be 'better equipped' to deal with life. It was earnestly naïve, but disarmingly so, a vulnerability with which – we now know – so many people could identify.

As Diana left the *Guardian*, people emerged from offices to get a glimpse of her. Spotting a burly computer manager peering out of the window, unaware she was still in the building, the most photographed woman in the world walked up behind him. Tapping him on the shoulder she innocently inquired: 'Have you got a good view?' Now that's style.

Michael White, *Guardian*

'SHE HELD ME SPELLBOUND'

The Princess of Wales glided through the door. She looked like a supermodel.

Tall, slim and beautiful and oozing this scent of her favourite perfume. 'Ah, ah,' she said, her face breaking into a broad grin. 'How nice to meet you, the man who knows me so well!'

Her sarcasm was not lost on me. It was the first time I had met her. And within seconds I had fallen under her spell – the toss of the head and the gentle dip of her eyes that make any man or woman immediately feel the centre of her world.

She wanted to talk about the *Sun* and her beloved boys and express her fears about their future under media scrutiny.

Like many aspects of her life, the meeting was accompanied with its own drama. The original idea was for a quiet, private chat with her press secretary, Geoff Crawford, at Kensington Palace.

But he was part of her cunning plan, an ambush designed for maximum effect. He said: 'The boss happens to be in the office at the moment.' As if on cue, she entered the room like an actress striding on to her stage and held me spellbound.

In truth the whole world was her stage. Every niche, every corner where she saw suffering became her mission. She knew she could make a difference. And she did.

Her almost saintly powers brought a smile to the afflicted and her ability to attract a big audience raised millions of pounds for those causes close to her heart.

It should not be forgotten that she almost single-handedly saved the Royal Family by adding glamour and down-to-earth personality to the ailing House of Windsor. She was almost addicted to newspapers and magazines – but it was her public following that she cared about.

Diana wanted readers of popular newspapers like the *Sun* to understand her concerns for her sons.

She also wanted our support for her charities, to publicize her interests and help us raise money for her causes, which we did.

The Princess also sought advice about how to deal with the paparazzi. Knowing police feared an incident in London, I implored her to restore her protection.

She admitted other members of the Royal Family had appealed to her to have a personal bodyguard, but she insisted it threatened her new-found freedom.

Our second meeting was at a Pavarotti Concert of Hope concert in Cardiff to raise money for a children's hospice at Ty Hafan.

During the interval she flitted from guest to guest. I stood in a corner as unobtrusively as I could.

After the room had emptied she dashed across to say hello and asked where my wife was. I told her she had popped to the loo.

On her return the Princess said to my wife: 'I am longing to go as well!' Our last meeting was a lunch at Kensington Palace.

The bitterness of her marriage break-up had gone, her anger over Camilla Parker Bowles had subsided. She felt ready for a new beginning.

William and Harry dominated her life. She was grateful that their school lives had been unhindered by the press but she wanted more assurances as William approached his late teens.

Today the world is worse off. We have lost a remarkable woman – but her short life lives on in the thousands of people she touched.

Stuart Higgins, editor, *Sun*

'Shame, Anger and an Aching Loss'

Our relationship was always one based on drawing the line. It could not have worked for so long without it.

She, better than anyone, realized the power of pictures. They were the means through which she led her life. The way through which she could convey her messages, her passions, her happiness, her sadness, herself.

At times she was confused. And the line became blurred. But there was a standard of privacy and basic decency which did prevail.

The same, we now know only too sadly, did not hold true for those photographers called the 'paparazzi'.

For them the extra inch on the other side of the line was paved with gold.

Diana represented a giant payday, potentially worth millions.

I have been in countless situations where the paparazzi have swung into action.

They could swear abuse at her. They would provoke her. They put her children under intolerable strain.

She recently told me of her deep fears at the way in which the 'scum', as she called them, had chased her on foot, swearing 'F****** Princess! Who do you think you are?'

And she had jumped into a taxi, her head on her knees crying. 'Why won't they ever leave me alone?'

She knew the answer, but she had no solution. Those people did not have rules. They operated on the price of her immeasurable fame.

I had rules. She knew that was the only way I could operate. And the price of our friendship was based on that trust.

It began when she and Prince Charles chose me to photograph Prince William's christening at Buckingham Palace in 1982. It was a truly great honour.

She joked then how to keep William quiet during the christening, placing her little finger in his mouth, gazing at him with those gleaming blue eyes.

It was a love too which she gave, unconditionally, to so many children in the good and bad years ahead. I remember the Concorde flight back from New York in 1989 when she cuddled the small black child with HIV. It was a triumph, sounding round the world, sweeping away prejudice.

In Cairo she agreed to pose for me in front of the pyramids. I told her it would be 'the eighth wonder of the world'.

She understood the camera and understood the old cliché that a picture speaks a thousand words.

And I remember that sad message she conveyed sitting alone in front of the Taj Mahal. That single picture summed up every aspect of her broken dreams and shattered marriage.

In Zimbabwe, 1992, she visited a leper colony. The sheer joy on the faces of those ravaged and shunned people sent a message round the world louder than any before.

And I remember the quieter moments. The way she worked in a room full of people – touching everyone, squeezing an arm, patting a back, ready with a smile.

I have worked on *The Mirror* for 32 years. More than half of that time, I have focused my attention almost exclusively on one lovely face. Thanks to her I was awarded Royal Photographer of the Decade last year.

I called it 'a special relationship'. But it has not been an easy one. The turbulent facts of her marriage. The divorce. The scandals. They have pulled the line to breaking-point.

In the aftermath of this terrible day, I do feel shame. And anger. And an aching loss.

Only a few months ago we met at the Royal Brompton Hospital where we discussed about how best to photograph a group of desperately ill, heart-diseased children with her.

I asked her to wear a 'Heart of Britain' tee-shirt in line with our *Mirror* campaign. She thought and then slowly shook her head.

'It's better to show the children's faces,' she said, suggesting that we gather the children as a group – just as though they were lined up for a school picture.

And she was right. A wonderful photograph which expressed those little ones with dignity.

And that for me sums up Diana, Princess of Wales.

A woman with the common touch. With a natural ability to treat life's cruellest victims as human beings first.

A great ambassador for the nation. A woman of courage and kindness.

A deeply loving mother. A Princess for all time.

Kent Gavin, chief photographer, *Mirror*

'SOMETHING I'D ONLY EVER SEEN BEFORE FROM NELSON MANDELA'

Like most thirtysomething women, I grew up with Princess Diana. We were just 16 and discovering the other sex when she glided up the aisle in that Emanuel dress, and though my friends and I shrieked with laughter at the creases when she stepped out of the carriage, in those days we, too, dreamt of finding our fairy-tale prince as we clutched our commemorative wedding mugs. Some of us went to the hairdresser afterwards clutching magazine pictures asking shyly for a 'Lady Di' and our first highlights; others of us experimented at home with Sun-In. Following Diana's footsteps, we bought the pedal-pushers and the woolly jumpers patterned with sheep. Like Diana – and quite unlike what our mothers had told us – we gradually discovered that there was more to life than gilded carriages and bridal gowns, and that the best place to feel good might be the local gym.

As we got older, went to university, took jobs and even got married ourselves, most of us formed a love-hate relationship toward Diana, detesting what we saw of her as a control-freak, but impressed with her ever-changing image and the ways she embraced those with Aids or leprosy.

She made it all right to have eating disorders or need therapy – if someone that beautiful could have an image problem, then we had every right to be

124

screwed up. The stick-thin girl in our class whose mysterious absences we were never allowed to talk about, we all remembered with guilt. I was overseas when the famous Taj Mahal photo appeared of the lonely Princess, and a friend who had just broken up with her fiancé faxed it to me with the message: 'And I thought I had problems!'

But in an era when we were striving to become career women as can-do as any male, Diana was just too feminine and emotional. So in January, when the editor of this newspaper asked me to cover her trip to Angola, I had very mixed feelings.

When I told my friends where I was off to, they laughed, knowing me as someone more used to reporting on wars, with little patience for the media obsession with Di's latest look. Having seen first hand the terrible effect of landmines in Afghanistan and Mozambique, I cared deeply about the issue her trip was intended to publicize, although I feared it would be a vast publicity stunt. At the same time I was intrigued to have a closer look at this woman with just one CSE whose fans were so diverse that they even included my hippie friend Sarina who knits jumpers in Bolivia and always asked me to send pictures, and Tanya, one of my most dynamic friends, who is so ambitious that when we were students she had written a list of 10 things to achieve by 30, including becoming a company director and making her first million.

Standing in the baking sun at Luanda airport waiting for the Princess to arrive, I remembered the footage of Diana assisting the heart operation at Harefield in full make-up. I scowled, fearing this was going to be more of the same. I was pleasantly surprised then when she turned up in jeans, white shirt and no make-up, and consoled myself over how good she looked by snidely spotting the designer label. As she sped off in a Red Cross jeep, 40 cameras in hot pursuit, a bemused Angolan selling chewing gum tugged my sleeve and asked who she was. It took me a while to understand that after 35 years of armed conflict and civil war which had torn the nation apart, this was one of the few countries in the world where Princess Diana was not an instantly recognizable figure.

It was all the more remarkable then to see her effect on the hundreds of mutilated mine victims we were to come into contact with that week. She'd come, she said, determined to work, and work she did. The Red Cross whisked us from one hospital to the next, each with ever more horrific scenes of skeletal figures with missing arms, missing legs and half-blown off heads – victims of some of the 16m landmines scattered around the country. Many of the injuries were so gruesome that I could not look, despite years of Third World reporting. But Diana never turned her head away. Instead, she had something I'd only ever seen before from Nelson Mandela – a kind of aura that made people want to be with her, and a completely natural, straight-from-the-heart sense of how to bring hope to those who seemed to us to have little to live for. As I speak Portuguese, I interpreted for her a few times and felt absurdly pleased to have those familiar blue eyes turned on me, knowing I'd tell my friends they were even bluer than they appeared on television.

It was not an easy trip. Angola in summer is infernally hot and dusty; the streets of Luanda piled high with stinking rubbish and flies buzzing around us non-stop; every other person seemed to be an amputee, and yet I never once saw Diana express fatigue or ask for a drink. I was jealous as hell of her ability to stay cool and neatly pressed – a stark contrast to my own dishevelled appearance. Just how remarkable was her adaptation became evident talking to the royal hacks who sat in the bar of the Hotel Presidente every night, wistfully recalling previous jaunts to Klosters and Barbuda, and longing for the Diana of old who went to balls and banquets and wore Versace instead of flak jackets.

That trip wiped out all my past cynicism about Diana, to my own astonishment as well as that of friends familiar with my views. That Lady-with-the-Lamp performance wasn't just for the benefit of the cameras. Of course, she knew all right when there was a good shot to be had, always gravitated to the woman with twin babies and no legs or the cute young girl. But I wasn't sure it mattered, if these pictures made people back home like my own mum and dad aware of the reality of life in this forgotten nation.

Once, at a hospital in Huambo when the photographers had all flown back to their air-conditioned hotel to wire their pictures, I watched Diana, unaware that any journalists were still present, sit and hold the hand of Helena Ussova, a seven-year-old who'd had her intestines blown to pieces by a mine. For what seemed an age the pair just sat, no words needed. When Diana finally left, the small girl struggled through her pain to ask me if the beautiful lady was an angel. Could anybody have said no?

I thought of Helena when I woke up last Sunday to the incomprehensible news that Diana had been killed. At the end of the Angola trip Diana said that the lasting image she'd take away was of that terribly ill young girl. Both of them are dead now and my lasting image will be the two of them just sitting together hand in hand, finding peace. Diana wasn't my friend – I'd only met her that one week – yet I, like so many women, somehow feel that she could have been. At one lunch in Huambo that I'd sneaked into, Diana poured me coffee and insisted that I fill my plate from the buffet, saying, 'You're too thin.'

If I lived in England, I would have gone to lay flowers outside Kensington Palace and sign the book of condolence at St James's. Most of my friends went and told how moved they were by the peace of the place and how, instead of just biting their lips, they shed tears – in some cases the first time publicly in their lives, a fact which by itself shows me how much one woman changed a nation. My friend Tanya has blacked out her web site on the Internet, turning it into a tribute to Diana; Julie has cancelled her holiday to watch the funeral; Jane is to run the marathon for charity in her name; and Emma has named her newborn daughter Diana.

We don't feel ambiguous about Diana any more – she was a modern woman, always reinventing herself, balancing the demands of being a single mother and having her own life, and looking beautiful at the same time. We grew up with her and now we must grow old alone.

Christina Lamb, *The Sunday Times*

'HER INFECTIOUS SMILE AND GENUINE ENJOYMENT'

Like many people all over the world, I recall with gratitude and affection the few times I met Princess Diana.

Our paths crossed ten years ago, in January 1987, when my son Philip started at Wetherby Prep School at the same time as Prince William, and the Princess impressed me and many others for the first time.

Taking young children to school isn't the quality time you wish to share with them but there was rarely a morning she missed, come rain, shine or a long state banquet the night before. To our amazement and envy, she always arrived with William in good time, looking fresh, in casual clothes, exchanging nods, smiles and greetings.

No school occasion or sports day passed without her and it is well-documented how she out-ran us all (nearly) every time in the mothers' race. We remember her infectious smile and genuine enjoyment of ordinary things. My son and Prince William became friends and I wondered whether it would be possible for them to meet outside school. One morning the phone rang and a voice said simply: 'This is the Princess of Wales. Could Philip come and have tea with William?' This was typical of Diana's informal approach to life, though I almost choked on my muesli.

Where other royals would have delegated the arrangements to a secretary or nanny, she made them herself.

There followed a happy time when our boys met for tea, weekends at Highgrove or at our own cottage in the country. On more than one occasion a visit by William would be followed up by a thank-you letter or flowers with a personal note from his mother.

In summer 1989, undiscovered by the media, Prince William came on holiday with us. When he and I opened his suitcase, on top of his clothes was a big, jolly card wishing him a happy time, signed by 'Someone who loves you very much.' The thank-you letter I received, full of gratitude, kindness and warmth, is something I shall always treasure.

Long before this, the Prince and Princess of Wales attended a charity concert at the Royal Academy in 1985, and my son was chosen to greet the Princess with a posy of flowers, and my husband and I, two of our children and the nanny, were introduced to the royal couple. Princess Diana was charming to everybody but, typically, it was our nanny, standing modestly in the background, whom she addressed.

My heart goes out to Prince William. May he fulfil the promise he showed as an endearing young boy, and I pray that he will never forget his mother's shining example.

Dagmar Lowe, letter to *Daily Mail*

'A Reminder of Our Own Responsibilities'

What were the unique qualities of Princess Diana, which in sixteen years of public life attracted such attention, respect and affection?

She was a person whose life allowed her to mix freely with Presidents,

Prime Ministers and leaders throughout the world, and yet she was equally able to meet, listen and talk with people in all walks of life. From her privileged position, she developed a deep personal awareness, understanding and responsibility to help those less fortunate in life.

In particular, she identified herself with those who suffered with severe disabilities and personal difficulties (which we only too often conveniently forget). Those ill with Aids, leprosy, cancer, handicapped and seriously ill children are only some of those who received her attention and unlimited support. She was always ready to assist in raising charitable funds to help meet the needs of such people. But for her this was not enough, her spontaneous compassion and deep understanding took her frequently to bedsides to give words of encouragement and comfort to those in pain or dying.

Her very last mission was to visit Angola and bring to the attention of the world the ongoing horrors of children and adults who are being maimed by landmines.

Over the last ten years, Princess Diana was President of Great Ormond Street Hospital for Sick Children in London. As Chairman of this hospital, I was to meet her on frequent visits to this international hospital that treats children with serious, complicated and rare illnesses.

There were no formalities for such visits. While always taking a keen interest in the caring and research work of the hospital, she spent most of her time in the children's wards. On entering she would immediately sit on a bed and with a warm smile talk quietly to a sick child. Often there was a reassuring arm around the shoulder or a loving hug. When talking to groups of children, she would always kneel to speak to them at their level. There were always words of sympathy and comfort to parents and time to talk to doctors and nurses. Her natural kindness and brilliant personality left everyone encouraged. They were visits we all treasured. We shall greatly miss her.

Today we pause to mourn the short but full life of a remarkable person. She not only won the affection of all who met her but also of the millions who did not.

Tomorrow we must remember the values that she brought to our attention. Her qualities of compassion, understanding and care for those less fortunate, are surely the qualities we ourselves should try to show in our daily lives.

129

The life of Diana, Princess of Wales, should be a reminder of our own responsibilities to the world we live in.

Sir Brian Hill, Chairman Great Ormond Street Hospital for Children NHS Trust

A FANTASY
OF OUR OWN POTENTIAL
WHAT DIANA MEANS

AN ICON FOR THE MERITOCRATIC AGE

Icons have candles lit before them and prayers uttered. In the Eastern Orthodox churches they are still painted to a strict formula transmitted over the centuries so that what we see is not reality as we would perceive it but an abstract pattern of lines and colours making up a holy face and its enfolding draperies. It is the reduction of holy presences to a series of signs and symbols. People have always needed icons. They fulfil a basic human urge in which our strongest hopes, desires and aspirations find expression in potent images of the idealized person admired. Over the centuries that need has proliferated out from religion, whether pagan or Christian, to embrace the rulers and heroes of the secular world. Diana, Princess of Wales, was already an icon before her death propelled her into semi-beatification as the Queen of Hearts and the People's Princess.

Diana retained her hold through images of herself and certainly not through her spoken word. She was never a good public speaker – indeed she began with a dull, flat, barely articulate voice. With training, however, plus her own application, she was to make huge strides in her vocal performances. But for them, apart from the famous television interview, she will never be remembered. For that we must turn to the astonishing kaleidoscope of her images: fairy princess, field-worker, fashion model, loving mother, international playgirl and hospital visitor. No other member of the Royal Family in this century has ever achieved such complex iconic status. But what is so striking is that this was achieved not as in days of yore by deliberately set-up official photographs but by the clicking of the world's media photographers.

All through this century the royal image has been largely controlled by means of a succession of official image-makers. Sir Cecil Beaton was the greatest of these, able to bestow an aura of mystery, magic and romance on to even the most dysfunctional members of the House of Windsor. But it is not for any of her official images that Diana will be remembered, for they embody the Palace's view of how they wished her to be.

The earliest is the group by Snowdon taken before the wedding, two stiff unbending figures, Charles in his military uniform, she arranged in tiara, a figure from a pre-1914 royal court, with an ancient tapestry let down behind them. The most notorious official photograph was Snowdon's tenth wedding anniversary group taken in the grounds of Highgrove, a phoney picnic set-up if ever there was one. The Princess is seated smiling but tightly drawn into herself, the Prince standing behind with the two little Princes arranged as appendages. By then the marriage was in shreds and the photograph stands as an indictment of a system which would seem to sacrifice anything to maintain the façade. The media, when the photograph was released, were not taken in.

So official images will not figure among the enduring representations of her, nor will painted ones. Most of our monarchs can be encapsulated in one image: Henry VIII by Holbein, Charles I by Van Dyck, even the present Queen by Annigoni, but I doubt that we will ever picture the Queen of Hearts as depicted by Bryan Organ in the canvas in the National Portrait Gallery, a trousered figure seated before a door without a handle.

All of this only emphasizes that Diana was truly a child of her own time. Mass photography and filming may have killed her, but it also made her, and she was unashamed in responding to its possibilities in a way no other member of the Royal Family has ever done before. And as a result she has ensured her own immortality on the grand scale.

What was unique about Diana was that the camera loved her. She was clearly totally unaware of this when, at 20, the press took those first snaps of her at that kindergarten school in Pimlico, an awkward upper-class young girl caught with the light behind her, silhouetting her thin, long legs. Looking through the cornucopia of photographs, it was about two years into the marriage that she not only gained confidence but certainly realized that she was photogenic. From then on, I can't recall a single photograph of her where she didn't look ravishing, for her beauty blossomed and her sense of style developed as she moved beyond an initial royal make-over.

Looking at those earlier pictures, we sense an image to some extent imposed, what Buckingham Palace conceived that a Princess of Wales should look like. In many ways, it took up from where Princess Margaret had left off, an updated version of the romantic English rose look, a face with eyes downcast and shy amidst billowing tides of soft diaphanous fabrics. By the mid-Eighties that had been relegated to the ragbag as she set off to be the sleek, modern, fashionable young woman of a kind that must have evoked the ghost of Wallis Simpson at the back of some people's minds. Hers was a figure so perfect that it could wear the slinkiest, superbly cut dress with the minimum of jewellery. As a consequence Diana embodied a new phase, not only in the alliance of the monarchy and the press (which in other areas was fast breaking down), but with the world of fashion. In that progression Diana moved out of the insular mould of British royalty, whose clothes remain those worn by an endangered species, to join the ranks of the international glitterati.

That developing image could not have sat easily with the rigidly conceived and conservative stance of the Palace. The message that they gave out was also somewhat startling, as though under a royal version of Naomi Campbell lurked a Florence Nightingale. The Palace is always suspicious of fashion. What it has failed to take in is that fashion actually unites people and that interest in it is as fervent on the council estate as it is in Sloane Street.

To this was added a new ingredient in the composition of the icon, which was to prove an even more radical departure. Distance, above all physical and emotional, has always been *de rigueur* for any member of the Royal Family. Those engaged in that new academic subject, the history of courts, will no doubt tell us one day when those attributes of being royal were first formulated. Another, that no member of the Royal Family must ever smile in public, was also part of the etiquette of the pre-1914 courts. That has gone, but the rest remained until Diana dispensed with them in the Eighties. In looking at the endless spontaneous photographs of her cradling maimed, injured or dying children, bending to kiss an old person, shedding a tear with someone bereaved or holding the hand of an Aids sufferer, we see how she crossed boundaries. When they are set against similar film and photographic coverage of members of the House of Windsor performing similar duties one quickly realizes how enormously she had moved things on, giving the family a new humanity missing before.

Her loss in this sense is incalculable because there is no one else within the existing family who is capable of it. And what emerges from the astonishing and touching emotional tide which has engulfed the country since her death is that this is precisely what the public now expects from the monarchy. And that was what set her pictures apart from those of other members of the family. She was not forever standing bolt upright with her handbag on her arm extending a stiff gloved hand, but kneeling down to a patient, sitting on the bed and hugging them or lifting a child into her arms. Her sense of caring always shone through. What makes it more extraordinary is that the Royal Family has founded its public image for the majority of this century on the probity of its private life, presented in countless images down to the 1969 royal film as the ideal family. We now know that to have been a fabrication. The one person who could have made it a reality was Diana. That opportunity has now gone, seemingly for ever.

Saint or sinner? In her famous, indeed notorious, television interview she presented herself as a *Mater Dolorosa*, her huge mascara-etched blue eyes soulfully turned upwards to the camera's lens. She never concealed her indiscretions, and in history it is true to say that the greatest saints have also been the greatest sinners, so that the final images of her are less contradictory than at first glance they would seem – a good-time girl of the *Hello!* magazine-type romping with Dodi in the sea and the bejeaned crisp-shirted field-worker in Bosnia.

In terms of today's aspirations they are not as incompatible as a cursory glance would suggest. I caught Pamela Stephenson neatly summing up Diana as a 'fantasy of our own potential'. To millions of ordinary women of today, she offered the possibility that wearing a sexy dress by Versace was compatible with a commitment to the work of Mother Teresa. The one no longer excludes the other in the late 20th century.

This is a more than larger-than-life version of the old adage that those whom the gods love die young. Her iconic potency is infinitely strengthened by the fact that we shall never see her middle-aged or old. Like Marilyn Monroe, she will be eternally young, in her case a great beauty and a great humanitarian rolled into one. This is an image of untold power which will continue to haunt the monarchy in the years to come.

What is so desperately tragic is that if the marriage had held, the present events would have lifted the monarchy right back from where it had slipped and endowed it with a halo. As it is, the public is all too aware that they are mourning the loss of a Princess who exercised virtues absent from other members of the family. Indeed someone regarded, it would seem, as having let the home team down.

Alas, for them the pantheon of iconic images which will be enshrined in the public mind will be those which only highlight the monarchy's failings: Diana sitting alone before the Taj Mahal, those blue pools of anguish staring out from the television screen and almost any picture of her holding or hugging another human being in distress. The monarchy has been kept going in this century by its women being able to project a whole series of images to hold a mass public in a democratic age, as the embodiment of the state and as wife and mother. The age of deference has gone and Diana was an icon made for the meritocratic age we live in, for she asked for nothing on the grounds of being a Princess but believed her chief role was to be, above all, a human being.

Sir Roy Strong, *The Times Magazine*

Diana National, Diana International

'For God's sake let us sit upon the ground and tell sad stories of the death of kings.'

William Shakespeare, *Richard II*

1981

It was the wedding of the past and the future: the Radetzky March meets the *Tatler* cover girl – just what the disunited United Kingdom needed. But, as it turned out, the past and the future couldn't get along. And between them the present got lost.

1533–1536

Once upon a time, many hundreds of years ago, in a kingdom by the sea, there lived the fair daughter of a country gentleman. she took the fancy of a mighty and impatient ruler, became his bride, and promptly bore him a daughter. But after only a little while her husband the King, became vexed by her silvery lightness of spirit and her failure to produce a son. Her enemies claimed that she was enamoured more of her own self than of her liege lord, and was careless with her tongue, and even, some whispered, with her favours. A thousand days after her nuptials, she was brought before her peers and accused of treason for plotting the King's death and for sharing her bed with five lovers, including her brother and a court musician. Her persecutors implied that she was a skilled sorceress, accomplished in the dark arts. As a commoner, the musician was hanged; her brother and the other gentlemen of the privy chamber were beheaded. Two days later, the disposable Queen was herself sent to the block, and on the following day King Henry VIII was betrothed to his next wife, who died shortly after bearing him a son.

Diana Spencer was no Anne Boleyn, and her end was tragically accidental, not malevolently designed. But her sad fate belongs to the history of a monarchy littered with carnage and carnality. She was consciously selected for the purposes of dynastic reinvigoration, but the tonic proved too heady for the ancient body of the monarchy. It thrashed around with increasing desperation, seeking ways to subdue the feistiness of the elixir, or else to get it out of its system altogether.

This had happened before, and not just to Henry VIII. In the twelfth century, Henry II's marriage to Eleanor of Aquitaine made him the master of an enormous empire, which included most of western France along with England. But his consort was independent-minded as well as independently wealthy. She had been married before, as a teenager, to Louis VII of France, and had gone crusading with him in the Holy Land, where rumours spread that she had committed adultery. The marriage had been annulled, but by the time Eleanor became Queen of the Anglo-Angevin Empire she had evidently learned something about the cruelty of princes, for she made no secret of her anger at Henry II's infidelities. A bitter estrangement ensued, with King and Queen locked in a battle for the loyalty of their sons. Suspicious that Eleanor had backed them in a revolt against him, Henry had his Queen confined. But she prevailed, outlasting her husband and living to see her favourite son, John, become king.

At the end of the eighteenth century, Princess Caroline of Brunswick, chosen by George III for his son, the Prince of Wales, was repudiated by her husband after bearing him a daughter. (The Prince had had a prior, illegal marriage to a Catholic commoner, Maria Fitzherbert.) To his dismay,

Princess Caroline refused to disappear; instead, she conducted her own court and her own romances, becoming steadily more popular than the heir to the throne. Her trial before the House of Lords for adultery – essentially an attempt to rob her of her title – turned into a public-relations calamity, with vast, riotous crowds applauding Caroline and jeering at her husband.

Diana surely knew of these redoubtable predecessors. In a recent television interview, she made it plain that she saw herself as part of a tradition of 'strong women' destined to make the establishment lose sleep at night for fear of what they might do next. It was, after all, her spirited embrace of modernity that had made her useful to the guardians of propriety. Now they would have to live with it.

1961

Remember, both Diana and Dodi were babies of Suez, an event as traumatic for Britain as Vietnam was for America. Dodi was born into the Egypt of Naguib and Nasser, a country that had just deposed the playboy King Farouk. Diana was born into a Britain still licking its wounds from the worst fiasco of its imperial disintegration. In 1956, an Anglo-French military force, the rotten fruit of a secret alliance, had pretended to 'interpose' itself between embattled Egyptian and Israeli troops but had been forced into ignominious withdrawal after the United States made it clear that it was displeased with the gambit. The debacle disgraced the British Prime Minister, Anthony Eden, and left the country writhing in fury and humiliation, and with a long-term Egypt complex.

In 1961, when Diana was born, on the Queen's private estate of Sandringham, the strength of national tradition was still the balm for impotence. Superannuated brigadiers in Cotswold pubs consoled themselves with the truism that if the Yanks had the power the Brits still had the glory. Elizabeth II's annual Christmas message, transmitted to the Commonwealth after British digestions had dealt with the plum pudding, was treated as an oracle from the Palace – the royal equivalent of a papal *pax vobiscum*. The London *Times* still had nothing on its front page but dignified small advertisements and announcements; the Tory Prime Minister was the reassuringly avuncular and squirearchical figure of Harold Macmillan; the noontime entertainment on the radio was called, without a trace of irony, 'Workers' Playtime'; and the annual cricket match between amateur and professional cricketers at Lord's was called Gentlemen vs. Players. 'Coming out' was for debutantes, not gays, and it meant being presented to the Queen. Each year, troops of double-barrelled Henriettas and Lucindas dutifully followed the rituals of the Season, donning wellies at the point-to-point or straw hats and ribbons on the towpath – doing whatever it took to find the perfect Nigel or, at the very least, notch up a mention in 'Jennifer's Diary', the society column of the magazine *Queen* and the unofficial archive of the ruling class.

Diana might have followed this well-trotted trail from the Badminton Horse Trials to the Henley Regatta, but she didn't. Somewhere, beyond the clotted cream and the Hooray Henries, there was another Britain – a Britain that was sick of being divided into country-house masters and comical Cockneys. The sex scandals that mired the last days of the Macmillan government and the transfer of power from the Prime Minister's hospital bed to his designated successor, the fourteenth Earl of Home, only confirmed this Other England in its gathering contempt for tradition. It was fidgeting around in its chrysalis, and when it finally broke free of the drab casing it went in for a cultural make-over the likes of which had not been seen since the Edwardians. It was rowdy, inventively insolent, street-smart, and genuinely democratic. In Lindsay Anderson's insurrectionary fantasy *If*, it had already machine-gunned the public-school establishment. And now it was waiting for Diana – not that the little girl from the broken aristocratic household and the Swiss finishing school knew a thing about it.

1981

By the time she came along, kitted out in the standard Sloane uniform, her large eyes running for cover beneath her bangs, it was too late. The Beatles had come and gone. England's finest hour – the besting of Germany in World Cup soccer, in 1966 – was a distant memory. Labour Party governments that had tried to mantle themselves in the gaudy colours of swinging London found that they were themselves swinging from the rope of the ailing British economy. Promises to stand firm by the value of the pound sterling were followed repeatedly by devaluation, for which international bankers, a.k.a. 'the gnomes of Zurich', were blamed. Grim winters of strikes produced electricity blackouts, turning Yuletide cheer into bitter darkness. The 'pinko-grey' race, as E.M. Forster called the masters of the British Empire, found itself confronted by an Indo-Caribbean immigrant generation that had the cheek to answer back.

Into this dismal picture strode, 'like a colossus' (as she would be the first to say), the phenomenal person of Margaret Thatcher. Attempting to understand Princess Diana's appeal without taking that Prime Minister into account is like assuming that Glinda ruled the Land of Oz uncontested. For, by the time Charles Philip Arthur George and Diana Frances stepped out of the nave of St Paul's Cathedral into the sunlight and the cheers of millions, it was Margaret Thatcher who had annexed the idea of a revolutionized 'new' Britain within her steely grip. This was to be a Britain in which the worst thing was not, as Diana would later say, 'to feel unloved' but to be unproductive. Accordingly, the British welfare system was brutally deconstructed; its dependent charges were given a strong dose of salts that looked suspiciously like mass unemployment and were told in no uncertain terms to stand on their own two feet. Thatcher and her supply-side myrmidons danced on the grave of the 'nanny state'.

But Diana had *been* a nanny (as well as a kindergarten teacher), and had seen nothing wrong with what she often called TLC. After her marriage, she very rapidly became the antithesis not only of her husband and the well-starched custodians of royal correctness but of the Prime Minister. It was not simply that Britons chose between the firm and the gentle hand; it was rather that they craved both the spankings and the smiles, and in no particular order. When Maggie barked and commanded, the country stood at attention; when Di smiled that smile, the same country melted in a warm puddle of adoration. Both women were necessary for the rebuilding of national confidence. Maggie's warships recapturing the Falklands were a poke in the eye to all those who had for decades jeered at Britain as the sick man of Europe. Diana's jaw-dropping allure gave the lie to the hoary give that where other nations had sex Britain had hot-water bottles. She was the bare-shouldered beauty, but she was also Peter Pan's Wendy, ministering to an entire nation of Lost Boys.

Indeed, Diana's physical outwardness was both the triumph and the trouble. The Princess touched people, and not just metaphorically. When she laid her hands on the sick, and especially on victims of Aids, she was, perhaps without knowing it, tapping one of the most ancient rituals of royal magic: Thaumaturgy, or touching for the king's evil. Medieval kings, at their coronation (and on each subsequent anniversary), would extend their hands to those suffering from the disfiguring disease of scrofula. It was believed that through their divine appointment they were able to absorb the evil of the disease into their own bodies and exorcise it. This was the emblematic miracle of monarchy, distantly related to the Gospel of Jesus washing the feet of the poor. More than any of the Palace Windsors, Diana seemed to understand the incredible potency of the common touch.

But, of course, it was for the Prince to exercise thaumaturgy, not his wife. Increasingly, the Royal Family found itself struggling to preserve the mysteries of its authority against a rogue member who seemed to believe in the healing power of familiarity, and who gradually came to seek out rather than flinch from the flashbulbs. But even as Diana was becoming an adept at healing the wounds of the British body politic she was secretly doing hurt to her own. As her husband seemed, bafflingly, to reject her company, she turned gratefully to the embraces of her children and the British people, and returned those embraces with genuine spontaneity and warmth.

Which is not to say, as the unofficial obsequies are already doing, that Diana was a saint. On the contrary, the power of her appeal was precisely the vulnerable fallibility that became increasingly visible as the wide eyes got still wider in the bulimically shrunken cheeks. To the morning coats in the Palace, Diana the Martyr was an even bigger nightmare than Diana the Pop Idol. Hence the desperate tactic of Prince Charles's making an end run around his wife's mastery of the media and giving the notorious interview that effectively ended the experiment begun in St Paul's Cathedral. Diana's response was to out-confess her husband in a telegenic performance of stunningly well-coached artlessness, leaving no cliché of the self-esteem movement undeployed. And the great British public, which back in Harold Macmillan's tweedy age would have averted its eyes in the presence of psychological damage, now Felt Her Pain.

The mortification registered by the guardians of the Palace may have been a little disingenuous, seeing as they had (presumably) allowed the Prince to have his say, but Diana herself may have been just a little confused about what she had really wanted from all the exercises in truth therapy. For the rest of her brutally interrupted life, she seemed both to demand and to expect maximum personal freedom, along with continued public prominence. Her determination 'not to fade away' was in many respects admirable, but in the torrent of vilification currently raining down on the subhuman paparazzi it ought not to be forgotten that Diana did want both privacy and publicity, and the power to control which had the upper hand and when.

1997

In her last months, Diana seems to have understood – perhaps even welcomed the fact – that the role she was inventing for herself had no precedent in British tradition or public life. It's not hard to imagine the upper lips of those in the royal circle stiffening to the point of rictus as they contemplated the establishment of an alternative court, funded by their own divorce settlement, attended by global contingents of Beautiful People, and exerting a bewitching spell on the growing Princes. Anne Boleyn was sent to the axe for much less.

In the end, though, there was a contradiction (which turned out to be monstrously fatal) in Diana's sense of her plans for herself. For she badly wanted to be both Diana National and Diana International. The fallout from this was apparent in the notorious interview with *Le Monde*, in which she said that if it were not for the boys any sane person would already have fled the sceptred isle. And her choice of lover was destined, in the long run, to make her adoring British public become disenchanted. For the ghosts of Suez have not all gone away. Though the treatment of the senior Al Fayed at the hands of the British naturalization authorities was evidently not cricket, Diana's alliance with the family that bought Harrods, the retailing world's equivalent of St Paul's Cathedral, and then leased the Paris mansion of the despised, exiled Duke of Windsor would finally have been seen as an act of wilful de-patriation.

It's not a problem that she or Britain will have to face. She was certainly more sinned against than sinning, and there is nothing in the book of misdemeanours that a funeral in Westminster Abbey, the mausoleum of Kings, will not wipe clean from public memory. Normally, the great diapason of British ceremony could be relied on to rise, swell, and cover her astonishing, tragic history. But the argument between tradition and modernity that Diana was recruited to settle threatens to follow her noisily beyond the grave. There is a chance that for the first time since the death of Victoria the well-oiled machinery of the monarchy may actually stall on the phenomenon of the populist Princess. And there is the absolute certainty that as the last anthems are sung the paparazzi will begin to focus their long-distance lenses on the already ominously good-looking features of William the Fair.

Simon Schama, Historian, in the *New Yorker*

THE END OF CYNICISM

The crowds Diana has brought out on to the streets are revolutionaries without knowing it. Unlike revolutionaries in the past, they are hungry not for for bread or for the blood of their oppressors – but for intimacy.

The culture of intimacy is being revealed as a major force in many countries as well as in Britain. This has been a spontaneous revolt by an unofficial world on which there are not statistics, a world independent of armies and governments and technology, but to which anyone – however poor, uneducated or unattractive – can belong. It is a protest against the official world whose coat of arms is the stiff upper lip and whose rule is always to keep up appearances and do what is expected. The confrontation should not have surprised us.

The culture of intimacy is the opposite of the culture of cynicism which, until last Sunday, appeared unchallengeable in the West. The world is still full of people who have used cynicism as a raincoat to protect themselves from the cloudbursts of daily existence. And yet, this week even some of them have suddenly found themselves uncharacteristically touched by this tragedy, and felt some sympathy with the great upsurge of regret that Diana's smile has vanished.

Cynics do not smile as she did. In previous centuries, a cynic was a brave rebel against convention. But today you become one, first, from losing faith in yourself, and then from despairing of others, too. What you seek, above all, is not to relive the horrible pain of being idealistic and then disappointed, so you systematically extinguish hope.

You can have a certain amount of fun as a cynic, wielding mockery and parody, but you will get only limited consolation from wrapping your sadness in the jargon of post-modernism. At its worst, cynicism is a universal despair. At its best, it is an eternal procrastination: 'I'm very brave generally, only today I happen to have a headache.'

It is inevitable that cynicism should lose its attractions with time, because hope has always re-sprouted – politically even after centuries of brutal suppression and domestically almost every time a child is born or two individuals fall in love. Today, it may be coming back into fashion.

Tony Blair's refusal to wipe his smile off his face, despite the mockery of cynics, is one sign among many of a determination to discover new forms of courage.

The culture of intimacy is fuelled by this search. The audacity of the post-war generation expressed itself in the desire to be happy, and many still believe that the purpose of intimacy is happiness. But happiness is an outdated ideal. It is impossible to be happy when others are not.

Being useful to others is an alternative ambition, more difficult to achieve; Diana, who was not happy, intuitively adopted it – and the grieving crowds are silently applauding her. They are not making public speeches, because the culture of intimacy has beliefs about the art of attaining one's objectives which are genuinely novel. It grows from a conviction that, terrible and inflexible though the world is, it is possible for individuals to make a difference to it, personally to diminish its cruelty and misunderstandings.

Instead of seeking change as individuals, alone or in large groups, the most promising, dynamic unit of action is two people. The *tête-à-tête* is the new source of confidence, the refuge where people give each other courage, and where they create the mutual respect between the sexes which is the most original achievement of our century – even if we still have a very long way to go.

Respect has become the universal goal. Even in one of the poorest villages in the world, where the descendants of slaves live in shacks without furniture or water, when I recently asked villagers what they wanted most, they replied not money or power but 'respect'. Even the rich and powerful are hungry for respect, for neither wealth nor authority guarantees it any more. Respect is something any two individuals can create between themselves, by the way they treat each other and talk to each other. Diana's hug has become its symbol.

The culture of intimacy has not been taken seriously, because its aberrations have been more visible than its positive aspects. When personal relations and private problems become the priority in people's lives, it is natural for cynics to interpret this as another manifestation of cynicism, a distancing of oneself from more weighty political concerns.

And, indeed, preoccupation with the personal remains a form of withdrawal so long as it is based on introspection and degenerates into a search for the scapegoats whom one can blame for one's misfortunes. This dark side, the difficulty of being too close to others, is illustrated by Diana's outbursts against her nannies, employees, friends, mother and stepmother, quite apart from the Royals.

However, some people get tired of asking 'Who am I?', to which there is never a satisfactory answer. Then they ask, instead, 'Who are you?'

Interest in the private lives of public figures can be legitimate as well as prurient. It does not follow that someone who lies to his wife will lie in his other dealings, but it is relevant to one's judgment of him. The culture of intimacy extends far beyond scandalous newspaper stories. In British politics, it is perhaps best symbolized by Mr Blair working not at a desk but on a sofa – made for two, a place for conversation.

Then one realizes how absent from our institutions genuine conversation is, because we have built a state designed to restrict the need for it. In ancient times, political loyalties were personal; but the closeness was vitiated by nepotism and favouritism. The nineteenth century's solution was to make relations fairer by establishing impersonal rules, about which there can be discussion. That has produced a welfare state which is too cold, too impersonal. A cheque is inadequate consolation for misfortune.

Diana spotted the need for the reintroduction of human warmth into institutions which are ultimately forced to concern themselves more with their own efficiency than the vulnerability of those they are supposed to protect. The novelists who nourish our imaginations about the possibilities of intimacy are now being urged by some reviewers to abandon the 'neurotic school of fiction', to stop wallowing in the 'sewers of exhausted liberalism' and start conveying 'some of the magic as well as the bleakness of existence'.

In the theatre, Irina Brook's *All's Well that Ends Well* shows what new depths of emotion friendship between actors can achieve. In pop music, the dreadlocked Jazzie B of Soul II Soul, celebrating generosity of spirit, regularly reaches the Top 10. Oasis sing: 'I hate the way you are so sarcastic. I've tried to find a better way.' But most people still do jobs they do not enjoy, or which leave many sides of their personality untouched.

The culture of intimacy attempts to achieve what international power politics cannot; it is all about the crossing of frontiers. Where you are going matters more than where you come from. In this perspective, it is a tragedy of historic proportions that Diana has not lived to pursue her friendship with Dodi Fayed, whom the Arab world has made its hero. They bridged the gap between two forms of intimacy. Eliminating the mistrust between Islamic and Western civilization requires the multiplication of personal friendships, the establishment of emotional bonds, as much as political generosity.

It is no accident that a woman should have sparked this unofficial revolt against the official world held together by gentlemanly traditions fearful of emotion and its disorders.

But one should not assume that the official world, sustained by all sorts of vested interests, is about to collapse; nor that the culture of intimacy is about to become official. They exist side by side, and the future of both is uncertain.

Throughout history, ideologies have always developed in unpredictable ways: they can be implemented with compassion, or dogmatically, producing diametrically opposed results. Intimacy can as easily be a nightmare as a solace.

Diana's death has made us worry about what we have lost. But all is not lost. Whatever her weaknesses and illusions, she has at least made us think about our priorities.

Theodore Zeldin, historian, in the *Observer*

THE SAVIOUR SPURNED BY THE COURT

One must not allow the lava of sanctification to harden. Diana, Princess of Wales, always hated pomposity, distrusted the excessive ceremonial of the court, and had a gift for ordinary friendships. She would have found formal eulogies of her personality either tiresome or laughable. From the beginning we should try to remember her as she really was: a beautiful woman of her own time, resilient despite the many sad events in her life, an attractive and warm human being. She had real compassion for suffering, but also a knack for getting on well with all sorts of people. She was fun; she liked to laugh and to make people laugh; she believed in hugs and kisses, particularly for children and the sick. A lovely, friendly young woman has been lost to the world.

What mattered to her most was the future of her sons. When she married, she was very young, though her strong willpower must already have been present. Nobody nowadays would take on the role of the future Queen, which she very much wanted to become, without a real inner conviction. Quite soon she decided that she had something unique and necessary to give to the monarchy. She came to think that the Royal Family was failing to adjust to the post-war world, that its other members had lost touch with the age in which they were living and to that extent were losing touch with their people.

Diana's life cannot be understood without recognizing the pains that she had suffered at each stage of her life. Her childhood was made insecure and unhappy by the separation from her mother; she hoped above everything for a successful and warm relationship with her husband and with the Royal Family. That too failed her; no doubt her childhood had made it more difficult for her to create the kind of secure family life she so much wanted. Suffering can, however, develop strength in those who survive it. Her ability to communicate with people who were sick, disabled or dying, and to give them comfort, was a remarkable human quality. She used that gift, as well as her fame in the world, to help the suffering. The unhappiness of her childhood also helped her to be an excellent mother: warm, loving, caring and, in an important way, serious.

Diana had great gifts. She was largely unacademic; indeed she rather distrusted intellectual interests in case they got in the way of her strong intuitive sense. She was, however, very quick; she could be unpredictable; she had an ability to foresee how the public would react; she was nobody's fool, though sometimes she was thought of as such by those who mistakenly underrated her. She also had a mysterious 'star' quality which made her much the most famous member of the Royal Family in the postwar period. She also had a gift which has played its part in Tony Blair's astonishingly successful career: she could instinctively identify herself with the aspirations of her own generation. The children of the 1950s and 1960s seem to have abandoned the universal hopes and schemes of earlier generations. They no longer believe in Utopian systems of socialism or in any other political theories. They put their energy for doing good into particular projects. Tony

Blair was able to win the largest election victory of this century by his ability to represent these ideals. Diana's work to help Aids or cancer victims, or to outlaw landmines, had the same appeal. She also represented the Royal Family's equivalent of the 'new' in new Labour. She did not argue for a new monarchy altogether, but she did believe that the monarchy needed to adapt to the present. I am not sure anyone else in the Royal Family fully understands that, except possibly for Prince William, under her influence.

That is why the loss is so tragic, not only in personal terms, not only in terms of national grief, though that will be profound and long-lasting, but because Diana stood for something important in British national life and there is, for the present, no one who can replace her.

There have been three stages of a constitutional argument in which she was largely right but the court usually opposed her. The first stage was the period of her early marriage, down to the birth of Prince Harry, in which the young bride saw increasingly clearly how the monarchy ought to develop but was pushed aside as an inexperienced girl trying to influence an ancient institution which was determined to go on doing things in its own way. There was also some jealousy of her celebrity status. The people loved her.

The second stage, in the time leading up to the divorce, was one in which Diana was becoming increasingly effective with the public and increasingly aware of the issues about the future of the monarchy, but the cooling of the marriage and the eventual divorce were undermining her position. Some conservative courtiers were relieved when the divorce actually occurred; they regarded her as an uncontrollable 'loose cannon'. They would not accept that their attitude was already out of date, and that she had a better instinct for public opinion, on which all monarchs ultimately depend.

The third stage has been the one between the divorce and her death. Again, at first sight, the cause she stood for seemed to have been lost. Diana was engaged in making a new life for herself. As a single woman she was enjoying a much freer social life; as a public figure she was making her compassion practically useful; she was continuing to be an excellent mother. Everything was beginning to fall into place.

Interestingly, Prince Charles was also coming to be seen as a more human figure, and public attitudes to the Royal Family were starting to improve. She was probably also succeeding in her plans to bring up Prince William as a thoroughly modern future King.

Nobody can yet say whether the death in Paris will have brought to an end the warmth and modernization which was Diana's contribution to the history of the Royal Family. A lot will depend on how well Prince William is able to overcome the tragedy. He and Prince Harry have, in the most genuine way, the sympathy of the entire nation. Royal policy could now develop in one of two ways. It is possible that the court will make few changes, and that life at Buckingham Palace will go on as usual. In that case, the late Princess of Wales's attempt to modernize the Royal Family will have ended in failure. Things may change in Prince William's time, but that will be all that is left to hope for, and it could come too late.

Yet history does not usually work like that. It is shaped by great and tragic events. The courtiers will be as shaken as the rest of the country by the grief we all feel. They are human too, and subject to all the human emotions. When remarkable people die in old age, people grieve with gratitude for their achievements; when such people die in youth, people grieve with added pain for their lost hopes. The dead sometimes have more influence than the living.

The Princess hoped for a renewal of the monarchy and she did not want to wait for her son's time. She wanted it to be a strong institution, compassionate and contemporary. That was the core of her life's work. Her divorce at one point seemed to be the end of these hopes, or at least of her influence. Even that was not quite so. Her death could provide a new and powerful energy to advance her aims. She had been, I think, the most remarkable member of the Royal Family since Queen Victoria. She was sad, she needed to be helped, she was entertaining, she was loveable; but she was certainly not an ineffective figure in our national history. At the time of her death she was still maturing, and gaining in her understanding of the world; that we have lost for good, and it is a great deal.

William Rees-Mogg, *The Times*

THE TWO DIANAS

She was our greatest royal personality since Queen Victoria. She could have been the most valuable. Properly helped and guided, Diana's extraordinary combination of gifts could have transformed the relationship between royalty and the public, deepening and strengthening it and making it almost invulnerable.

But her royal husband betrayed her, and his family then closed ranks, robbed her of her status, downgraded her title and excluded her from their intimacy. With only a scattered family of her own, she was lonely, unadvised, unsupported and fragile. She looked for loyalty and was exploited. She sought affection and found greed. She asked for love and got only publicity.

Her death, far from being meaningless, was full of meaning, even symbolic. She was a martyr to a combination of evils: the coldness of royalty, the prurience of the public in demanding even the most intimate secrets of her heart, and the cruelty of the media in supplying them.

In a sense, then, we are all guilty of causing her death. But some are conspicuously more guilty than others. The countless millions who cherished her will not be content unless some effort is made to apportion blame, show remorse and learn lessons.

However, it would be wrong to see Diana's life as an unrelieved tragedy. In some ways it was a tremendous success story.

She was only six when her family split up. She did not know what it was to have a sustaining home; she had precious little formal education; she was barely out of her teens when she married an ageing Prince Charming who had already given his affections elsewhere.

She had a miserable childhood, a curtailed adolescence and a youth quickly overshadowed by alarming responsibilities, of motherhood and public duty.

The amazing fact is that she survived these burdens and misfortunes to become one of the most delectable creatures of her age. It was a triumph of human will – hers.

Providence gave her beauty, but it was she who contrived to project it until it radiated to every quarter of the globe. She was 'a gem of purest ray serene', lighting up the dusty corners of lonely hearts, dancing into and scintillating the lives of multitudes longing to be nourished by grace and charm.

The world craves glamour, and Diana supplied it, but in the only form in which it is universally acceptable: allied with seriousness and high purpose. People could see that she was not just a beautiful woman but a beauty who had suffered – her eyes said it all.

She appeared on the world's stage as one who had ensured a woman's habitual wrongs and had learned to identify with the wrongs and sufferings of others.

Here again, Providence gave her natural intuition. But it was her own wit and willpower which turned this gift into a formidable engine of mercy and benevolence, reaching out personally to the stricken in a way no government or aid agency knows how.

Diana used her body as she used her beauty, to bring alive her response to grief: the touch of her fingers, the warmth of her lips, her encircling arm, her wholehearted hugs, her lap ever welcoming for a sad and abandoned child, she was always ready to move close to those who were hurt to comfort them.

For Diana, there were no strangers. All humanity was her friend. The bereaved, the dying, the sick and homeless, the outcasts and the despised – these were her close friends. She treated them as allies in the veil of tears they shared with her.

Often she had nothing to give but her love and sympathy. But that was a great deal to those who received it and the hundreds of millions who witnessed, on television and in photographs, the sincerity of the giving and the gentle joy of the response.

She had the truly princely gift of making the most insignificant person feel important to her, the recipient of her undivided attention, no longer excluded and ignored but brought into the warm circle, welcomed, cherished, made much of and caressed.

Diana had the magic to persuade the oppressed and the suffering, if only for the fleeting moment of her visit, that the world is not wholly evil or indifferent, and that one great personage at least cared for them deeply – not as a statistic or a class or a race or a social problem, but as an individual human being. They looked into her eyes and saw not just compassion but genuine love.

To possess such a gift amounts to a kind of genius, and brings with it heavy responsibilities to use it fruitfully. And on the whole that is what the Princess did.

Of course, there were two Dianas. There was the pleasure-loving Diana, the irresponsible, ignorant and foolish Diana, who did silly things without thinking, who asked for advice and ignored it, who had an appalling taste in men and sometimes gave way to it – Jackie Onassis Diana who lolled sensuously on rich men's yachts, who rolled her eyes and indulged herself and manipulated people with her wiles.

But the other Diana, the good Diana, was also the real Diana, who ultimately came to the top throughout her rollercoaster life. This was the Diana who suffered and, because she suffered, cared; the Diana who acted and campaigned and who used herself, without regard to disease or danger, to the utmost of her energy and with all the gifts God gave her, in the service of the weak.

Part crusader, part Mary Magdalene, part Florence Nightingale and wholly woman – with all that implies in tenderness, sensuality, capriciousness, warmth and single-minded love – Diana was in some ways a lady from the early Christian past, a fun-loving Princess-turned-saint who might have figured in an illuminated martyrology, and to whom only a Fra Angelico or a Donatello could have done justice.

But simultaneously she was very much a figure of her time, an icon of the muddled and mystical Nineties, with her psychobabble and consultations with 'wise women', yet also with her passionate concern for health and fitness, a clean environment and a world free from hidden, deadly weapons.

She was thus the stuff of which legends will be made and tales told, who will live on in the memories and fertile imagination of the human race, all of whom she touched during her brief but fiery passage through this life.

She was unique, a phenomenon: she leaves a huge, aching hole in people's sensibilities. The real soap opera in which we live has suddenly lost its most memorable and attractive character.

The men and women who control the British establishment will now have to think hard about how to limit the damage. There is the crucial matter of the upbringing of Prince William and Prince Harry; the public will not relish the spectacle of the Prince of Wales's mistress taking up the role of surrogate step-mother, especially since Charles is now free to marry more appropriately.

Then there is the question of how the Royal Family as a whole, having lost its one pearl, whom it threw away, can re-establish its popularity. It will not be easy but it might begin with a few words of much-needed repentance.

Finally, the Government will need to consider, not in haste but as a matter of urgency, the rising public desire for some legal check on the intrusions into privacy which have robbed the nation of the brightest jewel in its crown.

We must not allow Diana to have died in vain. We owe it to her memory, which will remain fresh and fragrant in our hearts, to address these matters with deliberate speed and wisdom.

Paul Johnson, *Daily Mail*

A GLORIOUS FORCE FOR REPUBLICANISM

When it comes to 20th-century iconography, we really have been fed a load of old rope. One blurry man jumping on the back of a car containing another blurry man, who could be anyone from John Kennedy to Julian Clary. A space suit, allegedly with a man inside it, floating on the end of a cord over a cratered surface, allegedly the moon. But now, at last, this sad, glittering century has an image worthy of it: a wandering, wondering girl, a silly Sloane turned secular saint, coming home in her coffin to RAF Northolt like the good soldier she was.

Only one thing jarred: Diana's coffin was covered with the Royal Standard, not the Union Flag. In death the House of Windsor is eager to claim her; in life it had already frozen her out with a staggering mean-mindedness best seen in the stripping of her HRH style and the official removal of her name from the prayers said daily for the Royal Family by the Church of England.

Diana was once again the commoner she had always really so radiantly been. And like other commoner heroes, she made it clear that loving one's country and loving the sorry bunch of dysfunctional Graeco-Germans stuck on as an afterthought at the prow were two entirely different – and sometimes actually contradictory – things.

In the soft-focus shampoo commercials being churned out in such indecent haste, no glimpse of the other Diana has yet been seen. We have seen Diana the Good, Diana the Stylish, Diana the Dutiful. These were, of course, real and valid Dianas. But we have not yet seen the other great Diana – Diana the Destroyer.

And destroyer she has been, gloriously so, with bells on; the greatest force for republicanism since Oliver Cromwell. She leaves the Royal Family with one big ticking gift-wrapped timebomb of a farewell present: the fact that, for the first time, more subjects of the House of Windsor are against it than for it. When the BBC televised the flag and played 'God Save the Queen' on Sunday, it seemed almost ironic; you could almost visualize Diana's slow, sly smile and mocking, mischievous eyes. God Save the Queen? God *Help* the Queen, more like, especially if she's got Nature Boy and the Rotweiler as her great white hopes to look forward to on her deathbed.

Diana's was not the republicanism of economics and pie charts; it was, like all her politics, based on emotion and none the worse for it. Coming from one broken home, yearning to create a real one, she was treated by her husband and his parents with a level of deliberate exploitation, manipulation and deceit that would be dazzling if it wasn't so vile. It was a fairy-tale, all right – one scripted by the Brothers Grimm, or a version of Cinderella in which the unsuspecting, virtuous heroine was not plucked *from* isolation and cruelty as a reward for her beauty and purity, but rather condemned *to* it. Very soon – with the dry, very English, self-mocking wit which provided a welcome balance to her occasional over-emotional, therapized American – she was calling herself the Prisoner of Wales.

And from the scraps she was thrown, sitting there in her sumptuous scullery, she made a life: a real, well-lived, well-used life in which she visibly pushed herself from a state of bovine upper-class ignorance (the only qualification she took from Heathfield School was a certificate for Best-Kept Hamster) to a state of inquisitive, crusading sentience. And in getting herself a life – in *wanting* to know, in *daring* to look naïve – she showed the House of Windsor up for what it was: a dumb, numb dinosaur, lumbering along in a world of its own, gorged sick on arrogance and ignorance.

Above all, she showed up her husband, the supposed 'intellectual' of the Firm, for what *he* was: a third-rate mind with delusions of adequacy, a veritable human jukebox of philosophical clichés completely unable to concentrate or contribute to any cause for any length of time. (I always found the idea that Diana failed to provide the Prince of Wales with the intellectual companionship he craved a real scream – this was the man who turned to Camilla Parker Bowles, Dale Tryon and Selina Scott for solace! You'd get more cerebral stimulation from the Three Stooges.)

'She had an inquisitive, strong mind,' said Magdi Yacoub. She also had a real sense of duty and an enthusiasm which made it look more like a vocation than a duty. She showed up the House of Windsor's total lack of rapport with, or affection for, its people with cruel clarity; her amazingly busy life, and her desire towards the end to play as hard as she worked, made them look sluggish and moribund, uneasy with anything on less than four legs or two knees. She was a great republican hero because her very presence made nonsense of the idea that you can be Born To Rule; she, the outsider, took to royal life like a champion and for one brief shining moment made sense of it all while her husband, with every wince, flinch and faux pas, made it painfully obvious that he found it increasingly difficult to love his people or do his duty. She was a fresh, unpretentious breath of roll-up-your-sleeves, best-foot-forward Englishness amidst the Gothic gloom of our own House of Usher.

Diana went into her marriage with an open heart and high expectations; when it finally dawned on her that she had a gift, a gift for loving and being loved on a global scale, she offered it proudly to the family she had married into and now would try to make the best of. She really did want to make them look good. When, envious and fearful, they threw it back in her face, she turned. She didn't get mad, she got even. And she got even by making the House of Windsor look like the biggest bunch of bastards who ever wore a crown. She still hasn't stopped. She never will.

'Diana the Martyr,' Prince Charming used to taunt his troubled, needy young wife when she first started to reach out to the sick in order to heal herself, to the dying in order to understand her life. And now she is: martyred by metal piercing that beautiful body, a body which spent a lifetime being dissected as surely as any corpse up for a post mortem, and the bursting of that big brave heart.

If Diana had lived she might well have become – thanks to the incessant whispering campaigns of the Windsors and their media lackeys – a joke: Lady Diana Al Fayed, an Arab merchant's bit of posh, endlessly sunning herself on the deck of some gin palace hooked up in the Med, toasting herself until her skin lost its bloom and she lost her husband to a newer model. But her death has preserved her for ever at the height of her beauty, compassion and power. She will be the mourner at every royal wedding and the bride at every coronation. Her brave, bright, brash life will for ever cast a giant shadow over the sickly bunch of bullies who call themselves our ruling house. We'll always remember her, coming home for the last time to us, free at last, the People's Princess, not the Windsors'. We'll never forget her. And neither will they.

Julie Burchill, *Guardian*

154

Unusual Normality, Jetset Glamour

Ever since she first appeared on the public stage, Princess Diana has had a special meaning for women. Young girls have always dreamed of the perfect romance, and her engagement to Prince Charles in 1981 seemed to be an embodiment of the old song, 'Some Day My Prince Will Come'. Much later, as her marriage fell apart, she seemed to be living out another script, this time the Gloria Gaynor anthem for abandoned women, 'I Will Survive'.

In that sense, Diana's unhappy marriage charted a familiar course for millions of women and made them feel that, however disastrous their lives, they were not alone. That is why, as we've seen over the past two days, she was not a distant glamourous figure but someone with whom they felt an intimate connection. Her story, from falling in love with an apparently eligible older man to the misery of a marriage gone wrong, could be seen as a paradigm of women's experience in the late 20th century.

When her husband's family closed ranks against her, as they often do, she made it clear she was not going to go quietly. This was a key moment in Diana's presentation of herself as a contemporary young woman. Royal women have traditionally been expected to sacrific personal happiness for the greater good of the institution, as Princess Margaret did when her proposed marriage to a divorced man, Peter Townsend, was vetoed. Diana, more in tune with contemporary mores than her sheltered upbringing would have led anyone to expect, dramatically broke with convention and went public with her complaints about her husband's infidelity and lack of support during her struggle with bulimia.

Talking not just about her troubled marriage but about her eating disorder was unprecedented. During a speech at a charity event, she likened the experience of bulimia to wanting 'to dissolve like a Disprin'. Vulnerability is a very human quality and it turned her from a figurehead into a real peson. And if it lost her much of the protection of her royal status, it gained her the admiration of women. Few angry wives get the chance to air their grievances as publicly as Diana did with her *Panorama* interview, but plenty of women recognized the impulse behind it, as well as being able to imagine the years of slights and insults that had propelled her to take action. The comment that 'there were three of us in that marriage' hit home with many 'ordinary' women. Even the wrangling over her divorce settlement, which involved what are for most wives unthinkable amounts of money, was only a version of what they themselves had gone through on a much smaller scale. And she was, crucially, unashamed. She had been unfairly treated, knew what she wanted and set out to get it. All over Britain, women cheered her on.

In that sense, her story was extraordinarily modern – far too modern for an ossified institution like the House of Windsor to cope with. She took on causes (Aids, for example) that touched the lives of thousands of people, yet lay far beyond the range of charities favoured by other royals. She replaced the family's traditional mystique with something far more potent: a thrilling familiarity. While few of us know much about the Queen, Diana managed the trick of saying little – her *Panorama* interview excepted – yet placing so much of her private life in the public domain that complete strangers felt they knew her.

There is, inevitably, an element of fantasy in this sense of identification between millions of 'ordinary' women and the former wife of the heir to the throne. But it explains why so many women who had never met her, and who do not see themselves as royalists, were so profoundly affected by the news of her death. It's hard to imagine people being so moved by the demise of any of the other Royals.

What Diana brought to the monarchy was an unusual blend of normality – the young mother in jeans taking her boys to a theme park – and jetset glamour. Other women recognized elements of her everyday existence, seeing her as someone like them, yet they were also able to read about her in magazines like *Hello!* and fantasize about a lifestyle that would never be within their grasp. The envy that might have been inspired was tempered by the knowledge that her life was essentially a sad one.

From her parents' broken marriage to her own divorce and disappointments in love, the setbacks in her life were documented in a degree of detail unprecedented in a public figure with a quasi-official position. We know that her campaigning for a ban on landmines was carried on against the background of a lonely existence in Kensington Palace and of frequent separations from her beloved sons, which made her concern for the damaged and the underprivileged even more impressive.

What remained unclear, however, was what would happen to our feelings about her if – as seemed to be on the cards in the weeks before her death –

she finally discovered the happiness that had previously eluded her. How far did our identification with her depend on the knowledge that, for all the privileges conferred on her, she shared our everyday discontents and frustrations? The year after her divorce had been difficult and many women could empathize with that, recognizing the mixed feelings of sadness and liberation.

But we had become used to her as the battling Princess, bravely overcoming her demons in order to help others. Were we prepared for her transformation into a mature, self-possessed woman with a handsome, attentive playboy on her arm? Since the early hours of Sunday morning, we can only speculate about the answer. Her sudden death has fixed her for ever in our hearts as a young, beautiful, essentially tragic figure. It is easy to forget, in the numbed aftermath of her fatal accident, that there might have been a very different end to her story, that she was perhaps on the verge of emerging not just as a survivor of a failed marriage but as someone who had put the past behind her. And what an example that would have been for other women.

Joan Smith, *Guardian*

THE MODERNIZER

Walking each day this week past the scaffold platforms being erected outside Westminster Abbey and along the route of Princess Diana's funeral procession, mournfully smitten with the irony that here is the final opportunity for the cameras to consume her on our behalf, there is at least this comfort for the professional journalist. On this occasion, there is no danger of the metropolitan elite exaggerating the significance of the events of the week. For those of us who have lived in Britain only in the second half of this century, this is the most stirring news event of our time.

It is also an event whose meaning we will continue to unpack long after the funeral cortège disappears from public view, for it is rich in paradox. In her relations with the media, in the redesigning of her public life after the failure of her marriage, in her commitment to good works, Diana's conduct was both deeply sincere and yet calculating; not unlike Tony Blair's brief performance before the cameras when he mourned the loss of 'the people's princess'. The people have declared themselves with unprecedented emotional force, their bouquets of flowers weeping inside plastic bags at every makeshift shrine to the martyred Princess.

In all this, the sorry House of Windsor stands like a granite-walled Highland castle amid a sea of national emotion, which it appears unable either to comprehend or address. Prince Charles, as good a man to be king as any, if king we must have, looks tortured, like a man confined for a lifetime in a dungeon who is required suddenly to chat on a TV sofa.

It is, in our view, a misreading to say that the death of the Princess hastens the demise of the monarchy; the Princess's force in death as in life derives from the fact that she lived and died a Royal. Rather, it sharpens in an unanswerable way the point that the Royal Family has to learn how to talk to people, especially in front of television cameras. But to argue that they need to blub in the face of all disappointment, like Gazza or the silly sentimental rest of us, is to risk absurdity. If the Queen were able to summon her formidable reserves of self-control to speak plainly and calmly at Diana's funeral, she would also in her own way speak for the nation. What is not permissible in these babbling, over-photographed times is silence and the retreat behind the security fence – yet another paradox in the age of the hated paparazzi.

The debate about the media is, surely, wildly off-track. The paparazzi's repulsive baseness holds a mirror to nature where, if we are honest, we all see our intruding selves. We will change this only by an act of free will, not of pointless and ineffective law-making: that requires journalists and their employers to ensure that the existing code against long lenses, intrusion and harassment is made effective, which means harsher punishment, of the sort the City regulators are able to hand out to errant players. Accusing seven men of killing two people whose chauffeur was drunk and travelling at 121mph is politics, not justice.

Where in this can we find some encouragement for the future? The answer lies in the response to Diana's death, which has shown, even celebrated, the end of the age of deference, the triumphant confirmation that Britain is not and need not be a conservative country (where the Conservative Party is 'the natural party of government'), but a dynamic, liberal place, where our hearts warm to those who take risks, where the first test of an action's quality is its authenticity and the most vile of workaday sins that of hypocrisy. Diana could be both rich and deeply committed to the outcast, so long as she was authentic and open in both: hardly an unchallengeable stance, but it is the country's mood.

As such, she was a modernizer. This spirit of modernity insists upon equality of respect and rights for everyone and upon a passionate search to place political trust in the people, not elites. It will not tolerate the hypocrisy of political discourse about drugs or gay people; rank will not be pulled without merit; politicians (and the media) will not say one thing and do another or occupy a parliament run with such emotional blindness that two of its members have killed themselves in a year. This is the spirit of the dead Princess and it is the spirit of our country and our time.

New Statesman

THE LEGACY

What does the astonishing outpouring of grief towards Diana, Princess of Wales tell us about ourselves as a nation? First, perhaps, that at a time when everything in society is tending to fragment, we still share a common soul. Other recent events – such as the VE and VJ commemorations and the Euro 96 Football Championships – demonstrated, on a smaller scale, the nation's yearning to express its shared identity. The Prime Minister hopes to achieve something similar from the Millennium Experience, which we applaud; but that undertaking, planned for years, is knocked into a cocked hat by the extent and intensity of the nation's unscripted mourning for Diana.

In some ways, Diana turned her life into a critique of the British establishment. Even those of us who were, so to speak, Diana-sceptic during her lifetime must now humbly admit that her hold on the affections of the public was far greater than we knew. The funeral demonstrated what the monarch could be, if it was able to undergo the painful and uncertain process of modernization. The Royal Family themselves may or may not be stuffy, but the organization that surrounds them unquestionably is. In this, The Firm has become out of touch with modern business practice, with its emphasis on customer relations. Yet none of this detracts from another obvious lesson of the weekend – namely, that the monarchy is still fundamentally important to British life. It remains – again more than anyone could have imagined – the focus of national emotions.

In the middle of last week, one almost felt that the funeral would mark a turning point for British behaviour. There was a shrillness to the expression of grief on the part of a public which often did not personally know the Princess that was uncomfortable to those brought up in a tradition of British reserve. By her readiness to verbalize about the secrets of her health and marriage, by her adoption of the langugage of therapy, Diana herself sometimes seemed more at home in the culture of Woody Allen than that of the Royal Family. Last Saturday, however, few people could have failed to observe the decorum of the silent, soberly dressed crowds lining the processional route. The love that Diana so abundantly inspired should not be mistaken as an endorsement for every aspect of her personality. The words most frequently used of her last week were 'fragile' and 'vulnerable'; it was for her weaknesses as much as her strengths that people took her to their hearts.

Nevertheless, Diana's example could yet help to lead Britain out of its present identity crisis towards a new self-image for the 21st century. It is appropriate that this week should see the publication of a report by Demos, in furtherance of the Prime Minister's mission for the rebranding of Britain. Diana supremely demonstrated that messages of compassion and humanitarianism come well from British lips. The protocol and distance associated with the rest of the Royal Family go down badly in countries such as the United States and Australia; nor do they now satisfy the instincts of the British people. Britain has a long history of humanitarian campaigning, through figures such as William Wilberforce, Elizabeth Fry and Florence Nightingale. It is by recognizing this strand in our tradition that we, as a nation, can reinvent our own myth. In recognition of this, the Royal Family might well question whether the young Princes really need a career in the armed forces.

In the course of the week, Buckingham Palace became an object of criticism for the arrangements it contrived, in the face of unprecedented public displays of grief. It is worth observing here that the ceremonies at Westminster, on the day, were faultlessly appropriate and beautiful. This must surely have impressed television audiences round the world. It might also be noted that their natural focus was the abbey, just as the first place to which the Royal Family thought of going on the terrible Sunday when the news arrived was their church. Part of Diana's appeal in what is regarded as a post-Christian age may have been her apparent openness to the alternative spirituality represented by mediums and astrologers. But Saturday showed that a church service is still the means by which great hurts of national life can be healed.

Now Diana's charisma has been vested in her sons. Through them, the Royal Family have a second chance to redirect the enormous popularity that Diana could command to the ends of a stable constitutional monarchy. Perhaps, too, some of the pressure has been lifted off HRH the Prince of Wales's private life, and the public will learn to find compassion for a man whom they evidently feel to be remote and unlike them. In these ways Diana's legacy could be to leave the monarchy and the nation stronger than before.

Clive Aslet, *Country Life*

THE FUNERAL

'A New World, a Goddess, a New Kind of Heaven'

A sound like a distant shower of rain penetrated the walls of Westminster Abbey shortly before noon. It rolled towards us. Then it was inside the church. It rolled up the nave like a great wave.

It was people clapping, first the crowds outside and then the two thousand inside. People don't clap at funerals; and they don't clap because people outside are clapping. But yesterday they did. It was dense, serious applause and it marked the moment at which the meaning of what was happening on this incredible day was made plain.

It was the end of Earl Spencer's tribute to his sister, Diana, Princess of Wales, that had raised the emotional tension to this breaking-point.

He had launched another savage attack on the press, saying Diana had been the 'most hunted person of the modern age'. What brought gasps from the nave of the abbey, however, was the fact that he had also flung down a challenge to the Royal Family over the upbringing of William and Harry, pledging to Diana that 'we, your blood family, will do all we can to continue the imaginative and loving way in which you were steering these two exceptional young men so that their souls are not simply immersed by duty and tradition, but can sing openly as you planned'.

His voice stumbled and broke as he finished; and then the masses listening outside, who had been claiming their own place in this very public realm, broke into the abbey. The people wanted to make their feelings felt. It wasn't enough to be one of the millions on the streets of London. It certainly wasn't enough to be one of the 1 billion watching on television. They wanted to be in the abbey and the applause was their way of getting in.

The Queen sat immobile as the sound of clapping reached her. Her young granddaughters, Beatrice and Eugenie, joined in with the congregation. But the adults in the Royal Family froze as Spencer's words sank in. Had he hijacked the funeral?

Of course, I had expected this service to be emotional. It came at the end of a week of wonders in which some force of popular magic, some ancient religious impulse, had broken through royal reticence and protocol and demanded a voice. But I had not expected the sheer pressure and intensity of the occasion.

Yet, at seven in the morning when the privileged few journalists had started queuing to make sure of the best places in the north transept, it had felt like a party. The crowd pressing against the barriers in Parliament Square had been jolly, good-natured. They applauded and cheered two lorryloads of workmen who had feverishly been chopping down traffic lights to open up the approach to the abbey. They clapped the Westminster council workman who, fag dangling from his lips, had hoovered up the mess left by the men. And they watched the celebrities joining our queue to enter the north transept. Ralph Lauren, Lord Gowrie, the Emanuels, designers of Diana's wedding dress, and Esther Rantzen who performed her own quasi-regal walkabout.

But as the tenor bell sounded at 9.08 to signal the departure of the cortège from Kensington Palace, the atmosphere darkened. A silence started to spread. We all lowered our voices and the occasional ringing of a mobile phone started to sound like a gross intrusion.

At 9.30, they let us in. The first shock was that it was warmer inside than out – a reversal of the usual experience of walking into great churches. I looked up and realized that the air had been heated by the racks of television lights suspended above the arches of the sanctuary and choir. The lights glared almost blasphemously. But who could complain? We were there only as surrogates for the billions in the world outside.

After finding our places we waited for the nearby, significant seats to fill – the Royal Family facing the Spencers, and those seats just marked Mr Al Fayed, Mrs Al Fayed. It was strange seeing these big players in the week's news represented by plain printed signs among the massive clutter of colonial monuments.

A key element in the layout of the service became clear. Just as television audiences were not shown the faces of the bereaved families, so we, in the press seats, were placed at an angle that prevented us looking directly into their faces. Plainly the political issue of the week – whether to show a trembling lower lip or the stiff upper one – was being evaded. But, at least, we did not have the sweeping shots of architecture in which television indulged. For us it was all stillness and concentration.

Gradually guests started arriving, a hybrid bunch representing the cross-cultural force of Diana's personality – Queen Noor of Jordan, Richard Branson, Luciano Pavarotti, George Michael and Elton John. At 10, the organ started playing and the atmosphere intensified. Celebrity spotting gave way to a more concentrated mood. The abbey seemed to be filling to bursting. Attendants had to bring in stacks of plastic chairs. Michael Barrymore and Conrad Black, the newspaper tycoon – one of many strange matches – found themselves squashed deep into the aisle behind the choir.

The visiting clergy filled their seats in the sanctuary, among them George Carey, the Archbishop of Canterbury. For the next half hour his rather odd role was to lean forward repeatedly to look down the length of the church and then stand up as a signal to us all when the Royals or Spencer family came in. The Spencers provoked perhaps the most awe as they settled into their seats amid a sea of black hats and largely grey heads.

The Al Fayeds had arrived and I saw the startlingly diminutive pop star Bryan Adams shake Mohamed Al Fayed's hand – another strange match. Al Fayed himself, sitting close to me, looked stern and impressive, a compact figure of grief and, perhaps, anger. His painfully knitted brows were the clearest evidence of what must have been going inside the man.

On the television screen, we saw the cortège approaching around Parliament Square. Everything now changed. I heard a gulp, a snuffle. I looked round and handkerchiefs were out around me. At last this was no longer a party or a celebrity outing, it was a funeral.

The choir, as it led the coffin up the nave, was invisible to us. But its sound fell on us like a fine, silvery mist. Then, as the coffin approached us, we could hear the soft tramp of the pallbearers' feet and, finally, it came into full view and, with an awkward grating noise, was slid into place – at, for that moment, the centre of the world thanks to the television camera projecting from a gantry at the summit of the crossing, 100ft above the chequered floor.

The opening words of Wesley Carr, Dean of Westminster, were shocking – first because they signalled the start, at last, of the funeral narrative, and second because of the plainness of their contemporary vernacular: 'She met individuals and made them feel significant.' The pomp and pomposity of the setting was already being undermined by a new, more direct, more emotional culture.

'I vow to thee, my country. . .' filled the abbey like thunder and then, after Lady Sarah McCorquodale's reading, Lynne Dawson and the BBC Singers gave a piercing performance of the Libera Me from Verdi's Requiem. This was enough for me. It had been a long week. I wasn't sure I could bear to have my emotions assaulted further. Yet with Lady Jane Fellowes's reading, the whole world must have felt the shock. It was the voice of Diana coming from one of her surviving sisters.

Tony Blair was to signal the start of a central passage of quite unbearable intensity. He read from St Paul's First Letter to the Corinthians – 'And now abideth faith, hope, love, these three; but the greatest of these is love'. His reading was badly overstated, his pauses too plainly theatrical. But it worked and nothing could hold back those words.

At once, Elton John, from a grand piano on a platform just west of the choir, started singing his new version of 'Candle in the Wind'. I had been dreading this. To me it is an over-the-top song, sugary and obvious; and the new words were hopelessly clumsy.

But it worked. He understated the performance, drying out some of the song's syrup. I found myself crying, and the tears were now flowing all around me. One weathered reporter was surreptitiously brushing his cheeks and another was rapidly putting on a pair of unnecessary glasses. As the song finished, we heard clapping from outside.

And then came Lord Spencer. Besides discomfiting the Royal Family, he lashed all of us in the press seats – we were 'at the opposite end of the moral spectrum' to his sister – and he claimed for her a title that seemed to be higher than saint: she was 'human'. She spoke to the 'constituency of the rejected' but she could suffer from a 'deep feeling of unworthiness'. It was not a well-written speech, but it was brilliantly pitched. He knew, in speaking of Diana, he must speak not to just the abbey, not even to the millions outside in the streets, but rather to the billions who made Diana in life one of the most famous people in the world, and in death the most famous of all.

He was speaking to the globalized, electronically connected culture of which Diana has become the supreme star. This was the new culture that, with that wave of applause, invaded and claimed the abbey.

We could only, from that point onwards, calm down. The archbishop's bidding prayers were again plain and direct, though he followed the globalizing lead of Lord Spencer by asking everybody in the world to join in the Lord's prayer 'in whatever language we may choose'.

Finally, following the Dean's Commendation, the soldiers returned, again filling the cathedral with the strange soft rubbery stamp of their steps. The minute's silence was deep as they departed with Diana's body – you could feel it extending across the world – but interrupted by more snuffles and suppressed sobs in the north transept.

It was all more, far more than I expected. It was an event made by the incredible upsurge of popular feeling in Britain and around the world. Before she died, some may have been hoping that she would grow old, her celebrity would dim and she would be quietly interred in relative obscurity. Even when she died, nobody anticipated the scale of this popular rising.

It was only a week from that mangled Mercedes to the abbey. But it was a week in which a new world asserted itself and made a goddess out of one rejected, hounded, marginalized member of the British Royal Family. The abbey service was the elevation of Diana to a new kind of heaven. I'll tell my grandchildren I was there. But they won't listen. By then, it will seem so obvious to them: of course Diana changed the world.

Bryan Appleyard, *The Sunday Times*

'SUDDENLY PEOPLE WERE CLAPPING'

During the one-minute silence for Diana, Princess of Wales there entered my head a phrase used long ago by country folk after someone had died: 'She has gone home.' That restless, loving, homeless spirit had found somewhere to lay her head.

Absurd, you may say, to talk of someone who lived at Kensington Palace as being homeless. Yet in the essential meaning of the word, she was. And so, during that silence, it struck me that we were not only mourning her loss to us, we were also welcoming her home.

In truth, the arrangements made for her funeral in Westminster Abbey left us all free to interpret this event in any manner we chose. Never in its long history has the abbey opened its arms to anyone in such a wide embrace. This sepulchre of kings and poets and statesmen set aside the rules and conventions associated with it. When this service was first mooted, most of us had our own unflattering ideas of what the establishment would make of it. How entirely wrong we were.

There was a piano for Elton John. There was mention of other faiths. And in the opening prayer for her there was this striking sentence: 'Although a Princess, she was someone for whom, from afar, we dared to feel affection, and by whom were all *intrigued.*' That is an unusual word to find in any form of Christian prayer.

And finally, to all our surprise, there was the clapping that rolled towards us from the world outside and ignited in the abbey itself; something never heard there in modern times, and not likely to be heard again. We will come back to that.

Tribute is due to reverent and loving hands which arranged the order of service for this funeral. It was not only all-embracing, it was appropriate. When I heard that Elton John would sing, strong doubts arose in my mind – as might be expected of someone of my generation. When it came to the moment, his rendering of 'Candle in the Wind' seemed to me entirely fitting. More than that, it was a joy. It came so close to her. I fancy it moved many elderly and conservative hearts present in Westminster Abbey into totally unexpected trains of thought .

I watched the faces around me while Elton sang. All seemed content, and some found themselves caught up by it. Come to think of it, this was natural enough. For what they contrived so well to do was make this farewell to Diana from one of Christendom's greatest places of worship a close reflection of her life and spirit.

So often when the great and the good depart, the drums roll and the trumpet sounds. It is all very grand and eloquent and fitting, but it seldom draws us close to the spirit of the departed. Winston Churchill was one of the few to be aware of this. He took a close interest in his own state funeral and was anxious there should be hymns that people could sing and good melodies. He knew what a heavy hand solemnity can lay on the memory of the dead.

This funeral was arranged on altogether different lines. There were many moments during that hour inside and outside Westminster Abbey when all who knew Diana and loved her must have felt drawn closer to her. A skilled and forgiving hand had gone towards the prayer we said for all who mourn, prefaced by these words: 'Diana was not alone in losing her young life tragically. We remember too her friend, Dodi Fayed, and his family, Henri Paul, and all for whom today's service rekindles memories of grief untimely borne.

Perhaps we should pause there, and reflect gratefully how extraordinarily difficult it must have been to put together this form of service, itself without precedent, in a manner which would win approval from the Royal Family, the Spencer family, the custodians of Westminster Abbey's conventions – and from the nation itself.

And having it all composed, agreed and in print in the space of four or five days. We have lost many things that touched our pride in the last half century or so. But still, I reflected, as I watched the cortège leaving Kensington Palace on a screen before entering the abbey, we have this matchless touch for high ceremony.

The police outriders were sitting to attention on their horses. There was the slow clop, clop of hooves. How good the horses were, how dependable they looked. That bright, early autumn sunshine around the palace and the park was so evocative. Setting eyes on something beautiful that a friend will never see again always brings pain.

What we all saw from the moment the gun carriage set out from Kensington Palace was a revival of the old confidence we once had in our way of doing things, blended with something entirely of this age which caught the elusive spirit of Diana.

I remembered also that when Princes William and Harry were in London, she would sometimes emerge with them from Kensington Palace and, at their bidding, head for a hamburger. 'My sons,' I heard her say with motherly exasperation while we were working in Bosnia last month, 'seem to be hooked on McDonald's.'

Westminster Abbey is a place which makes prayer easier. The beauty of its stained glass and the soaring columns enter the spirit. How was it, though, for those outside? They had stood for hours, sleepless and with little food. At dawn they had felt the early chill of autumn. Their devotion, I thought at one moment in the abbey, reaches further than our own, those of us who have slept in warm beds and made breakfast. Many of them who could follow the service from screen and relay responded reverentially to what took place in the abbey. When we rose, they rose; when we prayed, they prayed.

And what, I wondered, was going through some of those minds. Many, I did not doubt, were grieving in the belief that Diana had gone for ever, and with the close of her earthly life, there remained nothing but dust.

When loved ones die, we draw about us such hopes as we can muster about a future life. Did some of the public grief we have been witnessing come from the absence of such hopes? Or was it the cruelty of a life so suddenly taken.

Prince William walked by with his head bowed low. Understandably, we have become familiar with that look in recent days. Of all the partnerships that this sudden death has severed, that between him, his brother and their mother was infinitely the most precious. So the prayer was well chosen: 'Lord, we thank you for the precious gift of family life, for all human relationships and for the strength we draw from each other. Have compassion on those for whom this parting brings particular pain and the deepest sense of loss.'

The burden on Prince William's shoulders will now rapidly increase. Part of it, I reflected penitentially, comes from journalists. He shared so closely his mother's apprehensions of the long lens. The cameras were there in the abbey, of course, at every vantage point and all-seeing, but immobile – and so I hoped, to people like Prince William, less intimidating.

Which takes us to the substance of what Diana's brother sought to convey to the congregation in the abbey, but even more to the world outside. Naturally one so close to her was able quickly to strike a chord. 'For such was her extraordinary appeal that the tens of millions of people taking part in this service all over the world via television and radio, who never actually met her, felt that they, too, lost someone close to them in the early hours of Sunday morning.' He was right also to dwell on Diana's God-given sensitivity, without which we would be immersed in greater ignorance about the anguish of Aids, the plight of the homeless, the isolation of lepers and the random destruction of landmines.

Right again about her sense of insecurity, which never left her. It was what her brother called this childlike sense of unworthiness, of rejection even, which gave such poignancy to the helping hand she sought to extend to others.

It would be happy if we could be left to dwell on these endearing qualities. Alas, no. They will be remembered, but not for too long. What will echo on, the world being what it is, are Earl Spencer's other words . . . 'the most hunted person of the modern age . . .'

It is no good turning away from what he said. We have to weigh it. 'She talked endlessly of getting away from England, mainly because of the treatment that she received at the hands of the newspapers. I don't think she ever understood why her genuinely good intentions were sneered at by the media, why there appeared to be a permanent quest on their behalf to bring her down. It is baffling.'

Then he pledged himself to protect her beloved boys, William and Harry, from a similar fate. In all, it was a lovely panegyric; and who better to deliver it? In the long run, brothers and sisters who grow up together come to know each other better than anyone else on earth. It also expressed better than anyone else could have the feeling in so many other hearts. Then there came to us in the abbey this distant rustle, this ripple of sound. It travelled on its own wavelength into the abbey itself. Suddenly people were clapping, it seemed to me with surprising confidence. There was none of that furtive looking round to see whether we should be kneeling, sitting or standing. The clapping took hold and it continued. And this was the more surprising because it was a congregation in which I thought the senior citizen was extraordinarily well represented.

What were we to make of it? Soon after leaving the abbey, an American television crew rushed up to me. What did *I* make of it? Were the Earl's strictures against the media justified? Should he have spoken thus in the presence of the Queen?

I felt in the wrong mood to deal with such questions seriously. 'He feels deep emotion on this subject,' I said off the top of my head. 'And not without cause. He had an embittering experience of his own with the press.'

Then, perhaps influenced by the spirit of the preceding hour, I found myself saying something like this. The tabloid newspapers have their faults, but they do not have hearts of stone. Were this entire tragedy to lead us towards – even a few degrees towards – gentler methods, especially towards the two sons that Diana so cherished, then there would be the makings of an appropriate memorial to her. What so many of us shared on Saturday morning was more than a farewell to someone we loved. There was also promise of a fresh beginning. It was a service from which it was open to all to draw strength as well as sadness.

After Lord Spencer had ended his homily to such unexpectedly enthusiastic applause, we moved into the hymn 'Make me a channel of your peace' with its final verse:

Make me a channel of your peace:
Where there is hatred let me bring your love,
Where there is injury, your pardon, Lord,
And where there's doubt, true faith in you.

It seems to me pointless to mourn for Diana without at the same time taking serious account of the example she set in certain important ways. As one of the prayers reminded us, she showed compassion towards people most of us do not have a lot of time for.

The Bidding prayer, read by Dr Wesley Carr, Dean of Westminster, gave the rest of us our marching orders. We were to remember her life and enjoyment of it with thanksgiving. We were to rededicate to God the work of the charities she supported. We were to commit ourselves anew to caring for others.

That leaves it open to everyone, including the tabloid editors, to decide, after all the tears have been shed, what influence she really exercised on our lives in her own, all too brief life.

W.F. Deedes, *Daily Telegraph*

JOURNEY HOME

There was the same intense, cloying scent – so like votary incense – from the flowers heaped all this week here at Althorp as swelled from the mound of blooms at Kensington Palace. But among the cellophane bouquets woven into the black, ironwork lattice of the main gates and stacked along the stone estate walls for 100 yards in each direction, were tributes clearly from cottage gardens. A giant sunflower was propped against a stone gatepost, beside bunches of old roses. A modest handful of pink and red sweetpeas, wrapped in tin foil, made a poignant nod to the Spencer sweet pea, identified by a head gardener at the turn of the century at Althorp, from which modern varieties were bred. Another small difference made this a gentler, more uplifting scene than London in mourning. Here and there, bumble-bees dipped into the petals, while butterflies rested on the white memorial cards.

On Saturday, it was a lonely walk through the lightening autumn countryside. Anyone who had driven up in the early hours found roadblocks restricting access solely to pedestrians over the last mile or so of road either side of the gates. The landscape looked in melancholy mood at the changing of the seasons, with haw-lanterns, sloes and elderberries glowing in the browning hedges.

There was not another soul on the road, although grain driers burning the moisture from the wet corn could be heard on farms alongside. The life of the city can be shut down entirely – shops just close and trains don't run – but the life of the country goes on. There were cows to be milked, too, that morning and the late harvest was still being gathered well into darkness the night before.

Several families and groups of friends were already outside Althorp's gates in the half-light, perhaps a dozen in all, having slept out overnight on the grass road-verge. As if a natural disaster had suddenly struck, most of them had merely grabbed the nearest warmth-giving items when leaving home – a quilt or an overcoat – and headed straight for the estate. Some were local people, such as the off-duty security guard from Towcester, and the woman from Rugby who had been given a special day off from her job at Tesco to be here, although she had never spent a night out of doors before. Others had expressly chosen to mourn here rather than with the millions in the capital. 'Steve', in his thirties, drove all the way from Devon, and spent the night on the cold, grass bank, explaining simply: 'It is more personal here.'

At dawn, the first members of the press appeared by the gates. A photographer from Rotterdam, newshounds from the Sunday tabloids, local newspaper cub-reporters, and a BBC TV cameraman who shared, in the spirit of the day, his precious Thermos of hot chocolate with grateful overnighters. All were amazed that, compared with the crowds in London, so few had come to witness events. No doubt some were discouraged by the roadblocks, and many would have waited to watch the service on television, but queuing for hours on a blank stretch of country road a few miles from their homes was probably too odd a notion for most local people to contemplate.

As we waited for the first news of the cortège's departure from Kensington Palace, crows wheeled silently above the massive, dark cedars on the knoll behind the gate lodge. When a group of elegant police horses with black-jacketed riders appeared there, it was easier to imagine that they were coffee-housing while a fox-holding covert was being drawn, and that we were eager foot-followers at some early season meet, than to believe that we had all assembled to honour a Princess's burial in the park.

The press corps, police and emergency services soon came in dozens, near enough outnumbering the mourners. The St John Ambulance brigade had asked for 200 volunteers – 600 turned up. There were farmers and housewives with their dogs from all the nearest villages among those paying their respects to the woman the regional paper claims as 'the county's princess'. A local, although less rural, quality of the Princess's appeal was explained to me by a young Asian couple, who came from the large community in nearby Leicester. The Royal Family had never been of particular interest, they said neutrally. Diana, however, had often toured India and Pakistan, and made her last great friendship with a Muslim, and so they had been drawn to her. She made them feel part of British life.

When the funeral procession began in London, there was total silence along this stretch of the normally busy Rugby-Northampton road. Only the eerie clip-clop of the horses drawing the gun-carriage and coffin, which echoed from dozens of small radios held by mourners all along the verges outside the gates, broke the silence. It was the sound of a ghost procession that seemed as if it would come round the corner any moment. Nowhere can Earl Spencer's address have been listened to more intently than at Althorp, where his disembodied voice could be heard describing the childhood joy he had shared with Diana playing here in the park.

It was then a long wait in hot sunshine until, shortly before 2pm, the maroon royal train passed by with a roar on the main line, just across the red-brown ploughed fields. There was another wait for the party to alight at

Long Buckby's small station and drive in a fleet of limousines to Althorp.

Prince Charles swept by and through the gates with little Prince Harry in one car, ahead in another was Prince William – his eyes still cast down as they had been on that long march to the abbey. But it was Lord Spencer who glared, bitterly, unmistakably, directly at the television cameras and protruding lenses with flashes firing in his eyes outside his own gates. Well he might. Here were the newspapers he attacked in his funeral address, who doled out the treatment that made Diana talk endlessly of getting away from England, the footsoldiers of the self-same editors whose admisssion to Westminster Abbey he had barred.

During the service itself, one man from a nearby village turned to a reporter from the *People*, standing just behind me on the bank, and asked quietly if he thought the Princess's death would herald a new privacy law. 'Nah. It will all die down,' came the bullish response. Indeed, police guarding the cortège's route were already being shunted out of line so that the cameramen could get their picture of its arrival. And, of course, here it was the ring of a tabloid stringer's mobile telephone that had earlier pierced the minute's silence.

Another wait for the cortège. A solitary young rider, Judy Holah, appeared at the edge of the field beside the crowds, having hacked the few miles across the ploughed bridleway from East Haddon on her elderly bay mare. She shared with me the memory that had drawn her here: seeing the black pony at the stables at Church Brampton, on which the young Diana had learned to ride.

Then the hearse arrived, flanked by police outriders. There was loud applause as they circled in a tight, formal manoeuvre and swept back towards London. The black gates opened. There was a sight of the bright, Royal Standard wrapped over the slim coffin, and the wreath of lilies, before they disappeared into the green, green fields behind. The gates then closed on the world, still watching in its billions. Behind the walls of an old English park is the most peaceful place on earth to rest.

The day left an abiding hope that the family's extraordinary bond with every aspect of county life – from its medieval roots, to the establishment of the Northamptonshire Imperial Yeomanry, to its involvement with Althorp and Pytchley Hunt, and the patronage of the Northamptonshire Cricket Club – will be strengthened by the Princess's burial at her ancient home.

'The thing about Northamptonshire is that it is blessed with a collection of houses that are still lived in by their families. We have Boughton, Easton Neston, Rockingham, Holdenby. It has kept its fabric. If Earl Spencer came back from South Africa, he would fit straight back in overnight,' said one local landowner.

The Earl himself wrote in an edition of the parish magazine, *The Brington and Nobottle News*: 'I am sure my medieval sheepfarming ancestors would not be remotely surprised to learn that their descendants are still to be found in the same part of Northamptonshire where they used to bring their flocks to graze.' Although those ancestors could never have imagined the scale of the drama, or tragedy, that has brought another of their own back to Althorp, they might take solace from the Princess's return to ground the Spencers have nurtured for generations.

Sandy Mitchell (additional research by Camilla Bonn), *Country Life*

Diana was buried in a private ceremony, attended only by her immediate family, on an island in the Oval, the beautiful ornamental lake in the park of Althorp House. The decision had been taken earlier in the week not to inter her with her ancestors at the parish church in Great Brington, so that, Earl Spencer has said, the grave can be 'properly looked after by her family, and visited in privacy by her sons'. Land on the island was consecrated for the purpose by the Bishop of Peterborough, the Rt Revd Ian Cundy. Public access to the grave will be allowed for a number of weeks each year.

The lake, to the north-west of the house, is surrounded by an arboretum, which includes oaks planted by Diana, her sons and other members of the Royal Family. This tranquil setting for the grave is overlooked by a temple brought here in the mid 19th century by the 5th Earl Spencer from the gardens of Admiralty House in London. Lord Spencer has announced that his family is considering the idea of erecting a monument to Diana outside the park walls.

Michael Hall, *Country Life*

BRAVELY SAID, BROTHER

The trouble is that I suddenly don't want to be part of journalism any more. Ruin and unemployment loom. It is my own fault, I suppose, for consuming too many media, but how else is a provincial to keep up? Now, though, the weight of it has toppled over and crushed the spirit.

For if Diana, Princess of Wales, was a candle in the wind, we media are the wind-machine. Our racket smothers the central sad simplicity of what happened. We are saccharine, self-regarding, neurotic and competitive; we waver between sentimentality, misplaced outbreaks of cleverness and dreadful plonking comments about The Culture and The People.

An agony aunt turns up in a tabloid castigating the idea of the Princes walking behind the coffin; once they have done so – with a dignity they will be glad of all their lives – the same writer pops up in a broadsheet to condemn tabloids which tell the Royal Family what to do. Another, who sneered incessantly at Diana in life, justifies a sugary volte-face by prosing on about the nature of myth. The vaunted mood of national unity is marred by class hostility as the pop papers wilfully misunderstand the usefulness to 'toffs' of a dark suit and a stiff upper lip, while the broadsheets wonder superciliously why the common people leave the Cellophane on their bouquets. (Easy. Cellophane and ribbons mean 'Look, I didn't nick these from the park, I paid good money for them, to prove I care'.)

Then the political writers break cover, with a graceless rant from an archetypal Tory boy in the *Sunday Telegraph* accusing Labour spin-doctors of somehow stealing Diana. Print sneers at television while watching every frame, television steals newspaper angles while sneering back. Talk Radio asks listeners to nominate an actress to play 'Di' in the biopic. Only Radio 4, an oasis of phlegm, decides that what the national psyche requires is a repeat of *The Winslow Boy* and Penelope Keith reading *Winnie the Pooh*.

All other news is drowned by the roaring of the wind-machine: even yesterday, plucky little souls attempting to interest us in Scottish devolution struggled like mountaineers trying to pitch a pup tent in a hurricane. Only the irreplaceable Terry Wogan struck a bearable note on Radio 2. 'Ah now, I'm like the rest of you, I want to keep on moping but we mustn't, must we?'

I hoped not to be part of this. The weekend mostly passed in what felt like a reasonably appropriate contemplative quiet, talking with my children, sewing and sorting and marking things for the new school term. Life far from cities and cathedrals was normal, if quiet and tinged with the universal sadness. The queue stretched a little way outside Saxmundham Market Hall to sign the book of condolence, everybody shut their shops and friends talked quietly about the senseless sadness of it all, and how it brought to mind past losses of their own. I would rather have left it there, something never to be forgotten but not to be harped on. However, with apologies, I am going to add my one last word. I want to defend Earl Spencer, all the way.

Some of the phrases used about his funeral eulogy have been extraordinary: 'calculated vengeance', 'brutality' and 'opening wounds'. He was bitter, they said, 'intemperate . . . divisive . . . ill-judged'. Irrelevant, too: just an 'expatriate uncle' from a 'dysfunctional family' which could offer little to his nephews.

Puzzled, I went to the tape and watched the Earl's speech again, just as we had watched it on Saturday, sewing name-tapes into school socks through a mist of tears. Had I missed something? Something to justify 'brutal, bitter, divisive?' No. All I could hear was a brother.

It is, these days, a largely unsung relationship: but several women said to me that last week they wished for the first time ever that they had a brother of their own. Even those with sisters said it. There is powerful, ancient comfort to be felt at the idea of a man – without the possessiveness of a husband or the authority of a father – defending and praising a woman strongly but without illusions: giving a tribute better than admiration, glowing with utter familiarity but untainted by the weariness and guilt of daily contact. I have three brothers and to me Lord Spencer sounded just right. Analysts may pretend that his words were political or iconoclastic: instinct accepts them as brotherly and brave.

What did he speak, but the plain truth? It is true that Diana's qualities did not depend on royal title alone. Cynics predicted that the fascination with her would diminish when she lost a part of that title, but it did not. She shone even brighter alone, more fascinating to worshippers and more comforting to those whose sadness she tried to alleviate. Why should her brother not say so? It is a fact: strange, but true.

And he did not, after all, gloss over other facts, such as her emotional vulnerability and her eating disorder. Stripped bare by grief, rejecting cliché and platitude, he spoke of his sister with the frankness which is a brother's privilege. We should be grateful to him. After a week of mawkish illusion in which every one of us constructed our own phantom Diana, Lord Spencer spoke of the real one. He affirmed the reality of the girl who kept her small brother amused on the long, gloomy train journeys between estranged parents, of the sister with a wicked laugh, of the chronically (perhaps sometimes annoyingly) insecure woman who yearned for love. No girl is a heroine to her brother, but there is great security in the fond, exasperated kinship of somebody who harbours no romantic ideas about you.

Nor was it disrespectful to promise his nephews that the 'blood family' of their mother would always be with them as a counterweight to royal life. The boys are Spencers, too. Their uncle spoke for half their lineage and half their temperament. As he did so there was a fleeting shadow of old Earl Spencer, who had his failings but whose cheerful disregard for strict dignity once charmed onlookers on Diana's engagement day. Remember him, beaming at the palace gates with his battered camera to take his own snaps? Why is it irreverent that with Diana dead, her brother should pledge himself to encourage her boys in her warm, instinctive style?

Every child has a right to its emotional inheritance from two families. The Earl explicitly acknowledged their Windsor heritage of duty and tradition, but firmly laid claim to his own side. His sister wanted them to have wide experience of people, to talk informally, to trust their feelings and let their souls 'sing openly'. If her siblings can further that aim, it is their duty: which of us – however much we like them – wants our children brought up entirely in our in-laws' ways and values?

In the same way, the Earl intervened to take Diana's body to safety on the lake island, defying those who wanted constant public access to her grave. That too was a brotherly act: the alternative posed horrible risks. The parallel, *pace* Simon Jenkins, is not with Churchill's grave but with that of Sylvia Plath, which to this day is still regularly claimed and ideologically defaced by those who think they revere her, but never knew her and care nothing for her living children.

All week we have been told that Britain is sloughing off the carapace of old formalities for an attitude more respectful of individuals, less like an army and more like a family (heck, even the army has just promised to be more sensitive to recruits). It is a very British irony that a belted earl, who heads a family in archaic precedence over his elder sisters, should be the figurehead of this change. But on Saturday, it seemed to me, the young Lord Spencer stood precisely where the nation stands: between tradition and modernity, the idea of 'great families' and the acknowledgement of plain family feeling.

He is not a diplomat, but he is her brother and he did a brother's duty. There is no need to look for a spark of hostility, still less to fan it with our wind-machines. The Prince of Wales is a just and gentle man. He will respect the Earl's claim. And if any royal courtiers dispute it, they have only to remember how the applause filled the parks and the streets and spread, in a shocking, liberating moment, right into the gloomy heart of the abbey. It was not for the gentle hagiography of Elton John that the congregation inside the building broke protocol and silence. It was for the authentic, irrefutable, unsentimental claims of a brother, and of blood.

Libby Purves, *The Times*

THE TRIBUTE BY EARL SPENCER

I stand before you today the representative of a family in grief, in a country in mourning, before a world in shock. We are all united, not only in our desire to pay our respects to Diana, but rather in our need to do so.

For such was her extraordinary appeal that the tens of millions of people taking part in this service all over the world via television and radio who never actually met her, feel that they, too, lost someone close to them in the early hours of Sunday morning. It is a more remarkable tribute to Diana than I can ever hope to offer her today.

Diana was the very essence of compassion, of duty, of style, of beauty. All over the world she was a symbol of selfless humanity. All over the world, a standard-bearer for the rights of the truly downtrodden, a very British girl who transcended nationality. Someone with a natural nobility who was classless and who proved in the last year that she needed no royal title to continue to generate her particular brand of magic.

Today is our chance to say thank you for the way you brightened our lives, even though God granted you but half a life. We will all feel cheated always that you were taken from us so young, and yet we must learn how to be grateful that you came along at all. Only now that you are gone do we truly appreciate what we are now without and we want you to know that life without you is very, very difficult.

We have all despaired at our loss over the past week and only the strength of the message you gave us through your years of giving has afforded us the strength to move forward.

There is a temptation to rush to canonize your memory; there is no need to do so. You stand tall enough as a human being of unique qualities not to need to be seen as a saint. Indeed, to sanctify your memory would be to miss out on the very core of your being, your wonderfully mischievous sense of humour with a laugh that bent you double.

Your joy for life, transmitted wherever you took your smile, and the sparkle in those unforgettable eyes. Your boundless energy, which you could barely contain. But your greatest gift was your intuition and it was a gift you used wisely. This is what underpinned all your other wonderful attributes and if we look to analyse what it was about you that had such a wide appeal we find it in your instinctive feel for what was really important in all our lives.

Without your God-given sensitivity we would be immersed in greater ignorance about the anguish of Aids and HIV sufferers, the plight of the homeless, the isolation of lepers, the random destruction of landmines.

Diana explained to me once that it was her innermost feelings of suffering that made it possible for her to connect with her constituency of the rejected. And here we come to another truth about her. For all the status, the glamour, the applause, Diana remained throughout a very insecure person at heart, almost childlike in her desire to do good for others so she could release herself from deep feelings of unworthiness of which her eating disorders were merely a symptom.

The world sensed this part of her character and cherished her for her vulnerability whilst admiring her for her honesty.

The last time I saw Diana was on July 1, her birthday, in London, when typically she was not taking time to celebrate her special day with friends but was guest of honour at a fundraising charity evening. She sparkled, of course, but I would rather cherish the days I spent with her in March when she came to visit me and my children in our home in South Africa. I am proud of the fact that apart from when she was on display meeting President

Mandela we managed to contrive to stop the ever-present paparazzi from getting a single picture of her – that meant a lot to her.

These were days I will always treasure. It was as if we had been transported back to our childhood when we spent an enormous amount of time together – the two youngest in the family. Fundamentally, she had not changed at all from the big sister who mothered me as a baby, fought with me at school and endured those long train journeys between our parents homes with me at weekends. It is a tribute to her level-headedness and strength that despite the most bizarre-like life imaginable after her childhood, she remained intact, true to herself.

There is no doubt that she was looking for a new direction in her life at this time. She talked endlessly of getting away from England, mainly because of the treatment that she received at the hands of the newspapers. I don't think she ever understood why her genuinely good intentions were sneered at by the media, why there appeared to be a permanent quest on their behalf to bring her down. It is baffling.

My own and only explanation is that genuine goodness is threatening to those at the opposite end of the moral spectrum. It is a point to remember that of all the ironies about Diana, perhaps the greatest was this – a girl given the name of the ancient goddess of hunting was, in the end, the most hunted person of the modern age.

She would want us today to pledge ourselves to protecting her beloved boys William and Harry from a similar fate and I do this here, Diana, on your behalf. We will not allow them to suffer the anguish that used regularly to drive you to tearful despair.

And beyond that, on behalf of your mother and sisters, I pledge that we, your blood family, will do all we can to continue the imaginative and loving way in which you were steering these two exceptional young men so that their souls are not simply immersed by duty and tradition but can sing openly as you planned.

We fully respect the heritage into which they have both been born and will always respect and encourage them in their royal role but we, like you, recognize the need for them to experience as many different aspects of life as possible to arm them spiritually and emotionally for the years ahead. I know you would have expected nothing less from us.

William and Harry, we all care desperately for you today. We are all chewed up with the sadness at the loss of a woman who was not even our mother. How great your suffering is, we cannot even imagine.

I would like to end by thanking God for the small mercies he has shown us at this dreadful time. For taking Diana at her most beautiful and radiant and when she had joy in her private life. Above all we give thanks for the life of a woman I am so proud to be able to call my sister, the unique, the complex, the extraordinary and irreplaceable Diana, whose beauty, both internal and external, will never be extinguished from our minds.
There was applause from guests.

READING BY LADY SARAH McCORQUODALE

If I should die and leave you here awhile,
Be not like others, sore undone, who keep
Long vigils by the silent dust, and weep
For my sake – turn again to life and smile,
Nerving thy heart and trembling hand to do
Something to comfort other hearts than thine.
Complete those dear unfinished tasks of mine
And I, perchance, may therein comfort you.

                                      Mary Lee Hall

READING BY LADY JANE FELLOWES

Time is too slow for those who wait,
Too swift for those who fear,
Too long for those grieve,
Too short for those who rejoice,
But for those who love, time is eternity.

                                      Unknown

I come here solemnly to pray not just for my beloved daughter, but for the others tragically killed and their families.

During the days after Diana's death I have been touched and overwhelmed by the cards, letters, flowers and gifts which I have received.

Each one is precious and warmly comforting to me. I don't know how I can start to thank you all collectively or individually for your kind thoughts and prayers. The cards now number 15,000.

Many of those kind thoughts came from mothers who have suffered, as I have, the loss of a child. The loss of a child is a mother's worst nightmare become reality, and is one that I had suffered before.

I know that grief has no agenda, no timetable. In life there will be dark tunnels with just the occasional rainbow. I also know that the ache will never go away, but that there will be gentler kinder days. Although my life will never be the same again, it can still be good. Sixteen years ago I received a letter from a Glasgow housewife. It said: 'Thank you for your altruism in giving your daughter to the nation.' I didn't really understand what she meant until Diana started to creep up on us into people's hearts.

A message from a schoolfriend of Diana's reminded me of the sunny days of living when she was a girl. She wrote of her memory of 'Diana's Scottish home on the Isle of Sell' and of a particular memory she had of myself and Diana together in a boat hauling lobster pots in on a warm and calm Scottish day. She said 'I remember the softness of the ripples on the water like silk. Wherever Diana is right now, I hope it is how it was then. I can't believe that it will be any different.'

Much has also been written about Diana's relationship with me – supposedly authoritative articles, but actually based on no knowledge or basis of facts. Such pieces made us both wince, but also gave us joy that we often met in so many diferent places without anyone ever knowing.

A sense of joy that we did it and no one ever knew. I recall with great pleasure, her telephone calls from all over the world, at all times of day and night; hearing so often her ready sense of humour bubbling over. And I would think then of the nine months before she was born, that time when she was completely mine.

For years before Diana's death, and indeed since she has died, I have had frequent requests from the media for interviews to speak about Diana. I felt as though I was being asked for my very soul, which couldn't be given, since it belongs to someone else. My treasured memories of her last days are not for sharing. They remain zipped up in my heart, along with treasured memories of all my children and grandchildren. Believe me, I am the proudest grandmother in the world.

No television pictures can tell the full story of what happened in London that day. I doubt even if I can be articulate about it.

I spent hours during the night in the grounds of Kensington Palace witnessing thousands of people so thoughtfully choosing where to put their flowers and light their candles, seeing tears pouring down the faces of every age, race and creed.

The hugs I was given, and so many people saying to me 'Thank you for giving us Diana, and thank you for being here with us tonight.'

I felt indescribable comfort in a warm, protective mantle, and my fear of how I would cope at Westminster Abbey lessened. The day after the funeral I awakened at my son's home to another day of cloudy skies, and thought back how Johnny and I had made that wee lassie who brought the spark into so many people's lives.

Charles asked if I wanted him to row me across to the island where Diana rests, and at that moment I declined. But later that morning, walking in the gardens, I was drawn to the lake. The boat looked overwhelmingly tempting, so I rowed myself across to the island.

As I rowed back I noticed a thin covering of weed on the water cut in two by the boat. I looked back and saw it join like a curtain as a lone swan glided past. At that point I could feel my beloved Diana was at peace. Her earthly life was short but complete. I knew then that all she had to was completed; that all was well. Very well.

Frances Shand Kydd, St Columba's Cathedral, Oban, Scotland

REFLECTIONS

Anyone who imagines that normal politics will be resumed after Diana's funeral is in for a shock. Like a landscape stilled by lightning, the country revealed by the public response to her death appears sharp and unfamiliar to the eye. The Britain that has been disclosed by Diana's death is not new. It produced the electoral landslide of 1 May. But it has not yet been fully mapped. It is hugely at variance with the picture of a culture that is rooted in the past.

It is not a country that reveres traditional values. Still less does it defer to any authority that seeks to impose them. It has accepted the challenge of modern times, which is the opportunity to invent one's life for oneself and its corollary, the obligation to show sympathy for those who come to grief through the absence of choice. It sees its own insecurities in the lives of those who have been excluded from the mainstream – gays, ethnic minorities, the homeless. It is a flawed country, but one in which cynicism about any kind of public action has not become an automatic reflex.

In mourning the Princess of Wales the country honours the memory of someone whom circumstances forced to author her own life, and who went on to claim that freedom for others. Is this the country whose prejudices tabloid newspapers are so anxious to flatter and politicians of all parties desperate to appease?

That country no longer exists. Those who think they speak for it today are comic figures. Nicholas Soames's attack on the Princess of Wales two years ago, in which he described her during a television discussion as a woman exhibiting the advanced symptoms of paranoia, was striking in its buffoonish insensitivity to the national mood. Doubtless Soames imagined that he articulated the unspoken prejudices of a silent majority; but the sentiments he expressed had long ago retreated to the fringes of British life. A silent majority existed in Britain, but it was instinctively liberal in most of its attitudes.

The Conservative's gawping incomprehension of the fears and aspirations of the liberal British majority cost them the election. Today they still appear resolute in their determination to occupy the impotent margins of British political life. William Hague's tribute to Diana, in which he managed to avoid any mention of her campaign on landmines – one of the causes on which her impact has been internationally acclaimed and may prove to be enduring – showed a misreading of national sentiment only a little less awe-inspiring than that of Nicholas Soames. It will be remembered as a defining moment in the demise of the Tories as a national party.

Labour's strategy for ending 18 years in opposition was based on the premise that British political culture is incorrigibly conservative. There was a good deal in recent political history that supported this strategy. The Conservatives had lost the understanding of enduring human needs that made them the world's most successful political party. In their ranting evangelism for free markets it had somehow escaped them that most people everywhere are intensely averse to economic risk. They scoffed at economic insecurity as an invention of the chattering classes. They disregarded mounting signs that they were perceived – not inaccurately – as a party ready to demolish trusted British institutions such as the NHS for the sake of an ephemeral economic dogma.

Most Britons care more about securing the future for themselves and their families than they do about rising incomes or expanding consumer choice. They see the quality of public services as an index of civilized life. They believe that moderating economic insecurity is one of the core functions of government. In appealing to those decent conservative instincts Labour was not only taking advantage of a momentous political opportunity, it was responding to the neglect of vital human needs.

But Labour's immensely successful election strategy has limitations if it is deployed as a basis for government. Britain today is not deeply committed to the institutions and values it inherits from the past. Except in regard to crime, where its concern with security leads to law-and-order attitudes, the British majority regards the assertion of authority with indifference, even suspicion. It wants to trust government, but only if it respects personal freedom, and is consistently competent in furthering it.

If policies promoting family values mean concern for the wellbeing of children they will have strong support. If they mean a rerun of Back to Basics they will soon be an object of public ridicule. If the war on drugs attacks the despair that drives people to addiction it will have some success. If it attempts to repeat in Britain policies that have already failed in America it will be a tragic failure. In these and other areas of policy, Labour had better get used to governing one of the world's most liberal countries.

The public response to the death of Diana is not a fabrication of the media. It is a revelation of the country we have become. The Princess of Wales will be remembered as someone upon whom circumstances imposed the necessity of self-invention. Her frail and maimed spirit became strong by surviving the breakdown of an archaic marriage. Her death has disclosed a country that is already more modern than its politicians have yet understood.

John Gray, Professor of Politics at Oxford, in the *Guardian*

'A Vast Amount of Unmastered Grief'

It was impossible to stand outside her death. Irony suddenly became impossible. People who went to bed on Saturday night thinking, if they thought about her at all, that she was a foolish and inconsequential woman – woke up on Sunday morning to find themselves ambushed by their own emotions. She died a horrible death which upset even those who had been unmoved by her life.

The emotions which overwhelmed the country were large but they were never simple. It was never just a national outpouring of grief. Sorrow is more intense when compounded of guilt, and ours was a guilty sorrow. We all had a hand in making the myths which killed her.

Our sorrow began with her and then ended back upon ourselves. When we mourned her death, we mourned our own. People wept for their own mothers and fathers, for lost children, as if all the unconsoled losses of private life had been suddenly allowed to seek public consolation. The people who placed bouquets on the railings of Kensington Palace might have been decorating their own family graves.

One lesson of her death is how much unexpressed sadness and loss there is in our midst, how much ache and loneliness. The churches do not seem to help. The therapists do not help. We talk and talk. It does not help. In millions of us there seems to be a vast amount of unmastered grief. Her death became the catalyst for these suppressed emotions because we knew she had felt them herself. Her often confused expressiveness gave us permission to break the Windsor code of stoic reserve.

Certainly genuine sorrow was mixed with mawkishness and self-pity. An older generation wondered whether the British had lost their proverbial self-control. But by and large the grief was restrained by a determination to honour her life and dignify her death. The campaign for a people's funeral for a people's princess became a great popular uprising, not just against the Royal Family but against the indignity of dying and the impoverishment of our rituals of commemoration. The public wanted something grand for her because they want something better for themselves than hospital deaths and dry-eyed cremations. The popular uprising which forced an unwilling monarch to pay public tribute to Diana was actually demanding the right to define the protocols of public mourning. And they were not demanding it just for her but for themselves.

The native British genius for the invention of tradition crafted her the kind of funeral which honours us all. For one hour life stood still in homage to life. Now that the gun-carriage and the lilies are gone, and the last electrifying notes of Taverner's *Alleluia* have faded away, we have had the catharsis which only great public ritual can provide; but we are also back where we started, with the reality of her death, and the eventual fact of our own.

Had she died as the wife of the Prince of Wales, her death would have occasioned only discreet and manageable sorrow. But she was never a safe and manageable figure. She was a scandal in life and in death, a woman who had died in the company of her lover, a defrocked royal princess who both embodied the aura of royalty and incarnated its failure as an institution. Because she was unique, no one knew how she should be honoured, and a mighty struggle took place for the symbolic appropriation of her memory. At the centre of it all, three great families – the Spencers, the Windsors and the Fayeds – duelled in public over the ownership of her symbolic remains. The 'blood family' claimed her; her putative adoptive family, the Fayeds, sought to convince us that she had almost been theirs; and the Windsors, baffled and battered, struggled lamely to say that they mourned her like the rest of us. While the three families struggled to control her legacy, two institutions – the modern media and the monarchy – fought to save their reputations from the stain of her death, and a third, the Labour government, discreetly manoeuvred to capitalize on the discomfiture of the other two. Watching this struggle was a force – the British public – which at the week's beginning hardly sensed its power and by week's end had swept all before it.

In Earl Spencer's thrilling defence of the claim of the 'blood family' in Westminster Abbey, a very British process of social alchemy took place. In life, Diana had shed the strangled accents of her class of origin for the mid-Atlantic idiom of stardom. In the brother's eulogy, she was reclaimed by her clan and simultaneously offered back to the world as their 'classless' Princess. When the Earl sat down, it was clear from the applause which began among the crowd outside and then spread through the abbey – to include the younger members of the Royal Family itself – that his words had succeeded beyond any imagining. The elder Windsors could only stare at the floor in silence, knowing that the Spencers had taken their revenge.

But it would be a mistake to suppose that either Lord Spencer or Diana ever represented a latent British republicanism. Their battle with the Windsors was a revenge drama, not a blow for constitutional change. If the country wanted a republic, it would not have mourned her with such intensity. In time, the public anger directed at Charles will wane as reality returns and people recall that divorce is too sad a business to be a matter of easy blame.

This struggle between the families to appropriate Diana's meaning was soon caught up in a real battle of institutions. The press began the week with the finger of blame pointed at them; by the end of the week, they had shifted it to the Royal Family. In turn the Royal Family was forced, in this ruthless struggle for legitimacy, to make humiliating ritual gestures. It is not clear that the public required the Queen to give a clipped eulogy to her former daughter-in-law, but the media, battling to salvage its own reputation, forced her into it to save theirs.

Luckily – and most unexpectedly – a third institution, the Labour government, intervened on the monarchy's side. At first, it did not appear to be doing so. When Tony Blair appeared on camera to praise the achievements of the 'people's Princess', his choice of words suggested that he sided with the people against the hard-faced family who had turned her out. But in insisting on a large public funeral, in urging the Royal Family to make a public show of their grief, he loaned them the formidable public relations skills which had won him the election. In the process, he managed the difficult feat of becoming a national rather than a political figure, so that no one – save a few resentful Conservatives – found it objectionable that a party political figure should be seen on television reading the lesson from Corinthians. In managing the monarchy's counter-attack, while simultaneously promoting himself as a national leader, and accomplishing all this without appearing to profit from national distress, Blair may have guaranteed himself the kind of hegemony which Margaret Thatcher enjoyed in the 1980s.

Yet, from the first morning, when cameramen found young black men weeping openly in front of Buckingham Palace, the public's reaction set the pace at which other institutions, the media included, reacted. Certainly the media sought to take control of the popular mood, with those nauseating headlines demanding that the Queen show herself to her suffering people. But the public saw through the media's attempt to turn the focus of attention away from themselves to the failings of the monarchy. Which is why, in the end, the public allowed the monarchy to regain the initiative, and why, just possibly, a repentant public may force a humbled press to respect the privacy of the grieving Princes.

Now that it is all over, will our anguish about fate and death simply retreat back to the inner recesses of our private lives? Will it ever surface again in such a tidal wave of emotion? And what, if anything, will be the political consequence of that moment of empowerment, that sudden determination by the British people that they – and not the families and the institutions – would shape the rituals of their Princess's passing? These moments of empowerment make revolutions and they have torn down the walls between empires and nations. They are the sudden eruption which tears asunder the damp cloak of acquiescence and fatalism. Everyone who stood among the crowds will long remember the quiet but dignified sense that the moment belonged to them. Such moments are quickly thrown away and the energies released are easily squandered. But if someone has the wisdom to put the people's sense of empowerment to productive use, the effects may last long beyond that extraordinary week.

Michael Ignatieff, *Prospect*

'QUIT MAKING SUCH A HASH OF THE JOB'

Of all the images evoked during the past week by the death of Diana, Princess of Wales, the one most likely to survive the passage of time is the startling response of the British people.

The queues of mourners at the condolence books, the massed bouquets outside Kensington Palace, the millions who lined the streets and applauded spontaneously during the most evocative moments of the funeral service – all these reflected a collective surge of national emotion that sent two clear messages.

One, of course, was an unmistakable message of affection for Diana.

The other, perhaps in the long run more important, was that while most Britons remain loyal to the institution of the monarchy, they believe that the Windsors need some instruction in how to run it.

Queen Elizabeth and her family had a chance to surmount years of bad publicity by leading the nation in a prolonged show of elevated bereavement. Instead, for most of last week they looked dottily remote and badly in need of the guidance that flowed up from the streets instead of down from Balmoral.

The source of Diana's remarkable hold on the public remains something of a mystery. Now, as exaggerated by an abrupt and senseless death, the adoration of Diana certainly partakes of the canonization that her devoted brother, Earl Spencer, warned against in what must surely be one of the most scarifying eulogies in Westminster Abbey's long history of royal ceremony.

In any event, the people seem unlikely to dwell on Diana's imperfections any time soon, because early and late in her streaking course from obscurity to madcap destruction she connected with the British people in a fluid way that the rest of the royals cannot master and, indeed, seldom bother to fake.

Queen Elizabeth, scrambling to catch up with a public that condemned her aloofness and absence from England's mourning capital, had invoked Diana's healing common touch in her remarks from the palace balcony on

191

Friday. She noted Diana's capacity 'to inspire others with her warmth and kindness'. She 'admired and respected' her former daughter-in-law, the Queen allowed. But Elizabeth could not quite bring herself to say she loved the woman.

Had the Queen made even so controlled an appearance earlier in the week, she might have deflected much of the criticism hurled her way in the final two days before the funeral. But over the years this particular queen had somehow forgotten how her father, King George VI, stabilized the House of Windsor by keeping his family in London to share the hazards of the Blitz.

Elizabeth herself began her reign with a large bank account of public affection. But that account was depleted by her zealous quest for privacy, her husband's ostentatious crankiness, her children's spendthrift indiscretions and her son Charles's idiosyncratic ideas about private behaviour and public duty.

Diana's death and the immediate worldwide audience provided a chance to replenish the account of public affection with which Britons yearn to endow their rulers. But instead of responding rapidly and in personal terms, the Queen and her family retreated to Balmoral Castle in Scotland, itself a historic symbol of royal disengagement, where Queen Victoria secluded herself for years following her husband's death.

It was this chilly detachment, as much as the family's rough treatment of Diana, that turned what could have been a moment of healing into a public relations hurricane.

By dawn Saturday, with a crowd of millions building in the streets, the Royal Family began to get things right. They stood in full public view to watch the casket pass bearing its three bouquets and the young Princes' heartbreaking card to 'Mummy'.

Prince Philip, unannounced, joined his son and grandsons to walk in the funeral procession, and for once his stern gaze and martial stride seemed not remote but of a solemn piece with the mood set by a slow-gonging bell and the tossing black horses.

Through Wellington Arch and down the Mall, it was at last proper Windsor gesture and pageantry. If television pictures were anywhere near an accurate gauge, an anger long pent seemed to seep from the crowd.

But while the streets were commanded in some measure by the Queen again, the church that has seen 39 coronations belonged one last time to

192

Diana and the odd-lot congregation left by her odd-lot life.

Britain's leaders listened with official guests, rockers, models and movie folk as Elton John – a courtier in the pop-culture world Diana adored – sang a keening ballad he had composed for another blonde prisoner of fame, Marilyn Monroe. As for Lord Spencer's raw and passionate eulogy, the British press and eventually the historians will be chewing it for a long time.

He strafed nearly everyone except the irresponsible driver who sped his sister to her death. His flogging of the press was predictable, but it was his 'blood family' challenge to the Windsors over the raising of Diana's Spencer sons that will be remembered. His meaning, barely veiled, was that the Royal Family has an obligation to protect Prince William and Prince Harry in a way that it never protected Princess Diana.

It is a warning that Queen Elizabeth and Prince Charles would be wise to heed. Their belated gestures let them squeak through the funeral with a fair chance to reclaim public affection, if not the worship now owned by a Diana who is already wrapped in legend.

Her burial ended one of those weeks when the British people seem to rise up as one to deliver an emotional verdict that confounds expectations. Perhaps Churchill's defeat after World War II was one such moment.

But this one, of course, is more primal than political. In the extremity of their mourning, Britain's citizens were exhibiting their desperate loyalty to the Royal Family and their desperate demand that this bunch quit making such a hash of the job.

New York Times

THE MIRROR OF OURSELVES

The subtitle on CNN was suddenly saying 'Princess Diana dead'. And for just an hour or so, it felt like November 1963. 'This will be a fixing moment in your lives,' I intoned to my two sons (I was thinking, naturally, about *her* two sons). 'You will always remember where you were and who you were with when you heard this news.' Princess Diana dead: it seemed brutally inordinate. Because Diana had never been hard news, until then. Diana, in every sense, had always been *soft*. For once I found myself longing for a euphemism: passed away, perhaps, or succumbed.

A sense of proportion would soon return. Or at least it would in my house. The true comparison, of course, is not with Kennedy but with Kennedy's wife. (And consider the passive figure of Mr Zapruder, his shutter innocently open on the grassy knoll, as opposed to the figure of Mr Rat, the paparazzo.) But in the immediate aftermath, one experienced the pity and terror associated with a major loss. You felt stunned from nowhere, as if something had veered in out of your blind spot.

The fatal ride has the quality of nightmare. What was it *like*, being driven by a vainglorious drunk at an insane velocity in an urban *tunnel*? With rising claustrophobia, the passenger will sense that a driver's mind is disorganized – that 'control' is in the process of being relinquished. And so it was. It makes your shins shudder to imagine the atrocious physics of the impact, as the Mercedes transformed itself into a weapon of blunt force. Next, the SWAT team of photographers and the final photo shoot. Whether or not the paparazzi helped cause Diana's death, they undoubtedly defiled its setting. They took pictures of the dying woman. How could they? But they did. And now the two sons, the Princes, face not only the loss of a loving and lovable mother but also a bereavement uniquely contaminated by the market forces of fame.

Let us for a moment examine the nature of Diana's fame. One might call it a collateral celebrity, because it relied on no discernible contribution (except to the gaiety, and now the grief, of nations). Lady Diana Spencer attracted the love of the introverted heir to the English throne. And that was all. Brightness of eye, whiteness of tooth, a colluding smile, a certain transparency, a vividness, an exposed vulnerability: it was enough for him, and it was enough for us. Madonna sings. Grace Kelly acted. Diana simply breathed. She was a social-page figure who became a cover girl. One can soberly assert that the Diana saga, in itself, was a non-story, remorselessly and fanatically annotated by our own projections and desires. Rather, *we* are the story. Equipped with no talent, Diana evolved into the most celebrated woman on earth. What does that tell us about the third rock from the sun?

She certainly believed she had a talent: a talent for love. She felt she could inspire it, transmit it, increase its general sum. It has been said about her (what *hasn't* been said about her?) that she adopted various charities as 'accessories'. But the causes Diana was most strongly identified with – Aids, hospices, landmines – demanded more than a reflexive commitment. There is no question that she made a difference to the homosexual community, in England and perhaps elsewhere; her support came at a crucial time, in defiance of tabloid opinion as well as royal prudence. Yet the fact remains that Diana was far less dedicated than, for instance, her one-time sister-in-law, Princess Anne, whose want of looks long ago consigned her to near total obscurity. Let's face it: we're a planet of looks snobs.

Diana could touch and feel; perhaps she believed she could heal. Watching her on television, jolting with tears as she listened to a speech praising and defending her work, one saw signs of an almost delusional inner drama. If power corrupts the self, then absolute fame must surely distort it. Her enthusiasms were crankish, hypochondriac, self-obsessive: aromatherapy, colonic irrigation, the fool's gold of astrology. Diana, I repeat, was 'soft' news. She causes sensations by wearing a party dress or by gaining a kilo of weight. She made headlines with every wave of her hand, every twitch of her eyebrow. This is why her death – her metamorphosis into hard news – feels so savage. Death has enshrined her and frozen her in time. It has also fulfilled her own prophecy. She *did* have a gift for love: look at the people in their millions, weeping on the streets of London. Diana was a mirror, not a lamp. You looked at her and saw your own ordinary humanity, written in lights. After all, everyone is a star, everyone is a prima donna, in the karaoke age.

On the larger scale. Diana's contribution to history is both paradoxical and inadvertent. She will go down as the chief saboteur of the monarchy. It wasn't just the divorce, the tell-all boyfriend, the married rugby star. She introduced an informality, a candid modernity, into a system that could offer no resistance to it; she had a beauty in her life that made them ugly.

Above all she will be remembered as a phenomenon of pure stardom. Her death was a terrible metaphor for that condition. She takes her place, among the broken glass and crushed metal, in the iconography of the crash, alongside James Dean, Jayne Mansfield and Princess Grace. These other victims, however, died unpursued. They weren't fleeing the pointed end of their own celebrity: men on motorcycles with computerized cameras and satellite-linked mobile phones. The paparazzi are the high-tech dogs of fame. But it must be admitted that we sent them into that tunnel, to nourish our own mysterious needs.

Martin Amis, *Time*

'To Mobilize the Love of the World'

She was beautiful – or at least she became beautiful – in the way that only the sad can be beautiful. If you look at her eyes, even in the most smiling of photographs, you see something resembling sorrow. It rarely dominates her appearance but it always lurks within it. At times her eyes turned hard and an excluding cold shone from them, a response to the brutalities of the world in which she found herself. But that was no more than armour, not the real self. The real self, the fragility of that real self emerged at the times when she could afford to let it. And it was then that the sadness became apparent. This look, a sudden access into the heart of a woman who came to realize that her vulnerability was her greatest strength, is the ghost of sorrow overcome, sorrow understood, sorrow acted on, sorrow not exactly defeated but invited on to the apron of the stage, and embraced there. In that act of courage, of allowing a profound sense of weakness and failure and doubt to emerge as part of the person she allowed the world to see, that sorrow became beautiful. Diana's beauty was the beauty of two things which her life combined: sadness and courage. Both were essential parts of her and neither triumphed over the other. That was why people loved her.

Looking back to the first moments in which she appeared in the newspapers and on the television, it is almost impossible to predict the trajectory which her life would follow. The Diana who died seems scarcely related to the Diana who was teaching at the Pimlico kindergarten in 1980. The first sight of her is of a person essentially untried, not yet subjected to the formative processes of life. It is a modern assumption that a person is made by their childhood and that life after childhood is no more than an acting out and fulfilment of everything that has been planted there in the first few years. If you were looking for evidence of the wrongness of that assumption, the life of Diana provides it. The 20-year-old who married Prince Charles in 1981 had known unhappiness enough. Her parents' divorce had been traumatic in the extreme. During it, Lady Fermoy, her mother's mother, had sided with Diana's father against her own daughter and he was awarded custody of the children. But how much of that past was apparent in the Diana with whom the Prince of Wales fell in love – 'whatever love means', as he said at the time in that chance, fateful, tossed-away phrase – in the autumn of 1980? She had suffered but the suffering had not shaped her. She had the air, in fact, of somone on whom life had scarcely impinged. Her uncle, Lord Fermoy, told the world that she was 'a bone fide virgin' and, however unfortunate those words, that was certainly the image she gave to the world and presumably to the Prince. Look at those photographs now of her escaping the duffel-coated photographers in the cold last months of 1980, and she looks as if she has yet to grow up. Her clothes muffle her body. Her haircut is page-boyish, making no claims, without calculation, innocent. She is the kind of girl which that kind of girl, from that kind of family, often is, at least in the sense that she is sweet, loving, gentle, generous and impotent.

Th assumptions of her background had given her little education, and no O-levels; had told her, however insidiously, that she was as thick as two planks; but had given her a flat and had pushed her towards cookery classes and a time as a nanny. There were hundreds of girls like her who felt that powerlessness was their natural lot, that their destiny was to be no more nor less than sweet, loving, funny, honest and, with luck, loved.

The track of Diana's history is a movement away from impotence towards power, from a suppression of hurt towards its expression, and towards an integration of personality in which the mobilizing force was her own innate courage. There were no landmarks here and her stepping out into that unmarked territory resonated for the simple reason that so many of her challenges were shared by the rest of the modern world. The search for self-esteem, the way in which self-loathing clings on doggedly for year after year, the need for a sense of authenticity and purpose: these are all things to which the age itself was alive. Not that one should depict her as too sombre or responsible. She loved a good time and was perfectly capable of behaving badly, of poking people in the Royal Enclosure at Ascot with an umbrella, or simply baiting the establishment. But these, too, were symptoms of the predicament. Diana's life was tragic, in the technical sense, because these universal human dilemmas were lived out by her on a huge scale. How easy it would have been for her, or perhaps for someone in her situation, to have succumbed to circumstance, to have suppressed agony, to have diverted her sadness and disappointment into sublimated and uninspected channels. But she did not and her refusal to bow down was, quite literally, on a global scale. She shook the monarchy to be herself. She set her own vision of what is good in life – it can be summed up in two words: emotional honesty –

197

against that of the alarmingly powerful institution in which she had become embroiled. And that, too, is why people loved her.

There is a dark period in the centre of her adult life when that first soft innocence goes and an armoured hardness takes its place. This is how people are when they are unhappy. They become drawn and their faces take on the appearance of a victim, more sinned against than sinning, suffering their circumstances rather than existing within them. There is a pattern here too. The early Diana seems to receive the world and does not mind that she is in a passive relationship to it. The middle Diana receives the world but resents what the world is doing to her. And the later Diana, who has visibly suffered, and whose sadness is now integral to her being, in the way one geological layer buried deep in a landscape will mould the form of whatever is laid on top of it, nevertheless moves beyond that victimhood. This Diana, the Diana that began to emerge in the last four years of her life, separated from the Prince of Wales, now gives out to the world, rather than simply receiving it.

The old Diana was in some ways an imploding being, dressed, extraordinarily as it now seems, in those pie-crust collars and in soft, utterly penetrable, flouncy layers. The new Diana, fuelled by the courage to love herself, even when stepping out into dangerous and unsignposted places, exudes a sense of self. Her way of walking changes. Her shoulders, rather hunched and pulled protectively around her when she was a young woman, now move back and out. She dares to show her beautiful self. She gives and gives and gives because she knows in giving she is strong. She believes in the power of love, to accommodate those whom most people wish to exclude; and, far from being as thick as two planks, she understands acutely the ability of her own presence, demonstrated by the sight of her intimate involvement in a hug or a kiss or a touch or a glance or a smile, to mobilize what might be called love, the love of the world, or at least the desire of the world to love and to show its love.

Her canvas was herself. She was her own work of art, and from being something which the rest of the world created, she decided from the depths of her unhappiness to become her own creator. And, in doing that, she became beautiful. That acquisition of beauty is in many ways the most remarkable thing about this life. It is the convention, the expected thing, that beauty declines. What nature gives, time will take away. Diana swam against that stream. And her acquisition of beauty was not as an external commodity, a thing to be got by surgery or couture or the gym, but, as anyone should expect of this woman, as an outward and visible sign of a new and inner grace. Of course, those other things played their part; of course, her natural intelligence guided her towards an understanding of what would work in her circumstances. Of course, she learned how to dress, how to have her hair cut, how, in short, to look, but that was not the essence of the change she wrought in herself.

Something far more significant happened to this person; and those who sneer at beauty of her kind, or even at the search for it, should at least attempt to understand that her life demonstrates that beauty is a profound and not a superficial quality. If you look at those early photographs of her as young woman or as a young mother, it is perfectly possible to imagine any number of paths which she might have taken. It isn't difficult to imagine several versions of decline, of implosion, of stultification, of loss of self, of loss of dignity, of loss of courage and of loss of hope for that young and vulnerable face. But Diana, so nearly broken by circumstances which, of course, had their own complex justifications and their own rationale, denied defeat and stared out, in the end, the possibility of her own collapse. Her beauty was her triumph. It was her badge of survival, her mark of courage and of her ability to accommodate her own sorrows. That, instinctively and perhaps subconsciously, is why people loved her: because she had come through and in the process had grown into someone quite different and much larger than the person she had been before.

Clearly she had fallen in love with Dodi Fayed. The clutching, dragging sadness felt by the world when she died was surely the result not, as the phrase goes, of 'the waste of a young life', nor anger that the photographers should have been chasing her, nor that the Fayed driver was drunk, nor that her sons were left motherless, but of the knowledge that this long hard struggle, so bravely and in some ways blindly fought, like a drowning person struggling for air, for the surface, for the light, should, at what looked like the beginning of an emergence, a coming out into that light, be cut off and shut down by the grim banality of a car crash. It is a disproportionate end to everything that went before. That is why it hurts. It hurts because we know about her. And it hurts because, in some ways some of us have never recognized before, we loved her.

Adam Nicolson, *Sunday Telegraph Magazine*

The Naughty Girl Next Door

Diana Spencer was nothing like as gifted as Judy Garland, nowhere near as sexy as Marilyn Monroe, but like those equally doomed young women, she had the power to touch us – that is to say, if one examines the response dispassionately, to make us feel sorry for her. She was a terribly mixed-up kid. We felt close to her (when we were not infuriated by her) because she represented in herself so many of the worries our own children are likely to foist upon us – disappointing school grades, anorexia and bulimia, unsuitable young men, a tendency to show off, a preoccupation with clothes and publicity, a rotten marriage, single motherhood and trouble with the in-laws.

Sometimes she went too far, as children do, and we were fed up with her. Sometimes we felt that she was deceiving us. She doth protest too much, we occasionally thought, when she complained about the attentions of the paparazzi. When, after so many years of burning extravagant candles at both ends, she died at last so squalidly that night, some of us for a moment thought, as the Friar thought about Romeo and Juliet, 'These violent delights have violent ends . . .'

But she touched us – that's the thing. As the Friar went on to remark, 'So light a foot will ne'er wear out the everlasting flint.' She was so lovely to look at. She appeared to be so shy. Like all our children, she seemed to float above the drab and everlasting flintiness of our ordinary lives. Time and again we found ourselves ready to forgive her, just as in the end we always give in and send our wayward offspring another cheque to pay the telephone bill; and we did it as always with a shrug of the shoulders that was part affection, part exasperation, part amusement, part forgiveness – and part pity. Even a doubter like me, when the news arrived from Paris that Sunday morning, felt the tears come to my eyes.

But then we saw in her too some larger allegory. She mirrored our personal anxieties, and the perennial anxieties of the young – for it is hard to believe she was 36 years old. She was a cliché of the age itself. Much of the angst of this troubled fin de siècle was indexed in her brief life. Wars and poverty, sickness and prejudice, uncertainty and despair – this daughter of an earl, this mother of a putative King of England was paradoxically farmiliar with them all: and when the end came, it was a properly symbolic end as, with her playboy lover, she was driven at midnight by a drunken driver much too fast in a Mercedes through a city underpass, pursued by photographers on motorbikes.

How sad! What a pathetic life, after all, enlarged for us all by unrelenting advertisement, blown up like a fictional drama so that it is already entering, before our eyes, the realm of myth – an apotheosis that in previous ages took centuries to happen. In the world at large, she is already on the way to join Elvis and Marilyn on a flying saucer somewhere: in Britain she is mourned with a hysterical intensity that seems pathological, ordinary people standing in line for seven or eight hours to sign a memorial book nobody is ever going to read, or preparing to camp out all night long to see the funeral cortège pass by.

Of course, this is partly a tabloid mourning, a tabloid sincerity, just as Diana herself had become a tabloid star – almost a fictional star. Since the days of Thomas Hardy at least, people have been moved to passionate sorrow by the death of public personalities they have never met, and who sometimes never existed. No doubt thousands wept over the fate of Tess of the d'Urbervilles when her story appeared week by week in the *Graphic* in 1890, just as truly as they wept for Diana when they read of her death in the *Sun* in 1997. They have been deluded into thinking they actually knew her by the tireless machines of the media, and they have cried for her as for one of their own children.

Then again it is doubtless partly mass hysteria – groupies genuinely mean it too, when they swoon in the presence of their idols, one scream leading to another, one pair of panties thrown onstage soon leading to a storm of votive lingerie. It is partly resentment against the in-laws. Despite late damage limitation from the Palace, many Britons see the British Royal Family as villains in this soap opera, stuffy and reactionary guardians of an old order into which Diana came as a lovely catalyst, only to be spurned as young heroines so often are.

But perhaps, I like to think, the death of Diana has acted as a kind of catharsis for her nation. This has not been a happy half-century for the British. It has been a time of frustration and febrile self-doubt. Most of the national institutions, from the monarchy itself to the BBC, have lost their old sense of confident authority. In an age when no island is an island anymore, the very national identity, once apparently so unassailable, has been whittled away. British traditions have been discarded, British values have lost their meaning. A great people seems to be in moral limbo.

With the death of a lovely if maddening princess, out it has all poured. Something, as the old song said, had to give, and perhaps this fantastic display of public grief, so vulgar in many ways, so unconvincing in others, has to it some spiritual element after all. Perhaps in their hearts – or so I hope – the British people see Diana as a fellow victim of degraded times, and have instinctively seized upon her death as the moment for a fresh start.

Jan Morris, *Time*

It is Time to Grow Up

The mood of the times is volatile, unprecedented and unpredictable. Commentators and politicians are asking one another, What on earth does all this mean? Where does it go from here?

Out there on the streets, queuing through the night for eight hours, these are not the usual royal freaks who camp out for any wedding, jubilee or coronation. These are not readers of *Majesty* who can quote every royal birthday. Many of them are surprised by their feelings. 'I'm not much of a royalist but . . .' 'I was never interested in the royals, but . . .' Even in the newsrooms, hardened old cynics are swept off their feet. Is this just a strange example of global hysteria?

The Royal Family are plainly at a loss to read the meaning of all this. They are behaving as if a revolution is taking place outside the gates of Buckingham Palace. And they may be right. Hiding away in their Balmoral fastness, it is as if they dare not face the people, cannot face the people, cannot fathom the mood and they fear that it could turn nasty. For there is a growing groundswell of indignation out there. Where is the Queen? Why has she sent not one word of a message of regret, sorrow or condolence with anyone, not least her subjects? Why does no flag fly at half-mast over the palace? Yes, the cognoscenti know that's because she is not in residence. But why is she not in residence? Dead bodies may not require company but people are saying that Diana has been abandoned, left alone in her coffin with the mourners in the Mall.

She who stripped Diana of her HRH seems not to trust herself to the mercy of the masses, spilling out their hearts and flowers at her gates. Her life of frozen duty, stony faced and grim, may be admirable and full of noble self-sacrifice, but those qualities are out of fashion. Now people blame her for being a mother who put her duty above motherhood, keeping up appearances against all emotion, and they blame her for the miserable, contorted, agonized heir she raised.

How are she and Prince Charles to compose their faces through this ordeal? Weeping looks like hypocrisy, but dry eyes look as if they feel less than their subjects. Already the unforgiving public blame the monarchy for Diana's pathetic love-lorn life. They took a young 19-year-old into their dysfunctional family, used her as a brood mare and ejected her when she couldn't bear it.

Joining the monarchy is seen now by the people as something akin to marrying into the Adams family. Hardly surprising they all divorce. Feminists at the time of the wedding wore badges proclaiming 'Don't Do It Di!'. Now the people on the streets feel they were cynically manipulated with the pageantry of an empty 'fairy-tale' marriage.

That may be brutally unfair. Diana was not a simple young thing. She was already deeply neurotic herself. The one thing she shared with Prince Charles, disastrously, was a calamitous childhood. But she is dead and pitied while Charles had to stand out there and shoulder the blame. The Diana myth is that the monarchy killed her. And now they fear the monarchy will destroy her sons too. The monarchy is turning into the people's enemy.

That may all be complete nonsense, but that is what a lot of the people in the crowds are saying, loudly. It's what the phone-ins are saying. Royal reality is whatever the people think it is. The myth is all. They have created the dead Diana in their image and they are busily remaking their view of the Royal Family in her shadow.

Royalty only exists as an emblem. It has no substance, no role, no objective reality. As Diana so naffly put it, they have to be kings and queens of the people's hearts, or they are nothing. There were deeply unpopular monarchs in the past – but those days are gone. The monarchy, surrounded by European republics, is here only on the people's sufferance now.

People are not much interested in dry issues of constitutional reform. There is no significant republican political project. But what if they take against the Royal Family as individuals? What if they dislike the heartless institution that destroys those who marry into it or are brought up in it? Out there in the streets, they may be turning against the monarchy itself.

Commentators have been asking what the monarchy can do to make itself loved again? How can the Queen make herself more like Diana, less like her frigid Christmas messages? No number of Saatchis or Mandelsons can spin a new story for them. Can they send Charles out hugging lepers, kissing babies at Great Ormond Street, laughing with children and old folk, weeping with the sick? It's too late to retrain his shy and awkward body language. No, the royal advisers will pin their hopes on poor young William. After all he looks like his mother. But the chances of him growing up in Buckingham Palace balanced, happy and sane seem remote, if not impossible. The mad media frenzy will never abate.

So what should happen now? Charles is a sensitive, thoughtful, if tortured soul. If he has been tormenting himself in recent days with guilt and regret, then he should look to his sons and wonder how they at least can be saved from his fate.

There is only one brave and noble thing left for him to. He must call an end to this pointless, painful, ignominious charade. In a few months' time he should renounce the Crown. He should recommend that the monarchy ends with his mother's life. The country should prepare itself to become a modern republic at a measured dignified pace, whenever that may be. After all, the Queen may live as long as her mother. Charles could be 75 when she dies and William 40. What are they to do with their lives, beyond suffer in public all these royal humiliations?

And for the rest of us, are we to live with the fairy-tale turned nightmare forever? We are infantilized by our obsession with this meaningless family and their myths. Moving though it is to see the whole world in tears, there is also something gravely distressing about such extravagant outpouring of passing and emotion on so empty a vessel as the Royal Family. Not even Dunblane caused such a national paroxysm. The pathos of Diana's story is dreadfully sad and the sight of her bereft children will be terrible to behold at the funeral. But the kindest thing for them would be to set them free from our unreasonable, insatiable emotional demands on them. Charles must know that better than anyone.

But it is we too who need setting free. It is time to grow up, into the 21st century; time to put aside childish things. We cannot live forever expending so much attention and emotion on myths and phantasms of no significance.

It demeans us. It demeans them. The anger of the people on the streets against the monarchy may be unfair, but perhaps at last it will break the spell and set us all free.

Polly Toynbee, *Independent*

POETRY

Goodbye Sunshine Princess

The dark lantern of world sadness has cast its shadow upon the land.
We stumble into our misery on leaden feet.
Our minds seek to comprehend the unknowable and our hearts seek to
Measure a tomorrow without the Sunshine Princess.
Her hands which had held bright tiaras and jewelled crowns,
Also stroked the faces of pain along Angola's dusty roads.
She was born to the privilege of plenty
Yet, she communed with the needy without a show of pompous piety.
Glowing in Bosnia, radiant at glittering balls,
We came to love her and claim her for her grace and accessibility.
Luminous always. We smiled to see her enter and grinned at her happiness.
Now the world we made is forever changed . . .
Made smaller, meaner, less colourful.
Yet, because she did live,
Because she ventured life and confronted change,
She has left us a legacy.
We also may dare . . .
To care for some other than ourselves and those who look like us.
And maybe we can take a lesson from her
And try to live our lives
With passion, compassion, humour and grace.
Goodbye Sunshine Princess

Maya Angelou

6 SEPTEMBER 1997

Mankind is many rivers
That only want to run.
Holy Tragedy and Loss
Make the many One.
Mankind is a Holy, crowned
Mother and her Son.
For worship, for mourning:
God is here, is gone.
Love is broken on the Cross.
The Flower on the Gun.

Ted Hughes

MYTHOLOGY

Earth's axle creaks; the
year jolts on; the trees
begin to slip their brittle
leaves, their flakes of rust;
and darkness takes the edge
off daylight, not
because it wants to – never
that. Because it must.

And you? Your life was not
your own to keeep
or lose. Beside the river,
swerving under ground,
your future tracked you,
snapping at your heels;
Diana, breathless, hunted by
your own quick hounds

Andrew Motion

SEPTEMBER, 1997

Whatever 'in love' means,
true love is talented.
Someone vividly gifted in love has gone.

You went down to St James's Palace
as night fell. Candles shone.
You saw a vast and passionate queue silently form,

as though History was a giant
shaken from sleep by Love.
Then you looked at your hands. Newsprint

covered them like gloves. England's crown
is rusting. The century bleeds to its end.
You stand in a queue in darkness, mourning

an unmet friend. The stranger beside you the same.
A million dying flowers smell like Fame.

Carol Ann Duffy

OBITUARY

Not since the heyday of Jacqueline Kennedy Onassis had there been an international icon to match Diana, Princess of Wales. Her picture on the cover of magazines was enough to guarantee sales worldwide, and no personality in history was ever the subject of more unremitting attention on the part of the paparazzi. In that sense, the fact that she should have met her death – with her new boyfriend Dodi Fayed – while apparently seeking to escape a motorcycle pursuit by photographers carries its own cruel irony along with it.

In an age when stars have become drabber and more ordinary, she achieved unrivalled glamour and respect. She developed from being a relatively unprepossessing kindergarten teacher into a stylish and beautiful young woman, always well dressed, and beloved for her gentle and loving nature.

The most successful princesses in history have been those who loved children and cared for the sick. The Princess enjoyed a natural affinity with both children and the sick. She devoted much energy to their care, in a way entirely in tune with the age. Her warmth and kindness found many outlets, particularly in regard to those struck down with HIV. She was spontaneous in manner, happily ignoring royal protocol to bestow a kiss on a child in the crowd, and writing letters to members of the public signed 'love Diana'.

Almost from the day she emerged into public life, the British people took her to their hearts. She brought to the Royal Family not only her very English beauty, but the enthusiasm of youth, combined with an innate dignity and a good-natured sense of humour.

She was not an intellectual: neither a good passer of exams nor a noted reader. But she possessed a canny and straightforward form of common sense. She listened and she learnt, and whereas she may have found her schooldays boring, she relished her role as Princess of Wales. She loved fashion and dancing, and pop stars and groups such as Phil Collins and Spandau Ballet. In the early years of her marriage she was as excited at meeting stars like Elizabeth Taylor as they were to meet her.

Though she was born into the far from stimulating world of the conventional upper-class girl, reared in the counties of Norfolk and Northamptonshire and veering in youth towards the world of the 'Sloane Ranger', her character had great possibilities for development, and develop she did, into a figure of international importance, confident of her place on the world stage.

She was given little support, it would seem, by her own family or that into which she married. Perhaps one of the reasons that the British public loved her as they did was that they always feared for her, and were concerned that she might be unhappy, while admiring her for being a fighter who refused to give up in the face of adversity.

The world's press loved her, too. Newspapers built her up into the epitome of a fairy-tale Princess. Occasionally they were fickle and turned on their creation, but it was generally more comfortable to let the world love her, and their onslaughts were accordingly short-lived. The press interest was relentless, however, and it began long before the engagement was in any sense firm. After her marriage, her every movement, her every outfit, her every mood, was the excuse for many column inches of press comment. She was a natural joy for photographers, being both photogenic and having an innate understanding of the needs of journalists. Her face could sell a million copies of any publication, and both they and she knew it. She adorned many a magazine cover by editor's choice, and once, memorably, that of *Vogue* by her own wish.

In this great love for a public figure there was bound to lurk danger. When she flourished the press supported her, but when life was dark it deserted her. In the summer of 1992, the forthcoming publication of a biography by Andrew Morton, a journalist from the lower echelons of the trade, caught the attention of Andrew Neil, the editor of *The Sunday Times*. Several weeks of serialization damaging to the monarchy followed. Despite complaints from the Press Council and pleas from the Archbishop of Canterbury, the campaign raged on. It could be seen as a major destructive force in the Princess's life.

Diana, Princess of Wales, was born at Park House, Sandringham, as the

Hon. Diana Frances Spencer. She was the third and youngest daughter of Viscount Althorp (later the 8th Earl Spencer, who died in 1992), and his first wife, the Hon. Frances Roche (later married for some years to the wallpaper heir, Peter Shand-Kydd). She became Lady Diana Spencer on the death of her grandfather in 1975.

Her Spencer forebears had been sheep farmers in Warwickshire, who settled at Althorp, Northamptonshire, in 1506. Cousins of the Spencer-Churchills, they included many connoisseurs and patrons of the arts. Having inherited a considerable fortune from Sarah, Duchess of Marlborough, they were able to spend large sums on antiquities, paintings and sculpture.

For many generations they served their Sovereigns, and the tradition continued. The Princess's father was equerry to King George VI and to the present Queen. Both her grandmothers, the Countess Spencer and Ruth Lady Fermoy, were close members of the court of Queen Elizabeth the Queen Mother, as were no fewer than four Spencer great-aunts. To her two sons, the Princess of Wales passed strong physical Spencer traits, considerably diluting the Hanoverian strain in the Royal Family.

While the Princess's paternal ancestors were representative of the Whig oligarchy of the 18th century, she also descended through several lines from the Stuart Kings Charles II and James II, who were not ancestors of the Prince of Wales. Other paternal forebears included the great Duke of Marlborough, Sir Robert Walpole, the Marquess of Anglesey (who lost a leg at Waterloo), and the Earl of Lucan, of Balaclava fame. On her mother's side there was Irish and Scottish blood, with a sprinkling of pioneer New England stock. Her closest relationship to the Prince of Wales was that of seventh cousin once removed, through their common descent from the 3rd Duke of Devonshire.

The Princess was educated at Riddlesworth Hall in Norfolk, and then at West Heath, a boarding school in Kent. She achieved no O-level passes. Later she attended a finishing school, the Institut Alpin Videmanette at Rougemont in Switzerland, for six weeks. Her childhood was somewhat unsettled and unhappy because of the separation of her parents when she was six, and their divorce in 1969. She had more natural affinity with her father than with her mother.

During the period after leaving school, the Princess worked as a nanny, a babysitter and a skivvy. She attended a cookery course in September 1978, and soon after this her father collapsed with a grave cerebral haemorrhage, from which it took him months to recover. In 1979 she worked briefly as a student teacher at Miss Vacani's dance studios. Later she was invited by friends to help at the Young England Kindergarten in Pimlico, where she was popular with the children. She worked at the kindergarten three days a week and at other times she looked after a small American boy.

In London the Princess shared a flat at Coleherne Court, Earls Court, with three girlfriends. They found her a kind and thoughtful flatmate, keen · on housework and evenings in front of the television, a lover of ballet, opera and cinema. She loved to dance and sometimes they returned to find her dancing happily around the flat. At the time of the pre-wedding press siege, these girls were to prove staunchly loyal allies. Fortunately, they were content to spend hours in each other's company. Years later, one of them, Mrs William Bartholomew, the former Carolyn Pride, was a source for the Morton biography of the Princess.

The Prince and Princess of Wales claimed to have met in a ploughed field at Althorp where Prince Charles was staying as a guest of Lady Sarah Spencer, the Princess's elder sister, in November 1977. The accepted version of the story is that Prince Charles and Lady Sarah were romantically involved, though not deeply so. The younger sister fell in love with everything about the Prince, was keen to be Princess of Wales, and saw in him a challenge.

She knew from an early age that she would have to tread carefully, and she never put a foot wrong. It was not until the late summer of 1980 that Lady Diana Spencer's name came to the attention of the world. The Prince of Wales was nearly 32 and the subject of his eventual marriage had been of consuming interest to the media for nearly a decade. Nor had he helped his difficulty by pronouncing that he thought 30 a good age at which to marry. As November 1978 loomed, the pressure increased. But he remained a bachelor, and there were times when he looked a less than happy man.

Lady Diana's appearance on the scene refocused press attention on the Prince's bachelor state. While a discreet and low-key courtship was executed in private, Lady Diana was pursued to and from work by determined cameramen and reporters and had to resort to complicated manoeuvres to rescue the last vestiges of her privacy. Her subtle handling of the press earned her not only universal respect but the real affection of these normally hard-hearted men. At one point after she had broken down in tears, a note of apology was placed under her windscreen wiper. But the press pursuit persisted to such an extent that Lady Diana's mother wrote a letter of appeal to *The Times.* Later the Queen was obliged to complain to newspaper editors through her press secretary. The Prince proposed early in February 1981.

The engagement was announced on 24 February, after which Lady Diana was better protected. From that day on she was surrounded by what she described as 'a mass of smiling faces'. Indeed the engagement was greeted with universal approval – though the Princess herself found her immediate premarriage days in Buckingham Palace both tense and lonely.

The Royal Wedding took place in St Paul's Cathedral on 29 July, 1981, by the shared wish of both bride and groom. Prince Charles ensured that it was a 'marvellous, musical, emotional experience', with three orchestras playing and Kiri te Kanawa (soon afterwards appointed a Dame) and the Bach Choir singing. Lady Diana chose her favourite school hymn. 'I vow to thee my country'.

Many heads of state attended, including nearly all the crowned heads of Europe, President Mitterand of France, and Mrs Nancy Reagan, wife of the then President of the United States. The King of Tonga required a special chair to be built to support his mighty frame. A last-minute absentee was King Juan Carlos of Spain, because of the decision of the Prince and Princess to embark on the Royal Yacht *Britannia* at Gibraltar. The wedding day was such that for a brief while it seemed that all strife was set aside, the sun blazed richly and, at the end of it, the police thanked the public for their vigilance, and, the public praised the police, and as one commentator put it, 'the world was a friendlier and easier place for everyone'.

The honeymoon was spent first at Broadlands, the home of Lord and Lady Romsey, and a favoured retreat of the Prince when he had stayed there with the late Lord Mountbatten in his youth. Then they cruised on *Britannia* in the Mediterranean. A long holiday at Balmoral followed.

Returning to London in October, the Prince and Princess took up residence at Kensington Palace and at Highgrove House in Gloucestershire. These were their homes for the next 11 years. Their first royal engagement was a 400-mile tour of Wales, the first such visit of a Princess of Wales for

113 years. The tour included a visit to Caernarfon Castle where the Prince had been invested in 1969. The Princess of Wales was given the Freedom of Cardiff, made her first public speech and spoke a few words of Welsh. Despite the ever-present threat of incendiary devices, the tour was a resounding success.

The Princess made an immediate impact on the world of fashion. The British fashion industry, long in a precarious state, was given a welcome boost by her arrival. Her style was fresh, attractive and original. She became the personification of current trends in British fashion, with felicitous results for the trade.

The Princess soon revealed a penchant for outfits of considerable glamour. On her first outing with her fiancé, she had arrived at Goldsmiths' Hall in a décolleté black taffeta dress, a considerable contrast to her formerly discreet image, which caused the octogenarian Lady Diana Cooper to joke: 'Wasn't that a mighty feast to set before a King?' Her wedding dress with its lavish detail and lengthy train matched the magnificence of St Paul's Cathedral and her going away outfit was chic and stylish. The fair fringe she favoured early in the marriage was widely copied for a time.

Very soon the Princess was pregnant, giving birth to a boy, Prince William of Wales, on 21 June 1982. A second son, Prince Harry, followed in September 1984.

In the early years of the marriage the Waleses normally undertook joint engagements. This was the period of the Princess's apprenticeship. But it soon became clear that of the two it was her that the public most wished to see, and Prince Charles was to some extent reduced to a male dancer supporting his glorious ballerina in her pirouettes.

While the popularity of his bride should have delighted him, it added a sense of pointlessness to his slightly frustrated life. Equally, he was irritated when he tried to make an important speech, and the next day the papers merely reported his wife's outfit. He failed to grasp that one of the things the world wanted was a recurring series of images of a young couple enjoying a happy family life. He always appeared reluctant in such photo-calls, fearing that this diminished the import of his more serious endeavours. The Princess, on the other hand, fulfilled all such demands to perfection.

The respective backgrounds of the Prince and Princess of Wales were an additional challenge in the creation of a happy family atmosphere. She had come from a broken home, while his upbringing had been formal to say the least. His early companion had been his nanny, and he lacked any close involvement with his parents.

The love of solitude to which the Prince adhered even after marriage, combined with his love of polo and hunting, inevitably left the Princess on many occasions without him. But both parents shared an adoration for their children.

Even as the world rejoiced on their wedding day, the Princess was aware that she had not entirely captured Prince Charles's heart. Yet she always felt that she would win him. He most probably felt that the marriage was akin to an arranged one, and some have said that he did not enter into it in the same spirit as his bride. When the Princess realized that Prince Charles was never entirely to reciprocate the love she felt for him, she, like many mothers, transferred much of her devotion to her sons.

The Princess celebrated her 21st birthday in July 1982, and that September she represented the Queen at the funeral of Princess Grace of Monaco in the cathedral at Monte Carlo.

The Princess was soon busily involved in the world of public duty. As the years went by, she evolved into a deeply committed member of the Royal Family. She swiftly became better informed – in the early days of her marriage a Fleet Street editor was surprised to hear Prince Charles explaining to her at lunch that Chancellor Kohl was the leader of West Germany. She also learnt the tricks of the royal trade, speaking easily to individual members of the public of all ages and possessing a good instinct as to what to talk about.

Yet in the early days she seldom made speeches in public, and when she did they were of the most formal sort. As she gained confidence, she began to write her own speeches, delivering them from the podium with calm assurance. She spoke of the importance of the family in everyday life, the rehabilitation of drug-users, and urged more compassion for those dying of Aids. When she and the Prince of Wales appeared together in television interviews it was not long before she was the more articulate of the two, leaving him almost monosyllabic, despite an earlier reputation for fluency.

The modern manner is for members of the Royal Family to be actively involved with any organization of which they are patron or president. Until she gave up most of her charitable commitments at the end of 1993, the

Princess was never merely a figurehead, but served directly as a fundraiser, promoter, chairman of meetings – and, of course, as public spokesman.

She gave her support to an enormous number of charities, in a wide range of fields. Among her key presidencies or patronages were Barnardo's; the Great Ormond Street Hospital for Children; Centrepoint; English National Ballet; RADA; the Royal Academy of Music; the Leprosy Mission; the National Aids Trust; the Royal Marsden Hospital; Help the Aged; and the National Meningitis Trust.

An exhausting round of overseas travel was also a feature of her marriage. Her first big overseas tour occurred in March and April 1983, when she accompanied Prince Charles on a visit to Australia. The infant Prince William went with them. They travelled extensively from the Northern Territory to Canberra, through New South Wales, Tasmania, Southern Australia, Western Australia, Queensland and Victoria. At that time the Australian Prime Minister, Bob Hawke, was a committed republican, but he was forced to concede that the Princess was 'a lovely lady'.

The Australian trip (followed on that occasion by 12 days in New Zealand) was the first of three such visits. In June they went to Canada where there was an outbreak of 'Di-mania', a 1980s equivalent of Beatlemania.

In February 1984, the Princess made her first major solo visit abroad, to Norway to attend a gala performance of *Carmen* by the London City Ballet. Arriving in the snow, she was at once dubbed 'The Snow Princess'.

In the spring of 1985 she and the Prince of Wales went to Italy, a 17-day tour which included a visit to Sir Harold Acton at La Pietra, and to the Pope in Rome. Venice was perhaps the highlight of the tour, and here they were joined by Prince William and Prince Harry.

In October the Princess spent two days with the 1st Battalion The Royal Hampshire Regiment (of which she was Colonel-in-Chief until she relinquished her military commitments on her divorce in 1996) in West Germany. Following their second Australian visit, they paused briefly in Fiji, and rested in Hawaii before visiting the Reagans in the United States. The White House dinner and dance was typical of the mid-Eighties bonanza-style entertainment favoured during the Reagan era, and the highlight of the evening was when the Princess accompanied John Travolta in a sensational dance to 'You're the One that I Want' (from the film *Grease*), an experience which both enjoyed and which served to resurrect Travolta's flagging career.

Other destinations during these years included Austria, Japan (where there was more 'Di-mania'), the Gulf states, Portugal and France.

In 1989 the Princess returned to the United States, this time for a less glitzy trip to New York, where she visited centres for the homeless and dying children in the Aids ward of Harlem Hospital. She was dubbed, in American parlance, 'Bigger than Gorby, Better than Bush'. There was a visit to Kuwait (where security was intense following the Salman Rushdie affair), and the United Arab Emirates. In June she and the Prince revisited Australia, and in November they went on a Far East tour, taking in Indonesia and Hong Kong.

Visiting Nigeria in 1990, the Princess saw much suffering at first hand, and pointedly shook hands with the chief of a leper colony. In May the same year she and the Prince paid the first royal visit to a Warsaw Pact country, when they travelled to Hungary. In October the Princess went alone to Washington for a ballet gala and to further understanding of Aids.

In November she and the Prince went to Japan for the enthronement of Emperor Akihito (a visit surrounded by controversy in Britain). There were also visits to Brussels, to British troops in Germany, to Prague, and to Expo 92 in Seville.

Besides the birth of her two children, there were other events of significance in her years of marriage. She much encouraged the union between Prince Andrew and her friend Sarah Ferguson, and she was delighted when they married in 1986. For some years they remained close friends and confidantes, and it was a cause of distress to her when that marriage came apart in the spring of 1992.

The Duchess of York had appeared to be a good ally at court, never as glamorous as the Princess, never likely to threaten her place in the esteem of the general public, but certainly her friend. But the arrival of the Duchess of York was, in retrospect, a damaging thing for the Princess of Wales, for she began to be tarnished by the new Duchess's fun-loving and sometimes irresponsible attitude.

The two may have seemed alike in character, but they were essentially different, the Princess being a great deal more dutiful and less interested in the perks. But the Duchess of York influenced her somewhat and it was during the time when they were close that the two then Royal Highnesses prodded their friends with the tip of their ferrule at the Royal Ascot meeting, one of a number of incidents that caused establishment eyebrows to be raised.

Each girl represented an alternative fantasy for the young: to be like the Princess of Wales was to diet rigorously and undertake regular aerobics. The Duchess of York, on the other hand, made few concessions and her attitude was more one of 'Take me as I am'. In 1988 they were both in Klosters when their friend Major Hugh Lindsay was killed in an accident skiing off-piste with the Prince of Wales. This tragedy long dampened the spirits of all three.

For many years a small circle was aware of the not altogether happy state of the Princess of Wales's marriage. Much was written about this over the years, but the situation continued until *The Sunday Times* adopted the story in 1992 and blew it up to sensational proportions. The public was left with another dream shattered, and the monarchy's image was tarnished.

The 1992 revelations suggested that the Prince and Princess of Wales had failed to establish a mutually happy rapport during their marriage. There were many obstacles to natural happiness. With nearly 13 years between them, they were almost of different generations, he being born in the late 1940s, she in the early 1960s. The Prince was always of a serious disposition, inflexible in his way of life, not noted for his willingness to accept change. The Princess was initially more light-headed, though she developed considerably in the first decade of the marriage. She certainly entered the union with a more generous heart than her husband, who did not disguise his anxiety that the taking of a wife was an additional burden in an already busy life.

Despite her enormous popularity with the public, the differences in their interests seemed to divide them increasingly as the years progressed. Though they were both energetically and successfully involved in public life, the framework of their home life gradually eroded. He began to entertain separately. She spent more time in London, frequently away from Highgrove. Their problems were the focus of more attention than any couple could bear. Not only did they have to face their respective difficulties, but they had to do so in the full blast of media attention.

The strain began to show. The Prince of Wales had resumed his earlier association with a former girlfriend, Mrs Camilla Parker Bowles. The

Princess's name was linked with those of two men nearer to her age, the Old Etonian James Gilbey and the Life Guards officer James Hewitt. There were clear signs of marital discord during a visit to India in February 1992, when the Princess spent time alone looking miserable at the Taj Mahal, and during a four-day trip to Korea in November that year, when the Prince and Princess, clearly unhappy in each other's company, were dubbed 'The Glums' by reporters.

By the end of 1992, speculation about the state of the royal marriage had come to a head, fuelled by the release of a tape of an intimate conversation between the Princess and James Gilbey. There was talk of separate living arrangements, and a suggestion that reconciliation was now impossible. In December, John Major confirmed to the House of Commons that the couple were to separate.

Separation did little to reduce public interest, particularly after the discovery in 1993 of another intimate tape recording, this time of a conversation betwen the Prince and Mrs Parker Bowles. In December 1993 the Princess tearfully bowed out of public life, severing her links with most of the charities she had supported and begging to be left alone by the press. In 1994 Prince Charles admitted his long-standing and continuing relationship with Mrs Parker Bowles in a television interview with Jonathan Dimbleby.

Despite her pleas for privacy, the Princess remained very much in the public eye. As she set about putting her life in order during the period of personal confusion that followed the separation – visiting gymnasiums one day and psychotherapists the next – her every step was dogged by photographers and reporters. Yet her relationship with the media was always more complicated than she was prepared to admit. She may have been unhappy about some of the press ambushes, and about speculation on her association with married men such as the art dealer Oliver Hoare and the England rugby captain Will Carling, but there were undoubtedly occasions when she courted the attention, in an attempt to influence perceptions of her marriage and its breakdown.

Nowhere was this more evident than in her extraordinary decision – taken without consulting the Royal Household or even her own advisers – to appear on a special edition of the BBC *Panorama* programme in November 1995. She spoke frankly about her unhappy relationship with the Royal

Family, her eating disorders, and her own and her husband's adultery. She announced her desire to be seen as 'a queen of people's hearts'. On 28 August 1996, the Prince and Princess of Wales divorced.

Throughout her marital difficulties, the Princess had remained devoted to her sons. After the divorce, when she and the Prince were given joint custody, she continued to invest considerable energy in their upbringing. She was an adoring mother, and there were many images of mother and children together, the most celebrated when the children ran to their mother's arms on *Britannia* after a period apart. The devotion was reciprocated, and her boys were a great source of comfort to her.

After her divorce the Princess made a return to public life, associating herself particularly with the work of the Red Cross, and taking a leading – and sometimes controversial – role in the international campaign to ban landmines. Earlier this year she auctioned many of her dresses to raise money for charity. She also seemed to find new happiness in her private life, spending much of the past few weeks in the company of Dodi Fayed, who died with her.

When she married the Prince of Wales, Diana said on television that she saw her life as a great challenge. Realistic though she was at 20 years of age, she underestimated how great that challenge would prove and at what cost to personal happiness it would be met.

The Princess made a lasting impression on the public. On the whole, they loved her; and even when she tried their patience, she remained a source of fascination. Outwardly shy, she had no lack of inner strength and common sense. Before her marriage she cast her head down, hiding behind her fringe. After the marriage she gained confidence, the head came up, and she began to acquire that star quality that drew all eyes in crowds and preoccupied fellow lunchers in restaurants. That quality, and that strength of character, saw her through her marital difficulties, and remained with her once the marriage was over.

Soon after her marriage to the Prince of Wales she was given the Royal Family Order by the Queen, but she was never given any other honours, such as the Grand Cross of the Royal Victorian Order, which she perhaps merited. On her divorce she assumed the title Diana, Princess of Wales, and remained a member of the Royal Family. She received various foreign orders on state visits.

P S

7 September

The News of the World today announces strict new rules in its dealings with freelance photographers all over the world.

We are determined that yobs with cameras masquerading as photo-journalists will be cut off forever from the respectable newspaper world . . .

Today the News of the World calls a halt.

We pledge not to publish any photograph unless it has been taken under the strict guidelines of the newspaper Code of Practice.

This forbids the taking of long-range photographs on private property and the merciless stalking and pursuing of people in the news.

In the coming days photographers and photo agencies around the world will be required to make these agreements – or we will ban them from our pages.

Furthermore, as the Royal Family struggles to come to terms with its devastating loss, the News of the World vows to CONTINUE its ban on publishing photos of Diana's grief-stricken sons, William and Harry, without their father's permission.

News of the World

8 September

Her biggest concern was always for her boys, William and Harry.

Earl Spencer was right to demand they are spared the same constant attention.

Nobody wants to see those two remarkable young Princes suffer any more than they are already. *The Mirror* will now work swiftly with the Press Complaints Commission to protect these boys from intrusive paparazzi photography.

It is what Diana would have wanted us to do.

Mirror

Viscount Rothermere, chairman of the Daily Mail and General Trust plc, said: 'I am, and always have been, an admirer of Diana, Princess of Wales, and nagged my editors to protect her so far as they could against her powerful enemies. In view of Earl Spencer's strong words and my own sense of outrage, I have instructed my editors no 'paparazzi' pictures are to be purchased without my knowledge and consent.'

Daily Mail

Spencer's bitter attack on newspapers will force every editor and every journalist to reflect deeply on the way they conduct themselves in future.

The Sun, for its part, has no intention of carrying photographs which invade the privacy of Princes William and Harry.

Sun

No pictures of the Princes William and Harry should henceforth be published if they are unofficial or paparazzi pictures. The Express, for one, will only publish pictures of the Princes now with the approval of their guardians.

No paparazzi pictures at all will be published in the Express. There are great complications in the definition of what is a paparazzi picture, but our working definition is that they are pictures taken by the specialist band of freelance cameramen whose stock in trade is to snatch celebrity photographs, often after prolonged pursuit and harassment.

Freelance photographs will be published only if the suppliers can show that they comply with our Code of Practice, which says that we will not take long-lens pictures of people on private property without their consent unless it is strictly in the public interest.

We will strengthen our own definition of private property to go beyond homes and gardens to include places where people clearly believe they are alone, even though they do not own the actual location.

Express